GREAT ✝ EXCAVATIONS

THE PUBLICATION OF THIS BOOK WAS MADE POSSIBLE BY GENEROUS
SUPPORT FROM THE RICHARD LOUNSBERY FOUNDATION

Tales of Early Southwestern Archaeology

1888–1939

GREAT EXCAVATIONS

MELINDA ELLIOTT

SCHOOL OF AMERICAN RESEARCH PRESS † SANTA FE, NEW MEXICO

SCHOOL OF AMERICAN RESEARCH PRESS
Post Office Box 2188, Santa Fe, New Mexico 87504
www.sarweb.org

Director of Publications: Joan K. O'Donnell
Editor: Jo Ann Baldinger
Designer: Deborah Flynn Post
Photo Researcher: Baylor Chapman
Indexer: Andrew L. Christenson
Typographer: Tseng Information Systems

Library of Congress Cataloging-in-Publication Data:
Elliott, Melinda.
Great excavations : tales of early southwestern archaeology,
1888-1939 / Melinda Elliott. — 1st ed.
p. cm.
Includes bibliographical references and index.
ISBN 0-933452-42-X (cloth). — ISBN 0-933452-43-8 (paper)
1. Indians of North America—Southwest, New—Antiquities.
2. Archaeology—Southwest, New—History. 3. Pueblo Indians—
Antiquities. 4. Excavations (Archaeology)—Southwest, New—
History. 5. Southwest, New—Antiquities. I. Title.
E78.S7E49 1995
979'.01—dc20   95-16579
CIP

Cover: Top left, Monument Valley, Arizona; top right, Pueblo del Arroyo, New
Mexico, 1991; bottom right, Long Wall at Chetro Ketl, New Mexico, 1991;
bottom left, Aztec, New Mexico. All photos © Bruce Hucko.

Printed and bound in the United States of America

To the memory of my mother,

Maxine Yeatman Elliott,

and to my grandmothers,

Pauline Hoss Elliott

and Lydia Arnold Yeatman

✝

Contents

Map and Illustrations

Pueblo Pintado, Chaco Canyon, 1920.

THE LURE OF THE SOUTHWEST'S PREHISTORIC PAST

THIS BOOK GREW OUT OF A DESIRE to learn about the adventures and discoveries of early archaeologists in the Southwest. The idea was to introduce the public to some of the region's scientific pioneers and their achievements at several landmark excavations. As a journalist, I aimed to tell these stories from and for the layperson's point of view. I also hoped to convey a sense of the romance and excitement that went into uncovering the Southwest's scientific and prehistoric roots.

Though they are no longer with us, the archaeologists described here became very real to me. I read their letters, articles, and reports, and was fortunate to meet many of their families, friends, and colleagues. Perhaps these pioneers in the science of prehistory would be pleased to know that even more real in my mind's eye became the vanished peoples to whom they devoted much of their lives—the Native Americans who inhabited the Southwest for centuries before the arrival of Europeans.

How could one not feel kinship with and admiration for these pre-historic Southwesterners? Visiting the ruins of their former homes and witnessing the objects they left behind—pottery, jewelry, and tools—one is struck by the aesthetics and perseverance of their ancient ways of life. No wonder Kidder, Morris, Hodge, and the other early archaeologists were drawn year after year to "dig in the dirt" at Southwestern excavation sites.

In some ways the prehistoric Indians were easier to understand and appreciate than the archaeological pioneers, much of whose work has been criticized by their modern counterparts. These early scientists of prehistoric America explored huge sections of ancient ruins, digging areas far larger than would be considered acceptable—or would be economically feasible—today. Often they were charged by sponsoring patrons or institutions only with the task of collecting specimens worthy of exhibit. As their methods became more scientific, they ordered, described, and classified what they found, and defined patterns of prehistoric life and culture areas. Such activities are now considered elementary.

Early archaeologists also engaged in some practices that today are considered objectionable. In particular, the excavation of Native American burials and removal of sacred objects—activities common in the early days of Southwestern archaeology—are now disturbing and offensive to many Indians and non-Indians alike. Such endeavors grew out of the nineteenth-century traditions of European antiquarianism and reflect the mentality of the time. Fortunately the trend has moved recently toward a more progressive science that advocates respect for the Native American point of view, an approach recently underscored by stringent legal restrictions as well.

Though we may look askance today at some of their practices, early archaeologists in the Southwest created something out of nothing. They lived and worked during a period when there were few, if any, standards for them to follow, a time when their task of necessity involved introducing a glimmer of scientific order where there had been none.

Often they bit off more than they could chew. This tendency showed, especially, in the lack of final reports on some of the most important digs or the decades-long intervals between their fieldwork and the publication of the reports summarizing their findings. In the days before "contract work" and "salvage archaeology," most of these men held demanding, full-time institutional jobs, in which they shouldered major administrative or teaching responsibilities in addition to their excavation and reporting work. They were overburdened but determined—*dedicated* is probably the better word—and nearly all of them completed their reports despite long delays.

As one would expect, many of the interpretations stemming from these pioneering excavations are now outdated. The questions asked then—"Who were these people? Where did they come from? Where did they go?"—are less sophisticated than the specialized focus and scope of modern research designs. The findings made by the pioneers are described in the following pages, but readers must know that much more refined and complex information exists about each of the sites. In some cases, the early hypotheses have been completely disproved.

It is interesting to note, though, that a number of the conclusions reached inductively by the pioneering archaeologists still hold. And much of the classificatory work they did still provides vital, solid foundations for modern archaeology.

Finally, to their credit, they wrote wonderfully interesting, lucid, even elegant discourses that are a pleasure to read, far surpassing much of today's archaeological prose. Contemporary archaeology is too often couched in incomprehensible high-tech jargon. May the pendulum swing back to the tradition of Kidder and his colleagues, whose willingness to communicate is evident in every well-turned sentence.

Because this book aims to take the reader on an armchair tour of several "Great Excavations," it by no means completely covers the geographical and cultural landscape of Southwestern archaeology. Readers who want the whole picture will need to investigate several prehistoric cultures omitted here—the Mogollon, Sinagua, and Mimbres, for example. Some of the obvious geographic loopholes are the Flagstaff and Little Colorado areas in Arizona and the Mimbres and Galisteo vicinities in New Mexico, and there are others. The coverage here is intentionally selective, providing stories of some of the most interesting excavations and excavators rather an exhaustive survey.

One constant concern of mine throughout the writing of this book was the absence of women's achievements. During the decades described here, several women financially backed archaeological projects but tended to keep a low profile. Archaeologists' wives, such as Madeleine Kidder and Ann Morris, often made significant but largely anonymous contributions to their husbands' work. Today things have changed, obviously. If a similar book is ever written about late twentieth-century archaeology, many of the chapter titles will contain the names of outstanding women archaeologists.

My final thoughts about the book are pleasant personal memories of the many friendly, patient, and helpful archaeologists who were willing to be interviewed for this project. A more cordial and committed group of professionals could not be found.

This book in no way reflects their current understanding of Pecos and the other Great Excavations. Nor does it cover the general scope, depth, or complexity of their knowledge about the discipline of archaeology. For that, the reader must turn to the archaeologists themselves and their immense literature. If this book provides a basic understanding of what the early archaeologists did and stimulates a desire to learn more about the intriguing prehistory of the Southwest, then its goal will have been accomplished.

In addition to my memories of the archaeologists who helped, I have several happy remembrances of fascinating journeys into the Southwestern archaeological landscape. One adventure in particular is unforgettable. In Tsegi Canyon on the Navajo Reservation, I retraced the footsteps of the Rainbow Bridge-

Monument Valley expedition participants. Accompanied by a good-natured archaeologist and a cheerful Navajo guide, I "discovered" ruins that stood in expectant silence, seemingly waiting for the return of their Anasazi builders.

At our campsite, iridescent hummingbirds hovered to sip from a waterfall flowing silkily over rough sandstone cliffs. At midnight the August sky blazed with silver trails of meteor showers. Archaeology in the field, I learned, could addict one with its magical blend of new experiences, sights, and awareness.

I wish all readers the same enjoyment of discovery should they ever explore the Southwestern sites of these Great Excavations.

Melinda Elliott
Santa Fe, New Mexico

ACKNOWLEDGMENTS

MANY DEDICATED AND KNOWLEDGEABLE PEOPLE contributed professional expertise and other assistance to the creation of this book. Among them I found a number of true Westerners, individuals who demonstrated their pioneer spirit through their appreciation of the history of the Southwest and its archaeology—and through their humanity, helpfulness, and hospitality.

Although most of the individuals listed below have the Ph.D. degree, that credential has not been appended to their names; all are experts in their own areas.

My first thanks go to the three original supporters of the idea for this project: Douglas Schwartz, president of the School of American Research; Jane Kepp, former director of publications at the School; and Jonathan Haas, former director of programs and research at the School. These fellow instigators encouraged me throughout the project, firm in their belief that the time had come for a popular history of the early days of Southwestern archaeology.

A special note of gratitude goes to the memory of the late Alan F. McHenry, who, as president of the Richard Lounsbery Foundation, supported this project with his interest and with a substantial grant from the foundation.

Once research was under way, several of the archaeologists described in these chapters provided personal accounts that enriched the written reports of their work. Their help was invaluable, their reminiscences were delightful, and the scope of their knowledge—based on decades of experience—proved immense. To these individuals I owe enormous thanks.

The late Watson Smith, though in ill health, generously granted a lengthy interview, as did the late Emil W. Haury and his long-time colleague, Julian Hayden. The late Al Lancaster and his wife, Alice, provided hospitality as well as an informative and enjoyable interview. Evelyn Brew, wife of the late John Otis Brew, graciously consented to an afternoon's discussion of old times; and Faith Fuller, daughter of Alfred V. Kidder, kindly spent an evening escorting me around Cambridge. Katharine Bartlett, former colleague of and secretary to Harold Colton, generously made time to share her memories of early days in archaeology.

Assistance also came from several archaeologists who studied with and worked for the men described in the chapters of this book. Thanks for extended and informative interviews that provided context for historical details go to David A. Breternitz, Alden C. Hayes, Richard B. and Nathalie F. S. Woodbury, and the late Robert H. Lister.

Archaeologist Andrew L. Christenson provided several valuable interviews, a field trip, and very helpful source material. Other archaeologists I wish to thank for their assistance and willingness to be interviewed are John Andresen, Helen Crotty, David E. Doyel, Frederick W. Lange, Larry V. Nordby, Stewart L. Peckham, Ann Rasor, Jack Smith, David E. Stuart, Tom Windes, Gene Worman, and Penny Davis Worman.

Wirt H. Wills, associate professor in the department of anthropology at the University of New Mexico, revealed the state of the art of Southwestern archaeology in a series of lectures that I was fortunate to attend.

Several archaeologists generously agreed to read the manuscript, in whole or in part, at various stages of completion. Thanks for this help go to E. Charles Adams, Jenny L. Adams, David Breternitz, Andrew L. Christenson, Al Hayes, Fred Lange, Keith Kintigh, Stephen H. Lekson, Albert H. Schroeder, Brenda Shears, Ann Rasor, and Richard and Nathalie Woodbury.

Unflagging professional support came from librarian Laura Holt and her assistant, Tracey Kimball, at the Laboratory of Anthropology, Museum of New Mexico, Santa Fe. Laura's help in several cases proved crucial, and without her resourcefulness the book could not have taken shape as it did.

Generous assistance with literature searches was supplied by archaeologist Curtis F. Schaafsma, curator of anthropology at the Museum of Indians Arts and Culture and the Laboratory of Anthropology, Santa Fe.

Archivist Willow Roberts Powers of the Laboratory of Anthropology willingly and competently assisted with several phases of photo research. Walter Wait and Henry J. Day of the Branch of Archaeological Management, Division of Anthropology, National Park Service, Santa Fe, also provided advice and archival photo resources. Special thanks go to Arthur Olívas and Richard Rudisill, photo archivists, Palace of the Governors, Museum of New Mexico, for wonderful help and amusing anecdotes.

Appreciation is also due the staff of SAR Press at the School of American Research. As publications director during the early phases of the project, Jane Kepp remained firmly committed to the book and provided helpful input on text and illustrations.

Joan K. O'Donnell, current director of the Press, skillfully steered the book through the publication process with the good judgment and finesse that are her editorial trademarks.

One of the most fortunate additions to the publications team was Jo Ann Baldinger, whose excellent skills as text editor brightened and fine-tuned the narrative.

The professional contributions of Deborah Flynn Post, art director and designer of this book, and Peter Palmieri, marketing manager of the Press, were essential and expert. To publications assistant Baylor Chapman go my thanks for her adroit detective work in obtaining photos and permissions—a tough assignment that she completed with impressive thoroughness.

Several family members and friends provided essential personal encouragement, computer assistance, weather reports, snacks, coffee breaks, good cheer, common sense, and long-distance phone calls. These special people include my father, Richard H. Elliott; my brothers, Bill Elliott and J. F. Elliott; and my friend Bill Murphy, of Dallas, Texas.

The late Ann Maytag generously made studio space available for the writing of several chapters. I am grateful to poet Peggy O'Mara for her confidence in my creativity and for her example.

The important contributors named here gave much to the author during this project; many others who assisted remain anonymous for various reasons. Appreciation goes to all who helped.

Although all of these individuals contributed to the creation of this book, the interpretations presented in these chapters do not reflect their views or their efforts. Any errors are the responsibility of the author alone.

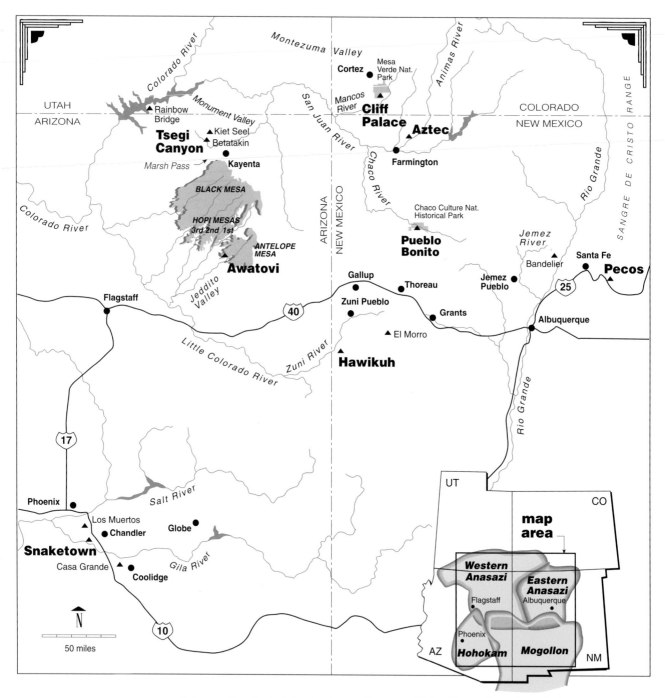

Major archaeological sites in the Southwestern United States. Inset: Boundaries of prehistoric Southwest cultural traditions. Map by Carol Cooperrider (based on a map in Lister and Lister 1983:21).

GREAT ✝ EXCAVATIONS

Cliff Palace, Mesa Verde, photographed
by William Henry Jackson in 1892.

CHAPTER 1

CLIFF PALACE

Three Generations of Exploration
at Mesa Verde

ON DECEMBER 18, 1888, Richard Wetherill and his brother-in-law, Charles Mason, came upon the ruin of Cliff Palace on the Mesa Verde in southwestern Colorado. Snow was falling softly as the two cowboys rode up to nearby Sun Point in search of stray cattle. From there they looked across the rim of Cliff Canyon to the west-facing prehistoric city.

The crumbling dwelling stood in a high, dry cave, nearly one hundred feet deep, carved by wind and water from sandstone deposited by an ancient sea. The silvery light of the snowfall illuminated the turrets and walls of the ancient town tucked away in its shadowy rock shelter.

With great excitement, Wetherill and Mason worked their way around the canyon rim, left their horses, and clambered down the steep cliff wall using a makeshift ladder created from tree branches. They found themselves standing in a huge building, partially collapsed, cobwebby, and blanketed with a centuries-old powder of fine dust from the adobe plaster covering the walls. The two wandered awestruck through a maze of towers, rooms, and passageways.

The rock overhang had protected the ruin from the elements for seven centuries. Within the deep rubble lay a wealth of beautifully preserved artifacts left by prehistoric people. Fascinated, Wetherill and Mason picked up and fingered the personal belongings of those vanished inhabitants: a stone ax, a *mano* (hand stone) for grinding corn, a sandal woven from tough yucca fibers, a broken wooden spindle, a drinking mug, a clay cooking pot.

Although Wetherill and Mason were cowboys, not archaeologists, their entry into the ruin of Cliff Palace set in motion events that would lead to many discoveries in Southwestern archaeology as well as enduring controversy over the Wetherill family's contributions to that then-budding science. During the next few decades Mesa Verde would become a symbol of the archaeological wealth of the Southwest, even as many of its treasures were carried off piecemeal.

In the late nineteenth century, scholars in East Coast museums and universities were slowly bringing archaeology out of the domain of amateur antiquarians and collectors and into the realm of legitimate science. These academicians, who usually had backgrounds in other sciences, occasionally surveyed, explored, and excavated ruins on major expeditions funded by wealthy patrons.

As part of this process, the field of archaeology became associated in the United States with the study of anthropology, another new science, which focused on the development and behavior of the human race. A few pioneers in the field, including some who had been trained on digs in Europe or the Middle East, realized that artifacts were more than admirable art objects or intriguing curiosities; they also offered clues to the evolution of human culture. These early archaeologists worked to devise methodical ways of removing ancient objects found at prehistoric settlements. The most valuable information, they believed, pertained to the on-site location and relationships of the excavated artifacts and architecture.

Nevertheless, the idea that information about prehistoric societies could be pieced together from objects found at archaeological excavations hardly affected the haphazard way excavations at that time were conducted. Most people searched prehistoric ruins simply in order to remove artifacts. In the Southwest, the region that, because of its dryness, contained many of the nation's best-preserved archaeological sites, local residents tended to view artifact hunting as a pastime and, occasionally, a source of income. Artifact-hungry museums and wealthy collectors encouraged the search for ancient treasures, paying good prices for the pottery, arrowheads, jewelry, baskets, sandals, and other items local people found at ruins. Spectacular sites such as those at Mesa Verde suffered particularly from the voracious artifact-hunting of these early years.

The public learned about Mesa Verde soon after Richard Wetherill and Charles Mason stumbled upon Cliff Palace on that December day in 1888. In fact, the Wetherill family introduced the enormous, ancient cliff dwelling to the world. Several anthropologists from the East had visited the Southwest previously, but their reports had not aroused widespread awareness of the region's archaeological wealth. The existence of Cliff Palace and the many other sites at Mesa Verde remained unknown to most East Coast scientists and collectors.

Despite an enduring controversy as to whether the Wetherills had "discovered" Cliff Palace—a debate raised by the indisputable fact that other Anglo explorers had entered some of Mesa Verde's cliff dwellings before them—it is clear that the Wetherills explored and dug at Mesa Verde more than any other nineteenth-century explorers. Their efforts to bring the ruin to the attention of the press, the public, and academic experts played a major role in stimulating enormous interest in the archaeological treasures of the Southwest. During the 1890s, no other Indian ruin so inspired the imaginations of people across the United States and Europe as did Cliff Palace at Mesa Verde.

The Wetherill brothers—Richard, John, Al, Winslow, and Clayton—were the sons of Benjamin Kite Wetherill and his wife, Marion, Quaker homesteaders in the fertile Mancos Valley east of Mesa Verde, the "green tableland" rising, at its highest point, nearly two thousand feet above the valley floor. Their ranch, named "The Alamo" for its spreading cottonwood trees, lay not far from the little pioneer town of Mancos, Colorado. The Wetherills' five sons and their daughter Anna, who became the wife of Charles Mason, grew up addressing each other with the gentle "thees" and "thous" of Quaker custom. Smoking, drinking, and swearing were forbidden. Yet the Wetherill boys' strong personalities, along with occasional disputes over cattle brands, and their determined efforts to publicize the ruins and remove the "relics" they found there, made them controversial figures in their local community.

For years, encouraged by their father, the brothers had brought home the artifacts they found in the ruins around Mancos Canyon, carved by the Mancos River, which cuts through Mesa Verde and spreads the fingers of its tributary canyons across the tableland. After the brothers explored Cliff Palace, they became much more serious about searching for and digging in Indian ruins. "For a number of years after that," recalled Al Wetherill in his autobiography, "everything else was of minor importance to us."[1] Al also reported that "over the long period of years [of exploration at Mesa Verde], John, Richard and I did most of the actual work. Charles [Mason] helped, as did Clayt and Win at various times, but we three felt that, somehow, the ruins were our personal responsibility."[2]

The brothers worked hard at exploration during the winter months, when their duties at the ranch were relatively light. By 1890 they had located and searched nearly two hundred Mesa Verde cliff dwellings. In the century that followed, archaeologists exploring the six hundred or so known cliff dwellings on the mesa would repeatedly find the names or initials of the Wetherill brothers scrawled in seemingly inaccessible caves.

As time passed, The Alamo fell into the financial doldrums common to small ranches in the area, and the brothers developed a four-point approach to economic survival—cowboying, outfitting tourists, digging and selling "relics" to collectors, and eventually trading with the Indians. The items that the Wetherills

Top left: The Wetherill brothers at the Alamo Ranch, c. 1893: (left to right) Alfred ("Al"), Winslow ("Win"), Richard, Clayton ("Clayt"), and John. Top right: Gustaf Nordenskiöld and his wife, Anna, 1893. Bottom: Richard Wetherill (seated at far right) with a group of tourists in the ruins at Mesa Verde, c. 1894.

gathered on Mesa Verde were kept in a barn at The Alamo, which the family turned into a casual museum. Sometimes individual prehistoric objects were sold. Other artifacts were assembled into collections that eventually went to the Denver Historical Society, the University of Pennsylvania Museum, and the Colorado State Museum.

Soon after Richard Wetherill and Charles Mason found Cliff Palace, the family began placing advertisements in newspapers announcing guided tours of the ancient ruins. The resulting publicity led to a kind of "artifact gold rush." Scientists, journalists, writers, artists, adventurers, millionaires, nobility, and ordinary people from all over the world converged on The Alamo and made the rugged, three-day pack trip on horseback to see the ruins. Between 1889 and 1901, Al Wetherill reported, "nearly one thousand people visited the ranch to see the cliff dwellings."[3] Visitors came away thrilled by the adventure. One of them wrote,

> Hurriedly unpacking, we hobbled the horses that were the most likely to stray far, and taking along our photographic kit, wended our way on foot toward that remarkable group of ruins ... which Richard has called "the Cliff-Palace." ... Surely its discoverer had not overstated the beauty and magnitude of this strange ruin. ...
>
> We observed in one place corn-cobs imbedded in the plaster in the walls. ... We found a large stone mortar, which may have been used to grind the corn. Broken pottery was everywhere. ... We also found parts of skulls and bones, fragments of weapons, and pieces of cloth.[4]

While white-throated swifts swooped and dived beneath the cave's overhang, the eager tourists roamed through the debris of Cliff Palace's two hundred rooms and nearly two dozen underground ceremonial chambers. The enclave was laid out like a vast, terraced apartment house, rising in eight levels from the edge of the cave to its back walls. Unlike many other ruins, Cliff Palace had no central plaza; but it did have odd features such as the tapered, rounded, three-story tower against the back wall of the cave.

Visitors peered into the dusty dimness of the ceremonial rooms, where the hard-packed dirt floors still held loops for prehistoric weavers' upright looms. They searched in wall niches for jewelry and fetishes and climbed through T-shaped doorways to enter ancient living rooms, many measuring no more than forty or fifty square feet. They ran their hands over plastered walls made of mud and sandstone blocks, hand-cut and shaped to fit by prehistoric masons. At the back of the cave, where John Wetherill once unearthed fourteen prehistoric mummies, the tourists found several ancient turkey pens, littered with feathers, droppings, and eggshells.

Early view of Cliff Palace, c. 1907.

At the time of the Wetherills' Mesa Verde explorations, no one had a clear idea of how old the ruins were or of the cultural development of the people who had built and lived in them. Subsequently, archaeologists would conclude that the dwelling was mainly constructed and inhabited by a few hundred people for about seventy-five to a hundred years in the 1200s and abandoned by AD 1300.

From their explorations and examinations of artifacts they found at such sites as Step House at Mesa Verde and later in the dry caves of Grand Gulch, Utah, the Wetherill brothers began to piece together rough hypotheses about the builders of Cliff Palace and the other ruins they explored. Richard and John developed the theory that two distinct groups of prehistoric Indians—a cliff-dwelling culture and an earlier, less complex culture—had occupied many of the same locations. Since the brothers found neither metal tools nor any sort of wheel among the ruins, they concluded that both groups were Stone Age peoples.

Making observations that foreshadowed future scientific discoveries, Richard coined the term "Basket People" to refer to the group he perceived as the earlier inhabitants. Beneath the remains of the cliff dwellings, he came upon small settlements of partially underground dwellings, which later archaeologists called "pithouses." The remains of the Basket People included little or no pot-

tery but many finely woven baskets created by the spiral coil method. Later, archaeologists would determine that rudimentary pottery had appeared among these people around AD 550. The Basket People also wove beautiful sandals with rounded or square toes; used an *atlatl*, or spear thrower, in hunting; and had skulls that were long, narrow, and undeformed by cradleboards.

The people who Richard Wetherill deduced were the successors of the Basket People left behind very different artifacts and architecture. Over the centuries, they developed spectacular cliff dwellings and, in open areas, many-roomed, multistoried pueblos of stone and adobe. Like most Southwestern cliff dwellings, Cliff Palace contained numerous circular underground chambers, most of which had built-in benches around the circumference and roof beams supported by pilasters. These underground structures resembled the ceremonial chambers of the Hopi Indians and, in the Wetherills' day, were often called *estufas* (literally, "ovens"), a term used by Spanish explorers who associated the underground rooms with sweat baths. Today they are commonly referred to as *kivas,* the Hopi word for "ceremonial rooms."

The cliff-dwelling people farmed plots of corn and squash with tools such as digging sticks; used the coil-and-scrape method to create clay pottery, which they painted white with black designs (they had no potter's wheel); hunted with bow and arrow; wore sandals that were fashioned with an indentation for the large toe; and flattened the craniums of their children by carrying them tightly strapped to cradleboards. Noting their distinctive artifacts and architecture, Richard Wetherill may have been the first to apply the term "Cliff Dwellers" to these later people.

Though many contemporaries scorned the Wetherills' ideas, reports of scholarly archaeologists who later worked in the area bore out the brothers' observations about an earlier, pithouse-dwelling culture succeeded by a group who built Cliff Palace and other major ruins. In fact, Richard's hypothesis of an earlier and a later group of prehistoric people continues to be recognized as a highly significant contribution by respected archaeologists. Years after the Wetherills' heyday at Mesa Verde, at a landmark conference held at the ruins of Pecos Pueblo in 1927, archaeologists officially accepted the use of the terms "Basketmaker" and "Pueblo" (the Wetherills' "Basket People" and "Cliff Dwellers"). Together the two groups constituted the *Anasazi,* who were at that time assumed to be the single cultural group of prehistoric Indians in the Southwest. The word "Anasazi" comes from the Navajo language and is often translated as "ancient ones" or, more literally, "enemies of our ancestors."

Among the tourists guided by the Wetherills were several notable scientists and writers of the day, some of whom published accounts of their explorations. One of the best-known of these early writings by an American is *Land of the Cliff Dwellers* by Frederick Chapin, who visited Mesa Verde in 1889 and 1890. Also significant were the popular and scientific articles of Dr. T. Mitchell Prudden, who first visited the Alamo Ranch in 1895, became a good friend of the Wetherills, and continued to explore the area for many years thereafter. Prudden noticed that numerous early ruins consisted of several rooms grouped around one pithouse-like structure, or kiva. He called such simple settlements "unit pueblos," and with that term contributed an important concept to Southwestern archaeology.

In the summer of 1891, the Wetherills outfitted and guided twenty-three-year-old Gustaf Nordenskiöld, who initiated the first scientific excavations at Mesa Verde and taught the Wetherills much in the process. Nordenskiöld, a Swedish citizen of Finnish descent, was one of the few Europeans to take note of and publish on American archaeology. He applied such basic practices as scientific note-taking, and he also made many fine photographs and meticulous drawings to serve as precise records of architecture, artifacts, and burials, and their locations at each site. His methods of unearthing artifacts were slower and more systematic than the rough pick-and-shovel approach to which the Wetherill brothers were accustomed. He taught them to work with smaller, hand-held tools—spades, brushes, small picks—and emphasized precision and caution. Nordenskiöld surveyed the numerous ruins on the mesa and marked the various structures by carving large, bold numerals into rocks. At the north end of Cliff Palace, his number "2" can still clearly be seen on the side of a boulder.

Nordenskiöld admired the beauty of Cliff Palace; from a distance, he wrote, it looked like "an enchanted castle." But, finding that the artifacts of Cliff Palace had been removed before his arrival, he spent little time there. With Nordenskiöld directing them, the Wetherills surveyed and dug at several other Mesa Verde dwellings, including Long House, Kodak House, Mug House, Step House, and Spruce Tree House. Nordenskiöld shipped home a collection of artifacts from the cliff dwellings, which is now at the National Museum in Helsinki, Finland.

Local citizens opposed the removal of these items to foreign shores and a brief court battle ensued, though in the end Nordenskiöld politely and quietly won out. The controversy led local women's groups in Durango to form activist associations, and eventually the activities of their Colorado Cliff Dwellings Association helped mobilize support for federal legislation to protect archaeological treasures from vandalism and exploitation.

After Nordenskiöld returned to Sweden in the winter of 1892, he wrote a book about his survey and excavations. *The Cliff Dwellers of the Mesa Verde, Southwestern Colorado: Their Pottery and Implements,* published in 1893, is still respected for the precision of its scientific reporting.

The Wetherills' work inspired controversy from the beginning, despite their association with scientists like Nordenskiöld. Because they were not formally educated, and because they helped private collectors who took artifacts for their own purposes, the Wetherills' activities were considered self-serving and unscientific. Like many early cowboys and tourists, they were accused of picking through Mesa Verde ruins carelessly and destructively.

The Wetherills later insisted that they attempted to treat the ruins with care, even in their earliest expeditions. Through techniques they learned from Nordenskiöld and other visiting scientists, note-taking, and attempts to excavate by methods they understood to be scientific, the brothers said they tried to win the respect of East Coast academics then developing the science of archaeology. In many cases, their efforts were rebuffed. "Although the influence of the work and deductions of the Wetherills has been widely felt, it has come to us mainly from the pens of others and through collections of artifacts in various museums," wrote scholar John Otis Brew in a landmark report published in 1946.[5]

However casual their digging may have been, the Wetherills' practices were hardly unusual for their day. No law forbade individuals or institutions from entering ancient ruins and unearthing and carrying off whatever artifacts they found appealing by any methods they pleased. Among hard-pressed homesteaders eking out a frontier existence, the land and its resources, including prehistoric ruins and their contents, were considered rightful sources of revenue.

Yucca and willow baskets found by Gustaf Nordenskiöld at Spruce Tree House and Step House, Mesa Verde. Plate 44 in Gustaf Nordenskiöld's "The Cliff Dwellers of the Mesa Verde" (1893).

Large spherical jar (canteen) found buried beside the ruins of Step House. Plate 31 in Nordenskiöld's "The Cliff Dwellers of the Mesa Verde" (1893).

Before the turn of the century, and in the first two decades thereafter, museums
and universities sent expeditions seeking the same goal as the local farmers who
dug for Indian pottery: to find the most exceptional, intriguing, and beautiful ancient artifacts at each site and bring them back for public display, and
sometimes even for sale.

Though the Wetherills undoubtedly had various motives in making their
collections (the first collection they sold brought them $3,000), they were not
alone in this pursuit. Other nineteenth-century individuals who became involved in the collection of artifacts included the wealthy patron of Southwestern
explorations, Mary Hemenway of Boston, who financed major archaeological
expeditions; Thomas Keam, an Indian trader in Arizona, who amassed large
quantities of Hopi material; and Robert S. Peabody, whose collection of archaeological artifacts eventually came to rest at the Phillips Academy at Andover,
Massachusetts. For the Smithsonian Institution, Colonel James Stevenson and
his wife, Matilda, collected enormous amounts of Pueblo pottery and other artifacts. In fact, most archaeologists of the day were either collectors themselves or
worked for collectors.

In 1906, as a result of concerned citizens' and scientists' protests about
abuses at sites such as Mesa Verde, the U.S. Congress passed the Antiquities Act.
The Act placed all prehistoric and historic remains located on government lands
under federal protection. That same year additional legislation placed the ruins

of Mesa Verde within the boundaries of a national park, the first dedicated to the preservation of archaeological treasures. Until the establishment of the Park Service in 1916, Mesa Verde, like all other national parks, was administered by the Secretary of the Interior.

O N JUNE 29, 1906, Mesa Verde became a national park, and Cliff Palace passed from the domain of its self-appointed caretakers, the Wetherills. By then, the family patriarch, Benjamin, had died, and the Alamo Ranch had finally gone bankrupt and been sold at auction in 1902. The Wetherill children had married and scattered from the homestead near the beautiful mesa where they had become famous.

Richard and John went on to work on other archaeological expeditions. They also maintained businesses as outfitters and traders to the Navajo. Until he was murdered in 1910, Richard owned a trading post at Pueblo Bonito at Chaco Canyon, New Mexico. Eventually John established his own post at Kayenta, Arizona, and from there he outfitted and guided many explorers. During the 1930s John assisted one of the last pioneering expeditions in Southwestern archaeology, the Rainbow Bridge–Monument Valley Expedition (see chapter 8).

Soon after Mesa Verde became a national park, a small band of U.S. government professionals — archaeologists and administrators — came to the "green tableland" to take up the challenge of managing the new park and overseeing the maintenance of Cliff Palace and the other ruins.

The number of visitors to Mesa Verde grew, in spite of the fact that no road extended onto the mesa, and a visit to the ruins demanded a tough trip on horseback of approximately thirty miles. It became obvious that the major ruins, especially the most popular ones such as Cliff Palace, could not absorb the stress of increasing tourism unless their crumbling walls were strengthened. Stabilization of the ancient buildings became the first imperative.

No one in the region had dealt with the sort of ruins maintenance problems that confronted the crews at Mesa Verde. The cliff dwellings were large, remote, perched in inaccessible locations, and uniquely constructed, so that patch jobs would look obvious unless they were thoughtfully done. Archaeologists at the park soon found that the task of ruins stabilization offered great opportunities for experiment, trial, and error.

The number one enemy of the adobe plaster and mortar in the walls was water. Over the years, every stabilization chief at Mesa Verde had to engineer ways to divert water from the crumbling foundations and floors of cliff dwellings. Crews also had to strengthen unsteady walls with new stones and mortar, and to reconstruct broken timbers in roof beams and deteriorating frameworks of logs and branches in ceilings.

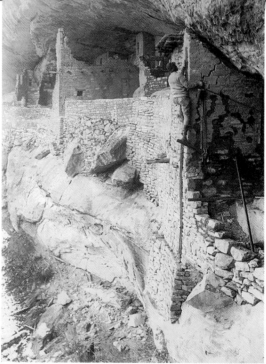

Top: Crew repairing the
north kiva of Balcony
House under the
supervision of Jesse L.
Nusbaum, 1910. At right:
Jesse Nusbaum bracing the
two-story tower at the
north end of Balcony
House, 1910.

The gaping holes in walls and towers presented special problems. What had these missing sections originally looked like? Early archaeologists wanted to restore ruins so that they appeared complete again. In later years the job of stabilization — keeping the ruins standing — was differentiated from that of restoration, in which workmen would actually reconstruct missing parts of structures. But when archaeologists first began maintaining the cliff dwellings, restoration according to the imaginative interpretations of those in charge was an accepted part of every job.

In 1908, the secretary of the Department of the Interior recommended ethnologist/archaeologist Jesse Walter Fewkes to oversee the work of excavation and maintenance at Mesa Verde. An employee of the Bureau of American Ethnology of the Smithsonian Institution, Fewkes had already explored and excavated Indian ruins in the region for more than two decades.

White-haired and sporting a neatly trimmed beard, Fewkes was a picturesque and reputedly eccentric figure, a Harvard-educated marine zoologist who started learning about Indians while pursuing zoological studies in California. He became involved in Southwestern ethnology, studying the culture, heritage, and lifeways of living Indian peoples, especially the Hopis. He evidently got on well with the Indians, for the Zunis and Hopis allowed him to make phonograph recordings of many of their traditional songs — an ethnological first — and the Hopi tribe granted him the honor of initiation into the Antelope and Flute priesthoods.

Though the Indians may have accepted him, among some of his Anglo colleagues in the Southwest, Fewkes earned the nickname "The Codfish" because of his straight-laced Boston manners,[6] and his tendency to go his own way made him unpopular with park management at Mesa Verde. While coworkers found him difficult, Fewkes apparently liked working with the public. One of his most successful efforts, initiated in 1915, was a program of evening campfire talks for visitors. Fewkes is perhaps best remembered at Mesa Verde for his work at Sun Temple and Fire Temple, which stood, like Cliff Palace, on the fingerlike extension called Chapin Mesa. He believed the Anasazi had held special ceremonial rites at these two sites.

Fewkes spent the summer of 1909 restoring and stabilizing Cliff Palace, partly to make the site a viable educational resource where visitors could learn more about the Indians who had built it. His crews cleared away rubble and fallen rocks, removed the dirt of centuries, cemented crumbling walls, and reconstructed some parts of the ruins, making Cliff Palace relatively safe for visitors.

In his 1911 report on the work, Fewkes criticized the Wetherills harshly for their methods of searching for artifacts. He was disturbed by the damage done by explorers and tourists, writing, "The ruin had been almost completely rifled

Left: Jesse Walter Fewkes in front of Mesa Verde's first museum. Right: Earl Morris early in his career as an expert at ruins stabilization.

of its contents, the specimens removed, and its walls left in a very dilapidated condition."[7]

Ironically, Fewkes's methods would in turn elicit strong criticism from later archaeologists and caretakers of Cliff Palace. Because his real interest lay in ethnology, then not viewed as separate from archaeology, his report contained more conjecture about cultural connections between the people of the Hopi mesas and the ancient cliff dwellers than it held archaeological details.

Fewkes made few records of what he found or what changes he made, omissions probably due at least partly to the lack of any standard method of stabilization at the time. He often resorted to fanciful reconstructions unsubstantiated by evidence of what the original building might have looked like. For example, at Cliff Palace he rebuilt the front left corner of the square "Painted Tower" at the dwelling's south end, seemingly without any concern for the building's original construction.

His reconstruction of Sun Temple, a ruin on Chapin Mesa opposite Cliff Palace, has been called "Fewkes' greatest enigma"[8] because later archaeologists found it so puzzling. At another ruin, he added a staircase where none had previously existed. Generations of archaeologists were forced to redo Fewkes's reconstructions based on their own guesswork about what he had constructed.

In an experiment that undoubtedly seemed sound at the time, but proved disastrous, Fewkes applied cement to the tops of walls. (The same technique would soon be tried by other archaeologists elsewhere in the Southwest.) The cement cracked and actually helped to channel the erosive water into the adobe and rock walls.

Fewkes's deep involvement in Indian ethnology and folklore led him into some mystical realms of experience. He wrote in some of his unpublished papers of his encounters with the "shades" of Indian spirits who, he said, sometimes spoke to him. Archaeological historians Robert and Florence Lister tell the story of this strange event: One summer evening Fewkes visited Sun Temple. Just after sunset he saw an apparition, which he later described as "an old man wearing the long abandoned kilt of a Pueblo priest." The vision spoke to Fewkes, saying:

> My ancient home for years is the great house now a ruin you call Aztec. ... This ancient pueblo, my former home, is being excavated and utensils and implements of my people are being brought to the attention of the world by an industrious and conscientious man of your race. I approve of his work.[9]

Fewkes must have interpreted this as referring to Earl Morris, a New Mexican archaeologist who was excavating at Aztec at that time. Twenty-five years after Fewkes worked at Cliff Palace, Morris would be entrusted with the job of stabilizing the Mesa Verde ruins once again, working with an expert field archaeologist, a local farmer named James Allen ("Al") Lancaster. Their task would involve repairing and redoing much of Fewkes's work.

I N 1934 the National Park Service recognized that Cliff Palace, by then known worldwide as the largest and most spectacular cliff dwelling in the American Southwest, again badly needed attention. After the first road onto the mesa-top park was completed in 1913, each year brought more tourists. In 1934–35 the park archaeologist recorded 21,842 visitors.[10] The mere vibrations of so many passing feet disturbed the ruin's fragile walls, many of which rested on terraces of soft fill and loosely packed rubble.

Natural forces—wind, freezing and thawing action, and burrowing animals—also took their toll. Moisture eroded and seeped into the adobe mortar, plaster, and porous sandstone blocks that made up the ruin walls. An ongoing worry was the unstable cave roof, which also was affected by moisture. Throughout Cliff Palace, there was a need for stones to be reset in walls, peeling surfaces removed and new plaster applied, shaky room walls braced, beams installed, and retaining walls built or reinforced.

An archaeologist from Santa Fe, Jesse Nusbaum, who had recently served as park supervisor, recommended Earl Morris for the job. Because he had stabilized Balcony House in 1910, Nusbaum knew just how difficult the task at Cliff Palace would be. At the time Nusbaum recommended him for the job, Morris was busy restoring the Great Kiva at Aztec National Monument in New Mexico, forty miles south of Mesa Verde.

Years later one famous archaeologist would remember, "Earl Morris was a bearcat for work."[11] In spite of this capacity for strenuous effort, Morris knew he would need extremely competent help if he were to continue operations at Aztec and also make the necessary stabilizations at Mesa Verde.

He wanted a man who could master the art of stabilization and then supervise the demanding and complex task of day-to-day work on ruins maintenance in his absence. By the 1930s, archaeological methods had emerged from the embryonic state of the Wetherill era and had outgrown their infancy, which marked Fewkes's early days at Mesa Verde. The architecture and artifacts characteristic of the Basketmaker and Pueblo cultures were better understood. Archaeologists now used methodical techniques to dig through the layers of debris and soil at prehistoric sites, and they kept careful records of the locations where artifacts were found. The man who helped Earl Morris would need to understand these excavation techniques.

Morris remembered Al Lancaster, the barrel-chested farmer he had met two years earlier at a dig at Lowry Ruin, thirty miles northwest of Mesa Verde. Lancaster's skillful work as foreman of the field crew had caught Morris's observant eye. He had demonstrated a homesteader's tenacity and grit, leadership, innate engineering skills, and two qualities in which he outshone virtually all other archaeologists for decades — a gift for accurate observation in the field combined with a highly developed memory.

The son of an unlettered Tennessee farmer, Lancaster had little time for formal schooling, though he managed to obtain an eighth-grade education. In 1919, when he was twenty-five, he moved with two brothers to the fertile Montezuma Valley in the flatland to the north and west of the Mesa Verde. Lancaster worked in the fields, did a bit of prospecting, and supplemented his income with manual jobs in the typical grueling battle fought by local farmers as they tried to make ends meet. He and his wife, Alice, lived near Pleasant View in a frame house that Lancaster built himself. Over the decades when her husband spent several months each year living at archaeological digs, Alice — a remarkable woman in her own right — plowed the beanfields, planted and harvested the crops, raised six children, served as the town's postmistress, and held a full-time job as a school teacher.

In some ways, Lancaster's background as a homesteader helped him develop his special archaeological skills. From his farmer's way of life he gained

Al Lancaster and his stabilization crew at their camp near Spring House, Mesa Verde, 1935.

an understanding of the long-vanished prehistoric Indians. Alden Hayes, a colleague who surveyed Wetherill Mesa on Mesa Verde with Lancaster, commented, "He knows how to think just like an Anasazi farmer."[12] Lancaster's highly observant eyes noticed changes in soil textures and traces of artifacts that textbook-trained archaeologists might miss. On site at a dig, he could spot the traces of a long-buried Basketmaker pithouse or Pueblo masonry wall, faintly outlined by indicators such as scattered stones and sherds on the surface. In her biography of Al and Alice Lancaster, Jenny Adams wrote, "His life experiences had left him with an uncanny ability to observe the smallest details and interpret them into workable definitions of prehistoric life."[13]

It was these valuable traits in the field that Earl Morris recognized. When Lancaster went to work for Morris at Mesa Verde, he was nearly forty. He proved adept at getting his crews of Indians and local farmers to work hard. His laconic orders in the field might begin, "Well, if it was me, I'd do it like this . . ."

Lancaster taught himself about the emerging science of archaeology, reading books when he had time, listening, and observing. Working with Morris at Cliff Palace and other Mesa Verde ruins in 1934 and 1935, he mastered masonry, the fundamentals of engineering, and stabilization techniques. Before that, he recalled five decades later, "I never put one rock on top of another."[14] Lancaster, Morris, and other pioneers in the field stabilized with hard, often visible, materials such as mortar, so ruins would hold up under visitors' wear and tear and the

Cliff Palace in winter.

erosive effects of moisture. They also rebuilt missing parts of structures, visualizing—based on their knowledge of prehistoric architecture—how the original must have looked. During the 1980s, theories of stabilization would change. Modern experts would switch to softer materials, such as adobe mud mixed to match the prehistoric masons' original material, and would aim to preserve the ruins without changing their appearance in any way.

Some of Morris and Lancaster's stabilization projects at Mesa Verde involved what one archaeologist termed "removal of Fewkes's eccentricities."[15] Morris carefully documented his work with "before and after" photographs and notes. At Cliff Palace, Morris and Lancaster gave special attention to the square structure known as "Speaker Chief's House," at the north end of the ruin, and to the four-story "Painted Tower" at the south end. The Painted Tower in Cliff Palace had been reconstructed by Fewkes, but Morris decided to redo the work. Inside the tower at the third-story level, a lovely, dark red, geometric design could still be seen on the cream-colored plaster. Lancaster and his crew "used white clay from McElmo Canyon and red ocher brought from Aztec by Morris to repaint the design,"[16] a series of triangles, lines, and dots.

A crack in the boulder on which Speaker Chief's House stood was jeopardizing the ruin. Lancaster brought in seventy tons of stone and cement and used these materials to build a foundation around steel I-beams and screw jacks that he placed underneath the boulder. Then the men built a masonry wall underneath the big rock to conceal their work.

Morris eventually moved on to other projects in archaeology, but Lancaster continued to work for the National Park Service at Mesa Verde, holding various titles but always carrying on his archaeological work—surveying, excavating, and stabilizing. He continued to develop the approach to stabilization that he began with Morris during the summer of 1934. Adams described his method:

> Every attempt was made to remain loyal to the aboriginal construction. Walls were rebuilt only when needed for retaining loose fill or for supporting other structures. Original building stone was reused until the supply was exhausted and then fresh stone was shaped to look aboriginal. Red adobe was packed into the joints and a thin coating was painted over the walls. As this aged, the new reconstruction was nearly indistinguishable from the ruined walls.[17]

When the Department of the Interior awarded Al Lancaster its Distinguished Service award in 1962, the document stated, "By 1934, his reputation as a master of ruins preservation was established." The citation continued, "Mr. Lancaster not only has developed unusual techniques to stabilize and preserve the classic treasures of prehistoric ruins in the Southwest, but he has also managed to excavate them so that they may be intelligently interpreted to the visiting public."[18]

As the decades passed, Lancaster helped to find, excavate, and develop many of the sites along the Ruins Road traveled by park visitors today. He also assisted several generations of archaeologists and their students. One of these archaeologists remembered the small hand tool for probing and uncovering surface remains that Lancaster carried with him everywhere: "Al had a little hand pick, all worn down over the centuries, and he'd take it out and quietly say, 'I'd like to do a little rootin' around over there and see if I can find a couple of wall corners.'"[19] Novices in fieldwork would watch in fascination as the sextogenarian's patient scratching at the hardpacked dirt gradually uncovered the tops of stones outlining a long-buried pueblo wall.

For many years after he retired from the Park Service in 1964, at the age of seventy, Lancaster went on working as a consultant, excavator, and stabilization specialist for archaeologists around the Southwest. Visitors to Cliff Palace today are witnessing one result of his years of dedicated work at the ruins of Mesa Verde.

Ruins of the mission church at Pecos,
New Mexico, c. 1915.

CHAPTER 2

PECOS PUEBLO

How A. V. Kidder Made Archaeological History

ARLY IN THE EXUBERANT TEENS of this century, two young men planted the seed of a historic archaeological expedition. On an all-day outing, Alfred Vincent Kidder and Kenneth M. Chapman visited the ruined pueblo of Pecos thirty miles southeast of Santa Fe, capital of New Mexico. Both Kidder and Chapman were to make major contributions to the sciences of archaeology and anthropology in the Southwest—Chapman as a scholar and authority on Pueblo pottery, and Kidder as one of the foremost American archaeologists of his time.

At Pecos Pueblo that day, they gathered broken pottery sherds strewn by the thousands among the rocks, wild verbena, and cactus overgrowing the ruin mounds. Beneath the mounds lay crumbled the remains of the pueblo's multistoried rock and mud dwellings.

The old pueblo stood at an elevation of seven thousand feet on a narrow, flat promontory, or *mesilla*, above the floor of the Pecos River valley—a spectacular spot set among steep-walled red mesas fringed with green stands of piñon and juniper. To the west, atop Glorieta Mesa, perched Las Escobas Peak; on the northern horizon rose the snow-edged rim of the Sangre de Cristo mountain range. The road that had once been the historic Santa Fe Trail passed by the mesilla's western side, winding from Pecos through the little settlement of Glorieta and on to Santa Fe. Only a few miles southwest and northwest of that modern town, ancient but still-inhabited Indian pueblos dotted the banks of the Rio Grande.

Serious archaeology had begun at the Pecos site before Kidder and Chapman's time, when Swiss-born ethnographer, archaeologist, linguist, and historian Adolph Bandelier explored the pueblo in 1880. His work was sponsored by the Archaeological Institute of America, an organization formed in 1879 to promote professional standards in the discipline. In 1881, the institute published Bandelier's report on the Pecos ruins and the surrounding valley.

The sherds Kidder collected on his outing with Chapman continued to intrigue the young archaeologist, and eventually led him to select Pecos Pueblo as the site of a major excavation. From the beginning, pottery was the key to Kidder's understanding of the pueblo's prehistory.

The fate of the Mesa Verde cliff dwellings in the late 1880s had underscored the need for archaeologists to investigate prehistoric Southwestern sites before they were ruined by treasure seekers. Stripped of its priceless artifacts before any archaeologist could thoroughly explore it, Cliff Palace at Mesa Verde symbolized the irreparable losses to science that occurred before the turn of the century and for years thereafter.

Urged on by many local citizens' groups and professional archaeologists, and especially by Dr. Edgar Lee Hewett, founder of the School of American Archaeology (now the School of American Research) in Santa Fe, Congress finally took action. In 1906 it passed the Preservation of American Antiquities Act. The act introduced a new era of preservation and scientific investigation at prehistoric sites in the Southwest by establishing a legal shield for sites on federal land.

In tandem with the move toward legislative protection of sites, universities and museums began training students in the most recent field methods of archaeology and anthropology. As a result, a fresh generation of professionals went into the field prepared to undertake major excavations and determined to make them "scientific."

A. V. ("Ted") Kidder's chance to dig at Pecos came in 1915 when, acting on advice from two of his graduate professors, Hiram Bingham of Yale and Roland B. Dixon of Harvard, the trustees of the Phillips Academy of Andover, Massachusetts, decided to sponsor long-term and thorough excavations at a Pueblo Indian site in the Southwest. Financial backing came from the Robert S. Peabody Foundation for Archaeology, formed in 1915 to support the new Department of Archaeology at the Phillips Academy.

The department appointed Kidder to lead the expedition, a choice also recommended by Dixon and Bingham. The previous year Kidder had received his doctorate from Harvard, becoming the first Ph.D. from an American university to write a dissertation based on Southwestern archaeology. By the time he received his degree Kidder had traveled widely, visiting archaeological sites in the Americas, Europe, and the Middle East. He had studied with several leading anthropologists and archaeologists of the day, including the Egyptologist George Reisner, who taught modern archaeological field techniques such as the systematic excavation method called "stratigraphy." In a class he took at Harvard with George Chase, Kidder had learned to analyze the designs and decorations on ancient Greek pottery.

Kidder chose Pecos Pueblo as the site for the Phillips Academy expedition. He first considered Aztec Ruins in northwestern New Mexico, but settled on Pecos because of its archaeological advantages: a very large trash deposit, a fascinating assortment of pottery, and its occupation in historic as well as prehistoric times.

Kidder believed that discoveries at Pecos might throw light on the prehistory of the entire Southwest. In those days, Kidder considered the Rio Grande a possible "avenue from Middle America into the Southwest"[1] along which corn, the mainstay agricultural plant in the New World, might have been introduced. Years after the Pecos Expedition, Kidder wrote that "the Pecos project was planned at a time when so little was known of southwestern archaeology that I believed it possible that the work might throw light on the origin of Pueblo culture."[2]

Of special interest was the potential for understanding what kind of connection existed among prehistoric settlements at Pecos and in the Galisteo Basin to the east and the Anasazi ruins along the Rio Grande. Kidder also wanted to know more about the relationship of the Pecos, Galisteo Basin, and Rio Grande pueblos to ruin sites to the northwest in the San Juan River drainage—sites that included the cliff dwellings at Mesa Verde, ruins in Monument Valley, and the massive structures at Chaco Canyon.

At Pecos, prehistoric Pueblo culture, Plains Indian activities, and Spanish and American history all mingled. The huge village, whose inhabitants were respected by the Spanish *conquistadores* for their military strength, stood at the entrance to a strategic pass through the mountains. Plains Indians came to trade with the pueblo's farmers and pitched their tipis just beyond the low rock wall surrounding the town.

By Kidder's time, scholars were bringing to light the pueblo's history during the Spanish period and the doleful story of the departure of the last inhabitants early in the nineteenth century. In 1540, when Coronado and his conquistadores ventured into *la tierra nueva* on their ever-more-desperate search for the fabled treasures of the Seven Cities of Cibola, they stopped at the pueblo, which impressed them with its size and fortifications. The Spanish called the town *Cicuye* (their mispronunciation of an Indian name).

During the next three centuries the Pecos people endured subservience to Spanish, and later Mexican, rule; raids by the Plains tribes; white man's diseases;

and internal strife—all of which extracted a heavy toll. A new wave of traders, explorers, and settlers—this time from the United States to the east—appeared at Pecos beginning in 1821, driving covered wagons over the Santa Fe Trail, which passed in the shadow of the pueblo. In 1838 the handful of surviving inhabitants of Pecos left their homes and moved west to join relatives at the pueblo of Jemez. Pecos Pueblo remained standing, an enormous, crumbling ghost town.

With so much prehistory and history lying beneath the surface of the Pecos site, the twenty-nine-year-old Kidder faced a monumental task. His nineteenth-century predecessors in the Southwest had focused less on formulating conclusions based on analysis of data than on collecting artifacts, studying living Indians, and speculating about their ancestors. Of necessity the goals of those expeditions included obtaining artifacts as compensatory "loot" for museums and private backers. Methodical fieldwork, analysis, and reporting of results were undernourished step-children of most expeditions.

A consequence of the lack of scientific method was that the dimension of time in Southwestern archaeology remained a mystery. No one had proof to verify any hypothesis about the age of Pecos or any other prehistoric Indian ruin of the Southwest. Defining the crucial factor of time became the challenge of Kidder and his generation of archaeologists in the field.

TED KIDDER'S CHARACTER and background suited him well for leadership in the next phase of the developing science of archaeology. His biographer, Richard B. Woodbury, wrote of the Phillips Academy trustees' decision, "The selection of Kidder was a vigorous expression of support to the new kind of archeology he represented, in contrast to the traditional excavation for the sake of collection."[3]

The son of a mining engineer with Bostonian roots, Kidder was born in Marquette, Michigan, in 1885. According to his colleague Gordon Willey, "Kidder's childhood and youth were extremely happy. One had only to listen to him tell of his early experiences to realize the warm and affectionate family atmosphere in which he grew up."[4]

Kidder was educated in Cambridge, Massachusetts, in Switzerland, and finally at Harvard, where he enrolled as a premedical student. Within two years, however, he had switched to a different course—archaeology. Later Kidder attributed his interest in that subject partly to "heredity" and partly to "conditioning."[5] As a boy, he enthusiastically read scientific reports his father received from the Smithsonian Institution, the National Museum, and the Bureau of Ethnology.

Kidder's career as an archaeological field worker began even before he graduated from college, during the summer of 1907, his junior year. Under the

Jesse L. Nusbaum (left) and A. V. Kidder above Spruce Tree House at Mesa Verde, 1908.

blazing Southwestern sun, he and two other Harvard students undertook a major project sponsored by pioneering archaeologist Edgar Lee Hewett. With virtually no training or guidance, the three young men made an exhausting, exhaustive, and fascinating survey of remote ruins in the Four Corners area of Utah, Colorado, and New Mexico. Kidder's companions were Sylvanus G. Morley, later an eminent Mayan archaeologist, and John Gould Fletcher, destined for a distinguished career as a poet and writer. Though Fletcher found he had no taste for the rigors of archaeology, Kidder and Morley were fascinated from the beginning. They formed a personal and professional friendship that became the nucleus of a group of men who directed Southwestern and Mesoamerican archaeological events in the 1910s, 1920s, and 1930s.

After that first summer in the Southwest, Kidder was "hooked" on the study of archaeology:

Kidder was one of the many men bred in the East who upon his first visit to the Southwest, in 1907, found himself under its spell. He was enthralled by its elemental exuberance, the incongruity of its young and old earth, its demands placed upon anyone who chose to be there at any season. Perhaps he could not have explained the appeal of the environment, but there is no doubt but that he could have stated the excitement he found in its archaeology.[6]

A few years later, in his doctoral thesis on prehistoric ceramics, Kidder included a chapter on the pottery he found while surveying New Mexico's Pajarito Plateau in the Jemez Mountains northwest of Santa Fe. In the thesis, which foreshadowed his contributions to archaeological method, Kidder moved into new intellectual territory:

> Kidder was formulating the basis for his analyses and synthesis of Southwestern archaeology, breaking with the tradition which looked upon all of the Southwestern ruins and their contents as fascinating relics of an undifferentiated, "far away and long ago" past and, instead, seeing them as unique expressions of different times and places in that past to be fitted together to tell a coherent history.[7]

The year that he received his doctorate, Kidder also made history in the field. During the summer of 1914, with Samuel Guernsey of Harvard's Peabody Museum, he investigated prehistoric rock shelters and pithouse remains in northeastern Arizona.

In the dry caves of the Kayenta/Monument Valley region, Kidder and Guernsey found many perishable yet wonderfully well-preserved artifacts, materials such as fiber, wood, and foodstuffs. In a report on investigations in another region, Kidder later described the state of preservation made possible by the dry cave environment: "One finds little things that bring back the ancient life with startling vividness ... a stirring stick still smeared with corn meal mush, a patched sandal, a cake of salt wrapped in corn husk."[8]

Kidder and Guernsey wrote landmark reports on their explorations, highly detailed descriptions of the habitations and artifacts of a prehistoric group whom Richard Wetherill and other Southwestern explorers had called "Basket People." (Decades earlier, the Wetherills and other early investigators of archaeological sites had found similar remains at pithouse ruins at Mesa Verde and in southeastern Utah.) The meticulousness and accuracy demonstrated in the Kidder and Guernsey writings evidenced the talent for scientific reporting that would make Kidder's later books archaeological classics.

Ann Axtell Morris, wife of archaeologist Earl H. Morris, later remembered young Ted Kidder as likeable, handsome, tall, and strong—"a Viking of a man."[9] Like the early mountain men and pioneers, archaeologists who were blessed with size, strength, and good health enjoyed a distinct advantage in the outback. It is no coincidence that several of Kidder's contemporaries, including archaeologists Morris and Jesse Nusbaum, were exceptionally strong physically. Kidder once wrote tongue-in-cheek of the two erroneous images of archaeologists conveyed in the media—"the hairy-chested and the hairy-chinned."[10]

Well-mannered and modest, educated into the Ivy League intelligentsia, Kidder personified the "gentleman archaeologist," a tradition that began in Europe, where interest in "antiquities" remained an upper-class pursuit. With Kidder's direction of the Pecos Expedition, Southwestern archaeology entered a golden era. Excavation took place in an expansive ambience of "relaxation, of freedom from pressure, of time illimitable, of unbounded opportunity for new discovery."[11]

Kidder's excavation, officially known as the Peabody Southwestern Expedition at Pecos, continued under sponsorship of the Phillips Academy from 1915 to 1929. World War I, in which Kidder served and saw combat, disrupted the fieldwork that had been planned for 1917–19.

Because the expedition lasted so long, it became a major chapter in Kidder's life and the lives of his family, who came out to live at the field site each summer. Kidder began working at Pecos fresh out of graduate school; by the time the excavations were completed, he was approaching middle age, his five children were growing up, and his scholarly career had entered mid-course.

Several of the archaeologists who contributed to the expedition at Pecos, including Carl E. Guthe, George C. Vaillant, and S. K. Lothrop, went on to successful careers in the discipline. Describing his professional crew, Kidder later wrote nostalgically, "Most of us were young and each us was working toward the common end of learning what we could of the forces that shape human destinies."[12]

The work crews at the dig included Hispanic Americans from the town of Pecos and surrounding areas, as well as some descendants of the Pecos Indians who built the pueblo. Among the crew was Gregorio Ruiz, son of Mariano Ruiz, who had worked for Adolph Bandelier.

Excavation began on a late spring day, June 6, 1915. In determining where to dig first, Kidder used old Spanish accounts describing the layout of the pueblo and the writings of Bandelier, as well as his own observations. The two largest buildings appeared to be the old pueblo at the northern end of the mesilla and, to the south, the seventeenth-century adobe church, built by the Pecos Indians under the direction of Spanish Franciscan missionaries.

The crumbling ruins of the church, whose mud bricks were dissolving in the elements, presented a special problem that Kidder dealt with by calling on an old friend, Jesse Nusbaum, whom he had met during his 1907 Southwestern adventure under Edgar Hewett, Kidder's former teacher. Hewett was then director of the Museum of New Mexico, which oversaw the Pecos ruins, and he arranged to have Nusbaum, an excellent carpenter, work on the badly needed stabilization and restoration of the mission church. Nusbaum later described his work routine at Pecos:

Altar steps of the mission ruin at Pecos during stabilization, 1915.

I started and went back and forth on my motorcycle. From the time the first homesteaders and squatters settled down the Pecos River, they pilfered timber for housing, sheds and corrals from the Pecos Mission. Its walls were rapidly crumbling and I put in concrete to slant it up and stabilize it.[13]

With Nusbaum handling the old mission, Kidder's main focus became the "North Pueblo." This ruin comprised the remains of a four- or five-story masonry apartment house called "the Quadrangle," which apparently was the structure that had impressed the early Spaniards with its size and defenses. Although the four-hundred- by two-hundred-foot ruin was their initial focus, the excavations took an unexpected turn when the pueblo's extensive trash heap, which Kidder had been eager to explore, yielded some dramatic finds.

Kidder knew that prehistoric Indians often buried their dead in "trash," which in Pueblo culture has sacred connotations because things that are used up are seen as returning to Mother Earth. Regarding Anasazi burial practices, one contemporary archaeologist commented that " 'trash' in one culture is not necessarily 'trash' in the same sense in another."[14] Because the graves contained pottery and other artifacts they revealed much about the prehistoric people, and the skeletal remains could be analyzed for clues to the population's life span, health, and diet.

Top: The Pecos ruin photographed from the air by Charles A. Lindbergh, 1929. Bottom: Pecos from the north, artist's reconstruction of the pueblo circa 1700 by Singleton Peabody Moorehead, published as figure 22 in "Pecos, New Mexico: Archaeological Notes" by A. V. Kidder (1958). The mission and convent are shown in the upper left.

On the surface, the very large rubbish deposit adjoining the main pueblo looked like a rock-strewn slope, extending out from the defensive wall on the east side of the mesilla for about a quarter-mile. Prehistoric inhabitants had tossed trash downwind over the embankment, and over time the debris had drifted into the gradually sloping deposit. As they dug into the deposit, Kidder's work crews turned up layers of decayed organic matter combined with wind-blown sand, charcoal and ash from prehistoric fires, and decomposed adobe mud. Like plums in a Christmas pudding, prehistoric artifacts were mixed in with the dirt.

The archaeologists were amazed when they discovered that the trash heap extended much further beneath the pueblo itself than they had expected. One section of the pueblo's defensive wall was actually built, not on solid ground as they originally thought, but on deep trash deposits. In fact, the trash came all the way up to the walls of the Quadrangle and turned out to be over twenty feet deep. Kidder wrote,

> We found that the whole broad terrace between the ruin-mound and the defense wall was made up of nothing but rubbish. ... We had learned early in the season that the refuse heap was very large, but this latest discovery showed that it was probably at least twice as extensive as ... estimated. This was the first of the long series of surprises which the Pecos work has furnished. Each one has proved the site to be vastly larger and more complex than had appeared from surface indications.[15]

Almost as soon as the workers' shovels penetrated the surface, a human skeleton came to light. This find was greeted with elation. Today, excavation of Native American burials is widely recognized as disrespectful, culturally discriminatory, and insensitive. But in Kidder's day, archaeologists considered burial excavation an essential part of the exploration of any Southwestern site. In fact, it was common archaeological practice worldwide.

After the discovery of the first burial, Kidder offered his workmen a cash reward for each additional burial unearthed. More than twenty burials had been found by the end of the week, and before long the number approached one hundred. Kidder had to rescind his offer of financial reward because, he later commented, the abundance of such finds threatened him with "bankruptcy."[16]

In all, during the first season the crews uncovered approximately two hundred burials. By the end of the expedition fourteen years later, the remains of more than nineteen hundred individuals had been found at Pecos, an especially high number compared to other sites in the Southwest.

During the 1920 season, Kidder invited physical anthropologist Earnest A. Hooton, of Harvard University's Peabody Museum, into the field at Pecos.

Hooton spent two months at the site, and a decade thereafter in his laboratory, examining and analyzing the skeletons. "Hooton's work there was one of the earlier examples of a physical anthropologist working alongside an archaeologist in the field."[17]

Including Hooton on the team was a step toward pan-scientific archaeology, an approach that remained important to Kidder throughout his career. "I still feel," Kidder said in an interview late in his life, "that the only way we are eventually going to get the real meat from archaeological work in terms of cultural development [is] by using … all the pertinent sciences … social and natural and environmental."[18]

The trash heap at Pecos offered more than burials and artifacts. Its undisturbed layers, deposited gradually over centuries, provided an excellent testing ground for Kidder's successful use of the then-innovative, now standard, field technique of stratigraphy.

American archaeologists of the day were familiar with the basic concept underlying stratigraphy, the idea of "superposition," which derived from the science of geology: The most recent material would be found on the top, and each underlying layer would represent an older deposition. Applying superposition to archaeology, the assumption was that objects found at lower levels predated artifacts found in upper layers. Excavators therefore dug carefully, making sure that layers remained clearly intact. They numbered each layer and labeled each artifact according to the layer from which it came. Thus, level by level, artifacts could be ordered from oldest to most recent.

The use of this method at Pecos marked the beginning of the period when Southwestern archaeologists began to grasp prehistoric time in terms of "relative chronology," in other words, what predated what. Because the upper levels of the site included metal objects, such as candlesticks, and other items that indicated historic times, chronological calculations could be made from recorded history back into prehistory.

Decades after Kidder's work at Pecos, archaeological commentator Walter Taylor wrote that the stratigraphic approach was perhaps "the most basic concept in the theoretical structure of the discipline."[19] Although the idea of sequential layering seems obvious now, in Kidder's time stratigraphic digging was regarded as an exciting experiment. Later archaeologists would refer to the "stratigraphic revolution" of Kidder's era, saying that the introduction of stratigraphy in the Southwest "initiated truly scientific archaeology in America."[20] Certainly without stratigraphy the study of prehistoric chronology in the Southwest would have no basis for precision.

The majority of nineteenth-century New World "antiquarians"—an ambiguous title that included archaeologists—supposed that prehistoric Southwestern Indian culture was not complex enough, nor had it lasted long enough, for stratigraphic efforts to be worthwhile. So, although archaeologists in Europe and the Mediterranean regions used the technique regularly, and a handful had tried it in the 1800s in the United States, at the turn of the century few American excavators bothered with it.

Then, just before Kidder began to work at Pecos, two archaeologists produced intriguing results with stratigraphy at New World sites. The pioneers were Manuel Gamio, who used the technique at excavations in the Valley of Mexico in 1911, and Nels C. Nelson, who applied it in the Galisteo Basin of New Mexico between 1912 and 1914.

Nelson's work marked a major scientific turning point in the Southwest. He later wrote to archaeological historian Richard Woodbury: "My chief inspiration to search for chronological evidence came from reading about European cave finds; from visiting several of the caves, seeing the levels marked off on the walls."[21] Woodbury described Nelson's work:

Digging a stratigraphic test.

When Nelson investigated the Galisteo Basin in the summer of 1912, one of his aims was the establishment of a chronology for the several types of ruins and numerous styles of pottery already familiar to those studying the ruins of the Rio Grande region.... None of the refuse mounds that were trenched in 1912 and 1913 fully satisfied him.... Late in the season of 1914 Nelson found a satisfactory deposit at Pueblo San Cristobal which showed no signs of disturbance in the 10-foot face that was cleared. He marked out a block 3 by 6 feet and dug it out in 1-foot levels, saving all the sherds encountered. Nelson comments that he did all the digging himself, not trusting to the care of his workmen. The sherds were classified into seven "types," each "sufficiently distinct" although admittedly arbitrary in definition; they were then counted and their numbers plotted by levels.[22]

Kidder followed Nelson's lead at Pecos. His workers used shovels to break ground and load "backdirt" into wheelbarrows, and spades to dig and then carefully smooth down, or "face," the sides of the trenches. The workmen created three-sided test columns in the earth, and the archaeologists then observed and marked stratigraphic layers in them. Unlike Nelson and other American excavators, Kidder defined the stratigraphic layers according to the natural layers appearing in the earth, rather than marking off the levels in arbitrary, uniform increments.

The archaeologists noted the positions of artifacts on a grid that they laid over the dig with numbered stakes, and on maps and plans of roomblocks, so that items could be located both vertically and horizontally—that is, in time and space. In creating this time/space framework for recording artifacts, the Pecos Expedition began to make scientific history.

Unlike modern-day archaeologists, who generally set out with a set of narrowly defined research questions to be answered and hypotheses to be tested, Kidder—like his contemporaries at other major excavations—began with an open mind, simply digging and carefully listing and describing everything he found. Right from the start, Kidder made detailed lists of his findings, which helped him begin to categorize the pottery and other artifacts. He proposed to gain knowledge of the vanished peoples of the Southwest by organizing, classifying, and comparing their "material culture," or artifacts, and their architecture.

Though he used stratigraphy in excavating all objects, Kidder paid particularly close attention when removing and recording pottery. Once organized and analyzed, the whole pots and hundreds of thousands of sherds gathered at the site began to tell the history of centuries of pottery making at Pecos Pueblo.

Above: Painted wooden ornament found c. 1915 in the Pecos mission ruins. At right: "Shelves of the workroom after a good day," a scrapbook photo from the Phillips Academy, Andover, excavations at Pecos.

The archaeologists bagged, boxed, and shipped tons of artifacts to the East for study during the winter months. While at the site, they also spent long evenings cleaning, classifying, and analyzing the finds. First, they examined each potsherd and matched it with others like it. Then Kidder, his wife, Madeleine, and his assistants detailed the attributes of the ceramics—their thickness, shape, decoration, color, and finish. The resulting categories showed how pottery had developed at Pecos over hundreds of years.

The Pecos potters had created a rich variety: plain cooking wares; early white-slipped pottery painted with black designs, called "black-on-white" by the archaeologists; and various glazed wares, including black-on-red, black-on-yellow, plain red, and polished black wares. These vessels were used for cooking and eating, and for carrying and storing food, water, and other necessities.

Eventually, Kidder and other archaeologists at the dig wrote extensive reports about the eight major categories of pottery found at Pecos. In his early conclusions, Kidder stated that

> work on these potsherds showed that there had been a steady and uninterrupted growth in the ceramic art of Pecos from the days of its founding down to the period of its abandonment in 1838. It was possible to establish eight major pottery types and to determine their exact chronological sequence, thus confirming and in many ways amplifying similar results then being obtained by Nelson at the ruins of the Galisteo basin a few miles to the west.[23]

Kidder later collaborated with ceramic analyst Anna O. Shepard, whose studies of the composition of clay and temper led him to conclude that early in their history the people of Pecos had imported pottery from the Santa Fe area, the Pajarito Plateau, and the Galisteo Basin. Kidder and Shepard summarized their findings in *The Pottery of Pecos, Volume II* (1936), presenting highly detailed analyses that superseded many earlier conclusions about the development of Pecos pottery. But it was the initial ceramic studies, done during the excavations, that permitted the identification of the relative chronological sequence of the ceramics.

This sequence provided the information needed for relative dating of artifacts and made it possible for Kidder to "cross-date" Pecos artifacts with those from other sites. A certain type of Rio Grande–style pottery found by Nelson in the Galisteo Basin, for example, could be compared with pottery found by Kidder at Pecos and dated as older, newer, or contemporary with it.

In addition to ceramics, Kidder's artifact lists contained immense quantities of other items removed from the trash and excavated blocks of rooms at Pecos. The archaeological cornucopia included household utensils such as *manos* and *metates* (hand grinding stones and grinding slabs); bone tools, such as knives, awls, and needles; arrowheads and hunting paraphernalia; bones of animals butchered for food; bits of clothing and sandals; hair brushes and personal objects; jewelry of turquoise, bone, and shell; bird bone flutes; and human skeletal remains and burial offerings from graves, including many whole pots, hundreds of clay pipes, and many human and animal effigies.

Using his observations of artifacts, and later of architecture, Kidder began to outline a sequence of changes in the way of life at Pecos over time. His findings showed that early explorers in the Rio Grande region of New Mexico, most notably Bandelier and Hewett, had been on the right track when they surmised that the Indian cultures there had, indeed, become more sophisticated and complex over time.

Eventually Kidder was able to compare and relate Pecos ceramics and architecture to those at other Southwestern sites. The prehistoric peoples of different geographic locations, it seemed, had different pottery styles, masonry, burial customs, and other distinctive traits. Based on their understanding of these traits, archaeologists created an overview of several prehistoric "culture areas" and defined the major cultural districts of the prehistoric Southwest. These districts were named after the river drainages: the Rio Grande, the San Juan, the Little Colorado, the Upper Gila, the Mimbres, and others.

Among these prehistoric culture districts, two of the most important were the San Juan district, which included the Chaco Canyon, Mesa Verde, and Kayenta ruins, and the Rio Grande area, encompassing Pecos Pueblo and the

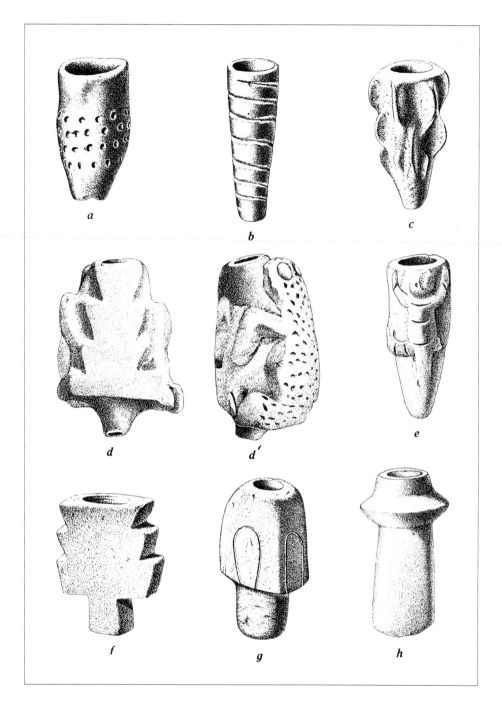

a

b

c

d

d'

e

f

g

h

"Pipes unusual in shape or decoration." This plate, showing objects excavated at Pecos Pueblo, originally appeared as figure 150 in A. V. Kidder's "The Artifacts of Pecos" (1932).

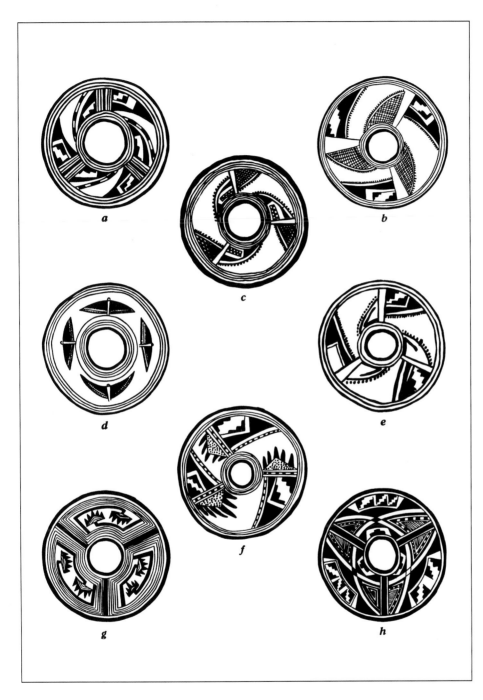

Bowl designs of the pottery type known as "Biscuit A." Figure 34 in Kidder's "The Pottery of Pecos," volume I, "The Dull-Paint Wares" (1931).

still-inhabited pueblos along the Rio Grande. The key concept explored by archaeologists became "relationships over time"—connections among artifacts, the various groups living throughout the prehistoric Southwest, and these peoples' patterns of settlement.

As the years passed, the Pecos expedition settled into its routine of camp life and archaeological work. For the Kidder family, Pecos was a glorious experience. "First, it was a grand place to be with kids," remembered Kidder.[24] Kidder's daughter Barbara remembered the family's home at Pecos: "Our house, our dear adobe house of three rooms front and three rooms back with a double sleeping porch to one side." At the beginning of each season, workmen pitched the expedition tents nearby, "in a remote corner of Forked Lightening Ranch," in the valley just south of the main pueblo ruins.[25]

Groceries, visitors, construction supplies, mail, and other necessities and niceties were brought to camp in "Old Blue," Kidder's trusty Model T. "It was a very famous car," Kidder remembered, on which Jesse Nusbaum had "painted on the back in large letters 'I do not choose to run in 1928.'"[26] Archaeologist Neil Judd later described Old Blue and its ilk:

> Its original floorboards had long since gone for fuel, but where Kidder wanted to go Old Blue found a way. . . . Model T's were everywhere in the 1920's. . . . Like Navaho sheep they stood well off the ground; they were designed to straddle high centers, to go where any other four-legged creature could go.[27]

At the dig the archaeologists, neatly dressed in business suits, made index cards with sketches and descriptions of each burial and wrote up their notes on each excavated room. Meanwhile, workmen with picks and shovels labored under the intense, high-altitude summer sun that turned them into bronzed athletes. They arrived at 7:00 A.M. to begin an eight-hour day for which they were paid $1.50. Horse-team drivers received double that daily wage.[28]

The archaeologists' family members were also put to work. Madeleine Kidder handled the enormous task of sorting the pottery sherds, which numbered in the hundreds of thousands. "I doubt if any other human being has handled so much broken pottery," Kidder wrote of his wife's efforts. "Her work required a thorough knowledge of types, an ability to judge as to what should be saved and what discarded, and a keen ceramic sense to recognize at a glance any sherd, no matter how small, which did not conform to local standards."[29]

Barbara Kidder remembered well her parents' daily work: "I loved watching the careful cleaning of a skeleton with pen knife and soft brush, Mother's hands fitting together fragments of a pot."[30] She recalled, too, evenings spent telling

Top left: Alfred Vincent ("Ted") Kidder, c. 1925, at the White House ruins at Canyon de Chelly. Top right: The four Kidder children at the Pecos mission church, 1924: Barbara, Randolph, Alfred II, Faith (in front of Randolph). At left: "Old Blue" and "Pecos Black," famous cars of the Pecos expedition, 1923.

Top: The 1924 excavation crew. Bottom: Crews at work at the Pecos excavation.

stories around the campfire, and afterward, "bedtime as the fire burned lower and the stars showed near enough to catch and the coyotes began their weird wild wonderful songs—the scent of juniper and piñon and the green grass that grew only under the eaves of the sleeping porch where the rain water fed it, and the moon and the quiet night."[31]

Kidder had planned to complete the expedition's work by 1922, but numerous unanticipated discoveries resulted in several seasons of additional digging. Excavating the many-storied stone and mud dwellings took years of patient, careful labor in crumbling and dangerous masonry.

There were major surprises during the second season of the dig. The North Terrace, a seemingly vacant area on the north side of the Quadrangle, was discovered to contain "forty rooms, a kiva, and no less than two hundred burials," Kidder wrote in 1924. "I believe ... that on the North Terrace lay the nucleus of the Pecos pueblo."[32] The buildings had not been constructed on bedrock, as the archaeologists had expected; instead, the top structures were "erected on the broken and tumbled walls of earlier houses, and ... these again had been built over at least two still more ancient ones."[33]

Slowly, a fascinating picture of many centuries of Indian life at Pecos emerged. Thanks to his meticulous stratigraphic records of the various types and styles of pottery at the pueblo, Kidder could date each architectural level according to its prevalent ceramic type. As the years passed, and in light of new scientific discoveries, analysis of the artifacts and architecture of Pecos led to conclusions somewhat different from those Kidder had first anticipated. New dating technologies indicated that building on the mesilla must have begun around the thirteenth century AD. The initial mesatop settlement on the North Terrace, which Kidder called "Black-on-white House" after its predominant style of pottery, was followed by construction of the multistoried Quadrangle, as people moved from earlier settlements in the valley to the mesilla's promontory, perhaps for defensive reasons.

Kidder used the chronology created from the pueblo's pottery to set relative dates for the architecture. Of the Quadrangle on the mesilla, he wrote: "The former straggling one-story community was pulled together, so to speak, during the first years of Glaze III. A compact, four-sided, multistoried pueblo was built around a spacious courtyard."[34]

The Quadrangle, the fortress pueblo described by the Spaniards, had apparently been built, not gradually like other parts of the pueblo, but in a very short period of time. Its construction date was eventually set at about 1400, an estimate still considered valid.

Danger threatened the expedition's workers as they cleared the Quadrangle rooms of their centuries-old fill. If not properly angled and reinforced, the freshly dug sides of the excavation trenches might collapse, smothering the workers in

A. V. Kidder (lower right) surveying trenches in the north midden at Pecos, 1915. Kidder is wearing a suit, as was customary for professional staff at the dig.

a deadly avalanche. Taking these perilous conditions and other factors into account, Kidder decided to content himself with only "a preview" of rooms in the Quadrangle.[35]

At times the archaeologists found the stratigraphy in the rooms in topsy-turvy disarray. Centuries before, the prehistoric occupants had dug in certain places—to bury their dead, or to remodel their homes. As a result, the oldest material sometimes lay on top, and the most recent on the bottom.

Kidder remarked in a later report that it was a good thing his staff had done their stratigraphic homework carefully while excavating the trash during the first season. "Without it," he wrote, "my colleagues and I would have been hard put to it to make any sense out of the horrible smash we had to deal with in the ruins."[36]

As the digging progressed, Kidder identified six architectural phases on the mesa top. He estimated that the multistoried Quadrangle and its neighbor, the "South Pueblo," had encompassed a total of about eleven hundred rooms. The Quadrangle alone had once comprised some 660 rooms, but his crews cleared only a small percentage of them.

Once excavations were completed, Kidder had the crews "backfill" the uncovered rooms. Refilling the rooms with the dirt that had been laboriously removed earlier left the ruin protected from the elements, as it had once been under the grass-covered and rock-strewn mound that nature had created over time. Like stratigraphy, backfilling became a standard procedure of professional archaeology.

When Kidder left Pecos, two-thirds of the ruin remained unexcavated. Nevertheless, at the time no other archaeological site in the Southwest had been so carefully and scientifically scrutinized.

Kidder's findings at Pecos inspired one of his lasting achievements, a volume titled *An Introduction to the Study of Southwestern Archaeology, with a Preliminary Account of the Excavations at Pecos,* published in 1924. It was "a book that was romantic but not ridiculous, scrupulously close to the facts but not a boring recital of them." [37]

The volume's introduction made a significant contribution to the growth of Southwestern archaeology as a science, and especially to the concept of Southwestern culture areas. Its synopses of the modern pueblos, their prehistoric counterparts, and the major prehistoric Southwestern cultural regions and groups have been used by every generation of archaeologists since its publication, and the study is still helpful to archaeologists today.

The Pecos expedition produced not only Kidder's classic but several other landmark reports. Earnest A. Hooton's monumental work, *The Indians of Pecos Pueblo: A Study of Their Skeletal Remains* (1930), traced the diseases, life expectancy, and demographics of the pueblo over time. Several other studies by scientists working with Kidder contributed significantly to ceramic analyses and ethnography.

In 1958, decades after the fieldwork had been completed, Kidder published his summary of the expedition's work, a thick volume with the modest title, *Pecos, New Mexico: Archaeological Notes.* Like his earlier works on Southwestern archaeology, *Archaeological Notes* remains a classic, exceptional in both scientific detail and literary style. Though the book was well received, Kidder felt it contained numerous shortcomings. In a review, his colleague Guthe wrote,

> Dr. Kidder, like all good archaeologists, suffers from a feeling of inadequacy—a conviction that the record should have been more complete. ... Yet the fact remains that it is a tremendous achievement to be able, after a lapse of thirty to forty years ... to incorporate in this report such a wealth of detail and significant factual data. [38]

Just a few years before the publication of *Archaeological Notes,* Southwestern archaeologists of the American Anthropological Association established the A. V. Kidder Award, presented every third year to one of their group "for eminence in the field of American archaeology." The award remains a symbol of professional respect for Kidder's achievements and contributions to the discipline.

Kidder had a few critics, chief among whom was an intellectually incisive iconoclast, Walter W. Taylor, who pointed out weaknesses in Kidder's descriptive reporting. In a 1948 publication, *A Study of Archeology,* Taylor debunked the work of the archaeologists of the early twentieth century as superficial and scientifically insubstantial. He argued that prehistoric cultures should be examined in terms of their "social processes" and organization, which he felt could be deduced from factors such as sizes of rooms, arrangement of roomblocks, and changes in pottery styles.

Though helpful to post–World War II archaeological thought, Taylor's comments seemed to some unnecessarily harsh. Many argued that he criticized early archaeologists without considering their work in historical context.

Archaeologist Watson Smith later described Taylor in his memoir:

I think that Walter Taylor was a very typical example of the angry young man in archaeology. Walter himself was a vivid, volatile person who had been a prisoner of war of the Germans, and it was always a puzzle to some that they let him survive because I am sure he was a very abrasive prisoner. Anyhow, the publication of this paper, which in some degree was indiscrete [*sic*] and brash because it named names, was sensational. It focused much of its criticism upon one of the most revered American archaeologists of all, Ted Kidder ... and it said almost in so many words that Kidder had really not carried out his scholarly obligations, and in effect pushed him aside as a fossil. I don't know whether Walter cared about this or not, maybe he did it on purpose. In any case, it did generate and point up very effectively the change that was rapidly occurring between the older generation and these new people.[39]

Some of Kidder's colleagues noted that the aging archaeologist appeared to have been deeply hurt by Taylor's critique, apparently viewing it as a personal attack that must have been backed by colleagues whom Kidder had trusted.

Taylor's work marked the beginning of a new era of controversy, change, and increasing sophistication in the intellectual development of archaeology. One unfortunate byproduct of this shift was that attributes Kidder displayed, such as modesty, good manners, and kindliness toward colleagues, seemed sometimes old-fashioned to younger scientists trying to make their mark in an increasingly competitive discipline. Nevertheless, Taylor did write in *A Study of Archeology* — along with his detracting comments — that Kidder was "the most influential exponent of the discipline active in the Western Hemisphere today."[40]

Among his many contributions to archaeology, Kidder led the effort to communicate and synthesize knowledge being gathered by his geographically dispersed colleagues. At the time that he entered the Southwest, its archaeological community was a small, far-flung cadre of explorers, who knew each other at least by reputation, and usually were personally acquainted.

An informal get-together that took place at Pecos from August 29 to September 2, 1927, became an enduring tradition in Southwestern archaeology. At Kidder's invitation, some forty archaeologists from all over the Southwest gathered at the Pecos camp to talk about their discoveries, setbacks, puzzlements, and challenges. Among the participants were numerous contributors to pioneering archaeology in the Southwest, including Byron Cummings, Emil Haury, Earl Morris, Frank H. H. Roberts, Odd Halseth, Burton and Harriet Cosgrove, Harold Colton, Paul S. Martin, and E. B. Renaud. As Martin wrote, "It was an historic event—unique, informal, and greatly inspired and influenced by Kidder's guidance and leadership—qualities that were strong but not tyrannical. Kidder never insisted on his point of view although he freely gave of his profound experiences."[41]

The atmosphere of that first Pecos conference blended levity with intellectual intensity. Besides enjoying each other's company, and exchanging notes and anecdotes, the participants found time to create a major archaeological breakthrough, the so-called Pecos Classification, which defined the prehistoric cultural periods that are still widely used in Southwestern archaeology today.

The first Pecos Conference, 1927.

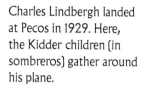

Charles Lindbergh landed at Pecos in 1929. Here, the Kidder children (in sombreros) gather around his plane.

The classification divided a thousand years of ancient human life into eight cultural periods, each with distinct characteristics. The periods were Basketmaker I, II, and III and Pueblo I, II, III, IV, and V, which referred to the prehistoric peoples called by early explorers "Basket People" and "Cliff Dwellers." (The Quadrangle at Pecos belonged to the last prehistoric period, called Pueblo IV.) The Pecos Classification may not have been the first effort to systematize archaeological knowledge, but it was the most comprehensive, usable, and enduring.

The archaeologists at the Pecos Conference also took note of a discovery in northeastern New Mexico in 1926 that extended the reach of their science much farther back in time than the early Basketmakers. Near Folsom, a cowboy named George McJunkins had come upon a prehistoric "kill site" left by ancient hunters. It contained ancient bison bones and uniquely shaped spearheads, or "projectile points." Later scientific investigation by the Denver Museum and by visiting scholars, including Kidder, confirmed that this site had been visited by human hunters probably about ten thousand years ago. The antiquity of humans in the Americas was established, and the Paleoindian period of prehistory was introduced to archaeologists.

In 1929, a second Pecos Conference was held, during which archaeologists glimpsed the technological future of the discipline when they viewed aerial photographs of Southwestern archaeological sites. The images were made at Kidder's suggestion by world-famous aviator Charles Lindbergh, who visited the Pecos site with his wife, Anne, that year. Lindbergh's work presaged coming decades in which aerial photography and, eventually, infrared remote sensing technology would provide detailed data on sites from the air.

It was not only aviators who brought news of scientific progress to those attending the second Pecos Conference. Dr. Andrew Ellicott (usually called "A. E.") Douglass, an astronomer, discussed his monumental discovery in dendrochronology, or tree-ring dating. Using a find of prehistoric wood made near Show Low, Arizona, Douglass had joined an already known prehistoric sequence of tree-rings with the modern tree-ring continuum. This breakthrough marked the beginning of absolute, or chronologically precise, dating of ruins in the Southwest.

The discoveries reported at the 1929 conference left participants with a heady sense of achievement. But a few weeks later, the efflorescent period of hope and expansion in archaeology—and in the nation as a whole—came to an end, as financial disaster hit with the stock market crash. That year also marked the end of Kidder's career in the Southwest. Kidder had signed on to work for the Carnegie Institution and moved to the East Coast. Though he devoted the remainder of his career to understanding the prehistoric Maya Indians and to administrative work at the Carnegie, toward the end of his life Kidder wrote that these pursuits had never replaced the prehistoric Indians of Pecos in his affections.

Excavations at Aztec Ruin, showing the
center and east parts of the north wing.

CHAPTER 3

AZTEC RUIN

Earl Morris Reconstructs
the Anasazi Past

I N 1911 a slender, dark-haired young man with an intense gaze boarded a
train in southern Colorado for a journey that would change the direction
of his life. On that train ride Earl Halstead Morris, then a college student,
met Edgar Lee Hewett, one of the leading archaeologists of the day.

Hewett was a controversial and influential figure, known as an institutional empire builder, teacher, lecturer, and legislative activist who had
been a driving force behind the Antiquities Act of 1906. He was the head of
two recently founded institutions in the territorial capital of Santa Fe—the
School of American Archaeology (later the School of American Research)
and the Museum of New Mexico. From Santa Fe he traveled widely, popu-
larizing the new sciences of anthropology and archaeology, and zealously
spreading the word about the need to preserve the Southwest's archaeological sites. Known by nicknames ranging from "Daddy" to "the Boss"
to "El Toro" (the bull), Hewett made at least as many enemies as he did
friends.

Some found Hewett offensively autocratic—and also slapdash in his
archaeological methods. Yet students flocked to his archaeological field
schools at the ruin of Tyuonyi, now part of Bandelier National Monument
near Santa Fe.

Soon after their first meeting, Earl Morris became Hewett's student
and thus joined a cadre of talented young people who began their careers

under the well-known archaeologist. Several of Morris's fellow students became his lifelong friends and colleagues, including A. V. Kidder, Neil Judd, and Sylvanus Morley. In the years before, during, and after World War I, these four men emerged as leaders in Southwestern archaeology. Morley expanded his activities to include prehistoric Mayan sites in Mesoamerica. Kidder, Morris, and Judd explored vast portions of the Southwest in some of the most extensive and ambitious excavations ever undertaken there.

Born in Chama, New Mexico, in 1889, Morris contributed to the circle of budding archaeologists the perspective of a native Southwesterner. His biographer, Robert H. Lister, wrote: "Earl was one of the few homegrown diggers with the training and inclination to push forward regional archaeology."[1]

Morris had begun digging artifacts at the age of three alongside his father, Scott Morris. Aztec Ruin, virtually in the Morrises' backyard near Farmington, New Mexico, was the largest of the dozens of prehistoric sites scattered up and down the Animas River in northwestern New Mexico.

Located on the west bank of the Animas about fourteen miles above its confluence with the San Juan, Aztec Ruin stood at an elevation of fifty-seven hundred feet on flat land surrounded by sand and clay hills. By the late 1800s, settlers had planted fields and apple orchards in the rich riverbottom soil around several ruin mounds, including a large, rectangular one, covered with overgrowth, which was called the "West Ruin." It covered over one hundred thousand square feet and encompassed more than four hundred rooms and nearly thirty kivas (though no one knew these numbers until after the pueblo was excavated).

The West Ruin faced southeast, with a three-story "north section" at the back, and wings of rooms extending along the west and east sides of a central plaza—a layout resembling the Chetro Ketl ruin at Chaco Canyon. The architecture was adobe and sandstone, which prehistoric masons had shaped into tabular building blocks. Ceiling entrances in the bottom-story rooms suggested to some a defensive design.

The prehistoric people had apparently chosen the site for its fertile, well-watered location. In summer the perennially flowing river gushed between banks shaded with willows and cottonwoods. Grasses and wildflowers grew knee-high, providing cover for birds and small game. The pueblo dwellers used the good river-terrace land to grow their crops of corn, beans, and squash, employing dry farming methods and also irrigating their crops with river water.

Nineteenth-century farmers also found the site appealing. Around 1876, settlers moving into the lower Animas River valley began exploring the many large ruin mounds in the flatlands along the river. They favored one spot for Sunday afternoon picnicking and digging for artifacts, a pastime later viewed as destructive pothunting, but then still classed as a harmless amusement. They named their favorite locale "Aztec Ruin," after the people they mistakenly believed had constructed the ancient buildings.

Reports by several early explorers had already put Aztec Ruin on the scientific map. In 1859 geologist John S. Newberry visited and later described the ruin's impressive walls, some of which rose to twenty-nine feet. Descriptions of Aztec Ruin attracted Lewis Henry Morgan, a scholar closely identified with the founding of American anthropology, who visited in 1878, accompanied by two grandnephews and two other students. The first anthropologist known to have visited the site, Morgan subsequently wrote eloquently about his exploration of the ruin, as did his grandnephew and student, William Fellowes Morgan.

In 1892 a party from the Phillips Academy of Andover, Massachusetts, which later sponsored Kidder's expedition to Pecos, surveyed the Aztec Ruin. In 1903 a visit was paid by Dr. T. Mitchell Prudden, who had explored archaeological ruins with the Wetherill brothers at Mesa Verde and elsewhere for years. Like Morgan, Prudden recognized the scientific potential of the ruins.

E ARL MORRIS GRADUATED FROM HIGH SCHOOL in Farmington in 1908 and enrolled as a psychology major at the University of Colorado at Boulder. He received a bachelor of arts degree there, and then a master's degree, also in psychology, in 1915. During those college years, he continued the archaeological explorations he had begun as a small child.

Aztec Ruin before excavation.

One of Morris's first professional archaeological opportunities came from Hewett, who enabled him to participate in excavations at a Maya site in Quirigua, Guatemala. Morris's involvement, as head of the last School of American Archaeology expedition to Quirigua, ended in 1914.

In 1913, also upon Hewett's recommendation, the University of Colorado funded Morris to dig at sites in the La Plata region of southwestern Colorado. Morris wrote:

> For years I had been gathering from stockmen who were familiar with the region, rumors of many small ruins in the mesa country between the La Plata River and Mancos Canyon, in Montezuma and La Plata Counties, southwestern Colorado. From these reports I believed that the district would well repay investigation, an opinion which was amply confirmed by the first brief season of field work. As a result the appropriation for 1914 was expended in continuing investigations begun the previous year.[2]

The La Plata work formed a foundation for a lifelong career of exploration and excavation in the Four Corners region. Morris would leave a pioneering archaeological imprint there, just as his friend Kidder did in the Rio Grande area.

Late in 1915, Scandinavian archaeologist Nels Nelson of the American Museum of Natural History came to have a look at Aztec Ruin. Earlier, Nelson had befriended young Morris, who was recommended to him by Hewett to help with a summer survey and ongoing stratigraphic work in the Galisteo Basin near Pecos Pueblo in New Mexico.

After examining the Aztec Ruin, Nelson returned to his post in the museum's Department of Anthropology. There he convinced administrators, including the museum's president, Henry Fairfield Osborn, and its director, Clark Wissler, of the value of "systematic exploration"[3] of the Aztec site. Nelson recommended Morris to direct the dig. Institutional wheels turned, and in the summer of 1916 the twenty-seven-year-old Morris found himself in charge of one of the region's major long-term excavations. Among the funders of the American Museum's Aztec expedition were Archer M. Huntington, heir to the Southern Pacific Railroad fortune, and financier J. P. Morgan.

Throughout the excavation Morris not only directed the digging but served as the only trained archaeologist, working mostly without professional assistance. His approach differed from the "expedition attitude"[4] typical of transplanted Easterners digging in the Southwest at the time. Aztec became his home, not just a place to visit during the summer field seasons. In 1920 he built a small house near the southwest corner of the ruins, and brought his mother there to

From left: Edgar Lee Hewett, 1912; Earl H. Morris; Nels Nelson.

live with him. Morris's goal was to uncover the entire pueblo and find out every-thing he could about it, rather than to fill in the gaps in a preconceived picture of the archaeological Southwest, as expeditionary archaeologists sometimes did.[5]

For Morris, his work at Aztec was an outgrowth of the lifestyle of his family and the neighbors with whom he had grown up. His crews were mostly Anglo farm people, some of whom he had known since his boyhood. "He had a group of local people," explained Lister, "the practical kind of people that he liked."[6]

Two of these men worked faithfully with Morris not only at Aztec but also on his later explorations in the Southwest. Oley Owens and Oscar Tatman were natives of the Aztec vicinity, and like Morris, hard workers who took an ener-getic, do-it-yourself approach to the problems of excavation. Earl's first wife, Ann, remembered that "Earl and Oley in the course of their checkered careers had acquired the art of stone masonry—which is just one of the hundred and seven professions an archaeologist should have at his fingertips."[7] She added, "Neither man knows what leisurely labor means."[8]

Among the adventures that Oscar and Oley shared with the Morrises, Ann recalled the men's excitement upon finding caches of artifacts: "Success takes men differently. Among Earl's most faithful diggers, Oley grimly snorts 'Got him!' Oscar yelps, and his son Omer tells his father, who paternally yelps for him. Earl himself just looks pleased, but so very pleased that you can read his pleasure all the way from his ankles to the back of his neck."[9]

On many of his archaeological explorations Morris drove an automobile known as "Old Black," a counterpart to Kidder's legendary Old Blue. Neil Judd remembered that the car, like Morris, would keep going no matter what: "Far out among the Lukachukai Mountains one day the dry sand proved too much, and Old Black burned out a bearing. Morris contemplated his predicament overnight and then replaced the bearing with a square of bacon rind and so finished the season. You don't get bacon rind like that any more!"[10]

Eventually Morris became one of the leaders of an informal group of "archaeologists, geologists, ethnologists, Park Service personnel, foresters, Indian agents, traders, [and] ranchers"[11] working in the Southwest. Archaeologist Watson Smith wrote that these people formed a "subculture." They "knew one another, either directly or by reputation and hearsay, and ... shared a community of interest based on their concerns with the country itself."[12] The group was forging an understanding of the roots of the Southwestern land, history, culture, and prehistory.

In the years after his Aztec work, as archaeology became increasingly scientific, Morris's rather freewheeling approach to exploration was often criticized, mainly because of habits formed during boyhood days of digging with his father. The Morris family lived the hard existence faced by many New Mexico settlers in the 1890s, moving frequently in search of employment for Earl's father. The boy grew up in mining camps and on homesteads where men had to build, repair, and invent everything from wagon wheels, to mining equipment, to irrigation systems. These experiences taught him much about self-reliance, independence, and long, hard days of physical labor.

In his spare time, the elder Morris took his young son exploring and hunting for Indian artifacts. Father and son dug without any scientific method, in keeping with the accepted custom of the time and place. These happy experiences with his father became all the more important to Earl Morris because of a great loss he suffered at the age of fifteen. In December 1904, a business associate shot and killed Scott Morris during an argument. Lister spoke of the impact of the killing on Earl:

> Earl and his mother became recluses after that event. I think it colored the rest of Earl's life.... He swore to kill the man who had killed his father. He wrote to me one time that he was on a hill watching this guy [the murderer].... [Earl] had found out where he was, and he had a rifle, and he had this man in the sight of his rifle.[13]

Morris held the man for a few heartbeats in the sight, but in the end, he told Lister, "I couldn't kill him." Still, to the end of his days Morris could not bear to hear the mention of the murderer's name.

Of Earl's lifelong habit of solitary roaming and digging for pots, Lister commented that it provided psychological relief, taking him back to happy childhood times spent with his father. "In truth, however, this digging was both a physical and emotional escape for Earl, a carry-over from his boyhood. Unquestionably, it was pothunting. However, nearly all the pieces recovered in this way were given to some scientific institution where they could be studied by anyone who desired to do so."[14]

Over the years, as a result of his wide-ranging digging, Morris created a collection of Basketmaker and Pueblo pottery that was an achievement in itself. Today, the Earl H. Morris Memorial Pottery Collection at the University of Colorado Museum at Boulder is still used by scholars for "comparative and innovative research."[15] Among the items in the collection is a prehistoric black-on-white ladle that Morris recovered while digging with his father at the age of three.

DURING THE PERIOD 1916–1921, when Morris excavated Aztec Ruin for the American Museum, he faced difficulties brought about by World War I, money shortages, and demands for higher wages from his crews. The initial budget estimate of seventy-five hundred dollars for the entire project proved completely unrealistic. Several thousand dollars were spent each season on everything from picks and shovels, to oats for horses, to payment for the work crews. Besides the administrative difficulties, the excavations themselves posed unique challenges.

During the first season, which did not begin until July 1916, large stands of thorny, densely tangled chico bush had to be burned to clear vegetation from the ruins. Pothunters had worked their way through the brush to a few isolated spots where they had left holes in the ruin, but for the most part the undergrowth had helped protect the mounds.

Aztec's private owners wished to preserve the ancient pueblo. In 1889, John R. Koontz, owner of the site, instituted a policy of keeping pothunting diggers out, and when H. D. Abrams purchased the land in 1907 he continued that approach. Abrams's sense of responsibility for the ruins was such that, while agreeing to let the American Museum excavate the ruins, he insisted that a collection of recovered artifacts be left at the site, rather than shipped back East.[16]

Though there were several mounds at Aztec, the expedition focused on the main one, the West Ruin. It presented a sort of archaeological jigsaw puzzle, with pieces indicating that two different cultural groups had lived there. Initial inspections of pottery and architecture hinted at connections with the Mesa Verde culture. Morris also anticipated that he might encounter Chacoan material, since the ruins at Chaco Canyon lay only sixty-five miles to the south. He did, in fact, eventually find evidence of such a connection. Many walls at Aztec, with their core and veneer masonry, looked as if Chacoan masons had built them. Morris wrote:

Top: Ann Morris (left) with Earl Morris, their daughters, and a nanny, c. 1935.
Bottom: Earl Morris (center front) with his work crew at Aztec.

There is no satisfactory building stone within miles of Aztec.... There are no thin laminated deposits whatever. To have shaped material thus either refractory or poor into walls of the excellence of many of the Aztec Ruin would have necessitated craftsmanship equally as good as any displayed in the walls of the ruins of the Chaco.[17]

The question at Aztec Ruin became: Did the Chacoan and Mesa Verdean occupations occur simultaneously, or were they completely separate from one another?

To serve as an advisor during the first season, Morris's mentor Nels Nelson arrived, fresh from consultations at Zuni, where Leslie Spier was completing a history-making analysis of ancient ceramics. Nelson had a strong influence on Morris, advising him on methods of stratigraphic excavation that could be applied to the Aztec digging. Morris viewed stratigraphy as the key to understanding the sequence of occupation by the Chaco and Mesa Verde groups.

Nelson suggested that Morris start with an exploratory trench, dug from the southeastern part of the ruin "toward the deeper mounds along the north side."[18]

In July, expedition work began at the southeastern corner of the West Ruin house complex itself. Morris probably was disappointed that his pothunting instincts were held in check while Nelson undertook to trench the seven-foot-deep deposits of the southeast refuse dump. Nelson hoped to establish a relevant chronology through stratigraphic analysis, wherein older materials, if undisturbed, were beneath more recent deposits.[19]

During this endeavor, Morris began training his crews in both digging techniques and ruins stabilization, which he was literally inventing as he went along. Stabilization work included repairing the crumbling walls and pouring a cement slab to protect a roof from moisture.[20]

The main tools of excavation were picks, shovels, and screens.[21] Morris also used not only the mainstay of the archaeologist's tool kit, the trowel, but many improvised implements as well. He regarded archaeology as an art, and of the archaeologist's tools he wrote, "There are almost as many different kinds of picks and shovels as there are of artists' brushes, and each one is shaped for a definite and specific use.... And if ever the touch of the master is needed, it is in archaeological excavation."[22]

That first season, excavators also worked on the south side and the east wing of the pueblo. Three kivas were cleared that season. One of the most interesting features at the site, a sunken circular area in the southwest section of the plaza, was left alone, though it looked promisingly like the so-called "Great Kivas"

Top: Excavations in the east wing of Aztec Ruin. Bottom: Corrugated pot in situ in room A-14 at Aztec.

which had been noted in early excavations at the Pueblo Bonito ruin in Chaco Canyon.

The administrators at the American Museum were satisfied with Morris's 1916 efforts: "The combined results...were sufficiently substantive to assure continuation of the work the next summer. In Wissler's view, the excavation and restoration of the Aztec Ruin would be a noteworthy monument to the American Museum of Natural History."[23]

After excavating during the summer of 1916 Morris returned to Columbia University, where he was working on a doctorate, an undertaking he never completed. To pay for that winter's studies, he "sold the museum a collection of San Juan pottery, which he and his father had acquired over many years of digging."[24]

The summer of 1917 marked the first full season of excavations at Aztec. In the spring of that year, the United States entered World War I, and a pall was cast on the dig. Morris himself was eligible for the draft, though in the end he did not have to serve.

The crews began uncovering burials this season, an activity that Morris had been eager to begin because of the amount of artifacts he knew he would find in association with the graves. In the east wing, where Chacoan masonry had been found, the crews dug in thirty rooms. The finds helped Morris revise his original ideas about the site. Previously, he had thought that two groups might have lived in segregated but contemporary enclaves. Now, on the basis of stratigraphic evidence that helped him to analyze the time sequence of architecture and ceramics, Morris arrived at some new, tentative conclusions.

> Applying the Nelson stratigraphic principles, Morris concluded that Chacoans had come and gone before Mesa Verdians [sic] moved in. The interval between the two occupations must have been substantial in order for the large volume of trash to have accumulated. With only four rooms thus far studied with demonstrable layered deposits of what appeared to be Chacoan material below Mesa Verde material, Morris admitted the evidence remained inconclusive.[25]

The year 1918 marked Morris's largest-scale excavations. It also brought him an increasing number of administrative problems, irritations caused by his sponsors, and excavation challenges.

Because his crews complained, he raised their wages from $2.00 to $2.50 a day; he was then criticized for drawing men away from the important wartime harvest work. The secretary of the San Juan Council of Defense and the county agricultural agent "lodged a protest with the American Museum over the $2.50 daily wage that was being paid laborers at the site." They argued that the wage

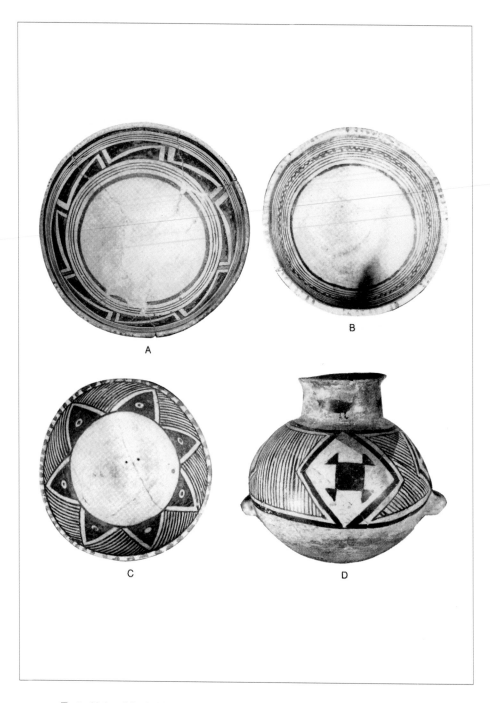

Typical Mesa Verde black-on-white ware from Aztec Ruin. From "Aztec Ruins on the Animas: Excavated, Preserved, and Interpreted" by Robert H. Lister and Florence C. Lister (1987).

Decorated interiors of bowls excavated from Aztec Ruin. Figures 63 and 64 in "Notes on Excavations in the Aztec Ruin" by Earl H. Morris (1928).

was so much higher than the local going rate that it "lured farm hands away from activities, such as haying, which were essential to the war effort." [26]

Finding himself the subject of a major local controversy, Morris had to make it publicly clear that none of his men would let their work at the dig interfere with farmers' needs for them as harvest laborers. A visitor reported that Morris also wisely hired the son of the local sheriff, who had been part of the opposition.

Meanwhile the American Museum, without notifying Morris, sent B. Talbot Babbitt Hyde, one of the heirs to the Babbitt soap fortune, to work with him at Aztec. Talbot Hyde and his brother Fred had backed earlier archaeological explorations at Pueblo Bonito in Chaco Canyon and elsewhere. Hyde, an Easterner born to wealth, and Morris, a Westerner imbued with a pioneer's independent spirit, clashed on various points of administration and excavation. "Hyde acted as sort of a spy," Lister explained, by informing the museum that "Earl wasn't doing it right. He [spent] more time putting pots together than ... writing reports." [27] In fact, Morris was the excavation's Jack-of-all-trades, supervising and digging during the day, and performing dozens of other tasks in his so-called leisure time.

In 1918 Morris began excavation at the back of the pueblo, the north wing where the walls stood tallest and the fill was deepest.

> At the end of the effort, Morris described the [north wing] excavation as the most difficult of his experience. The earth's crust was as hard as the masonry stones, and beneath it was a mass of stone, fallen timbers, and dust in which was blended a filthy amalgam of decayed and desiccated snakes, badgers, and rats. Worse [sic] of all was the miserable condition of bulging, cracking, and distorted walls. All the unpleasant fill had to be removed in order to reach floor level of the first story. [28]

Ceramics that Morris designated "archaic" (later identified in the Pecos Classification as late Basketmaker or early Pueblo) turned up in a northeastern area. These added another dimension to the pueblo's gradually emerging history, indicating habitation before the time when the Chaco-like walls were built.

With the encouragement of his mentor, Clark Wissler, Morris maintained a relationship with astronomer A. E. Douglass. When Morris and Douglass first met, the astronomer was devising a system for precise dating of prehistoric ruins using tree-ring samples taken from ancient wood found at archaeological digs. In 1918 Morris sent Douglass some wood specimens from Aztec Ruin, and the following year Douglass visited the excavation:

> Douglass's trip to the Aztec ruins in New Mexico in August of 1919 led to a significant change in the collection of archaeological beam speci-

mens. The Aztec sections previously examined had come from a pile of loose timbers, giving no indication of their original source. Douglass recognized that the location of the samples in the ruins would provide important information both for his own work with tree-ring chronologies and for archaeologists' desire to date the site. To this end, Douglass and his colleagues began using an instrument which bored into prehistoric beams *in situ* and obtained tubular cores one inch in diameter. These samples provided accurate ring records without sacrificing the structural integrity of the ruin.[29]

It was Morris who invented the tool that improved the quality of the core samples, and his work paid off richly. Shortly after the end of the 1919 season, Douglass sent Morris remarkable news. Though he still had only a relative time line, Douglass was now able to provide comparative dates for timbers from both Aztec and Pueblo Bonito at Chaco. The core samples indicated that the Chaco ruins predated Aztec by forty-five years. This finding helped Morris in his effort to visualize the sequence of occupations at Aztec.

During the seasons of 1919 through 1921, Morris began to organize his copious notes and to catalog materials and photographs. The number of tasks facing him as the only professional archaeologist on staff grew. But while the workload remained immense, his budget was reduced, as the American Museum began to wind down its support of the expedition. Diggers continued to explore areas of the north, south, and east wings. Entering the previously untouched west wing, they found, in just a few rooms, a large number of burials accompanied by Mesa Verde pottery.

Important finds also turned up in the courtyard. Early in 1921, excavations in two kivas, identified as "P" and "Q," revealed abundant Chacoan remains below Mesa Verdean artifacts. These superimposed kivas reinforced Morris's belief that Chacoan people had been the first to live at Aztec and were followed, after an interval, by a Mesa Verde group. In the spring, Morris found more Chacoan artifacts beneath the courtyard's hardpacked surface. His finds "showed Morris that from the beginning of explorations at Aztec Ruin he should have looked for superimposition in the courtyard. ... Diagnostic potsherds scattered at lowest depths further convinced the young archeologist that Chacoans had been there first and for a considerable interval."[30]

In February 1921, work started on the Great Kiva, no doubt spurred on by Morris's competitive spirit. He had known since beginning the excavations that the depression on the southwestern side of the plaza quite likely was a kiva similar in size to the Great Kivas at Pueblo Bonito. The news that his friend and colleague Neil Judd was considering excavating another such structure at Bonito in the summer of 1921 impelled Morris to uncover "his" feature first.

The Great Kiva at Aztec, like those at Chaco, was an example of large, elaborate, ceremonial architecture. With an inside diameter of forty-one feet, its many remarkable features included four massive, roof-supporting columns; two large, vaultlike pits in the center of the circular underground room; and a series of fourteen raised alcoves around the central chamber. Because it was surrounded by well-developed remains of Chacoan habitation, Morris was reasonably certain that the Great Kiva at Aztec had been built sometime late in the Chacoan occupation.

Morris speculated that after the Chaco people left Aztec, the Great Kiva stood empty. When the Mesa Verdeans arrived, they altered the structure to suit their style and used it until "its enormous wooden roof caught fire and collapsed. Whether that conflagration coincided with the final abandonment of the pueblo is unknown."[31]

In 1922, before Morris could excavate the entire ruin, the museum ended its support of the expedition. Morris's involvement at Aztec did not cease, however, and in 1923 he became the custodian for the National Park Service of the newly created Aztec Ruins National Monument. That same year he brought his new bride to live at Aztec. Educated, pretty, and vivacious, archaeologist Ann Axtell Morris provided a lively balance to her husband's intensity and seriousness. She participated wholeheartedly in the next phase of Morris's work, wide-ranging excavations in the Southwest and Mesoamerica, and recorded her archaeological adventures in one of the most enjoyable anecdotal accounts of early Southwestern archaeology, *Digging in the Southwest* (1933).

Kiva with burned roof, Aztec Ruin.

Chaco-style pottery from Aztec, 1929.

NOTHING MORRIS UNCOVERED at Aztec rivaled the Southwest's most spectacular artifact finds, such as those of George Pepper at Pueblo Bonito in Chaco Canyon shortly before the turn of the century. The digging at Aztec did reveal thousands of items from everyday life, however, and many of the most interesting came from burials.

In the 1910s and 1920s, the practice of digging burials was common, and seldom, if ever, questioned by those in the field. Like the widespread collecting and selling of artifacts piecemeal, excavation of prehistoric burials was then neither illegal nor professionally dishonorable, though today public opinion has turned against the practice, and it is now forbidden by law.

Unearthing the burials was tricky work requiring care, patience, and the tolerance of unpleasant conditions. Many of the graves had been disturbed, and the remains scattered by animals, weather, and occasional relic hunters.

In his later writings, Morris reported on more than 140 burials that his crews excavated at Aztec. These were found mainly in the floors of abandoned rooms, with an especially large number in the west wing of the pueblo. Morris provided individual descriptions of the burials in his third report on the excavation, published by the American Museum of Natural History in 1924. His text included carefully noted details, accompanied by a chart of the types of burials and associated artifacts. Along with data on architecture and ceramics, these descriptive records on burial customs helped him to define the development of ancient life at Aztec.

Several of the graves revealed fascinating circumstances and artifacts. Burial 100 contained the remains of an old woman with a pointed stake driven through her pelvis—a find imaginatively reported in local newspapers as a "witch execution." The discovery of an exceptionally tall (6'2") male buried with much regalia, including a coiled basketry shield, was titled by reporters the "Grave of a Warrior" (burial 83).

Doorway feature, Aztec Ruin, c. 1950.

In the grave Morris recorded as "Burial 27, room 139, North Wing," excavators uncovered the remains of a teenaged girl, badly injured before death. The girl had suffered a shattered pelvis and broken arm, which prehistoric healers had attempted to set with wooden splints.

One of the first burials excavated (number 16, room 41, East Wing) probably excited Earl Morris as much as any find during his nearly five-decade archaeological career. This skeleton of an adult male had been buried with an unusual amount of finery:

> An astonishing quantity and variety of objects accompanied the remains. A large globular vase, the first object found, was resting against the breast of the adult in the southeast corner. When it was raised a mass of olivella shells was visible beneath it. The skeleton had been completely covered from throat to thighs with beads, abalone shell, and mosaic pendants. There was also an olivella shell anklet on the left leg. In the southwest corner there was a veritable heap of pottery vessels, bowls, large and small, mugs, and bird effigies. In one of the latter there were approximately 31000 [sic] tiny black disc-shaped beads. A line of vessels was continuous along the west wall. Near the northern end lay 200 quartzite arrowpoints, in a heap as if spilled from some container. A large bowl and vase were adjacent to the west half of the north wall. Charred and broken bird bone tubes, beads, turquoise inlay, and mosaic fragments were scattered everywhere.[32]

Much Mesa Verdean pottery was found in burials. But according to the accompanying ceramics, only a handful of the graves were Chacoan.

During the Aztec dig, numerous other kinds of artifacts besides pots came to light:

> Diggers found many shreds of textiles, sandals, matting, cord, rope, buckskin, and even a fragile section of fish vertebrae, in addition to fine specimens of nonperishable stone tools, arrowheads, beads, and tiny pieces of turquoise. One unique kind of artifact recovered was what Earl surmised were snowshoes. These were oval frameworks of a size suitable for footgear crossed by one taut lacing of yucca fiber and another looser one, the space between being filled with cornhusks or bundles of grass.[33]

As at all digs, the uses of various odd artifacts were never determined, and archaeologists speculated about them long after the digging ended. For example, excavators found small stones with cords tied to them, about which one archaeologist later wrote, "These may have been used as plumb lines."[34]

Aerial view of the restored ruins at Aztec National Monument.

MORRIS AND OTHER ARCHAEOLOGISTS RECOGNIZED that the prehistoric towns at Aztec and Mesa Verde, and at Kiet Siel and Betatakin at Navajo National Monument, represented a flowering of Pueblo culture. The apartment-like structures rose a few stories in terraced layers, with masonry walls built of sandstone or cobbles and adobe. After the 1927 Pecos Conference, archaeologists placed these ruins in the time period known as Pueblo III, which they later defined as lasting through the twelfth and thirteenth centuries.

As a self-taught engineer, Morris could appreciate the construction expertise evident in many of the rooms and kivas uncovered at Aztec. One West Wing room, number 156, called the "painted room" in newspaper accounts, especially impressed him:

> Much of the original plaster of this room was unblemished. A red wainscoting reached from the dirt floor to a height of approximately three feet five inches. Above that, walls were whitewashed to the ceiling. Nine

sets of three red triangles extended from the junction of the wainscoting to upper white walls. The underlying earth-colored plaster was composed of clay tempered with sand. The pale red color seen in this and other protected patches came from solutions made from disintegrated red sandstone applied as washes over the earth-colored coat. White plaster streaked by seepage from above was made from impure gypsum from nearby deposits. Two straight clean pine logs a foot in diameter spanned the ceiling, on top of which was a pole layer of six sets of three cottonwood saplings. ... White hand prints were daubed on beams in several places. Morris believed the room was of Chaco construction, but masonry-sealed doorways pointed to a later Mesa Verdian occupation.[35]

Because he admired the construction work he found in the Great Kiva, Morris became intrigued with the idea of reconstructing it. Some of its features would have represented engineering feats even in modern times. Among these were the kiva's four pillars, which he calculated must have supported a roof weighing ninety tons or more.

Morris invented stabilization and reconstruction methods during the American Museum expedition that enabled him to reconstruct the Great Kiva a decade later. In 1934, under the sponsorship of the National Park Service, with funding from the Public Works Administration, Morris set about rebuilding the kiva so that it would appear just as it had in ancient times. It was a painstaking endeavor that tested his engineering skills and eye for archaeological detail.

He later told Robert Lister that he had based the entire reconstruction on archaeological research. "I didn't guess at a thing," he said. Lister commented,

> I think Earl felt, in order to preserve the Great Kiva that it was a good idea to restore it. ... He felt that one of these [Great Kivas] should be restored so that the public would realize the magnitude. ... You don't get this feeling from going to Pueblo Bonito or Chetro Ketl or Casa Rinconada. Such unreconstructed sites look like holes in the ground.[36]

By the time he began rebuilding the Great Kiva at Aztec, Morris was working under Kidder at the Carnegie Institution of Washington, D.C. That organization "loaned" him to the National Park Service, the agency in charge of both Mesa Verde and Aztec Ruin. While he was reconstructing the Great Kiva, Morris also took part in stabilization projects at Mesa Verde's Cliff Palace and other ruins.

Years later, when less invasive approaches to ruins stabilization became the norm, reconstructions such as Morris's work on the Aztec Great Kiva would be eschewed by many younger archaeologists. However, the project won the respect of Morris's contemporaries. In an interview several decades later, Kidder

Top: Temporary storage shack in the plaza of Aztec Ruin during the Hyde Expedition excavations. Bottom: The Great Kiva at Aztec Ruin seen from above, before completion of Morris's reconstruction.

commented, "One of the most remarkable things that has been done in the Southwest is [Morris's] restoration of the Great Kiva there. That's a thing that everybody ought to see—most impressive . . . an astonishing thing."[37]

BY THE TIME Morris's excavations for the American Museum were officially completed in 1921, nearly three-quarters of the Aztec Ruin had been explored either completely or in part.[38] But the unexcavated parts of the ruin represented a major disappointment to the young archaeologist, whose goal was to excavate the entire site.

Morris worked painstakingly to piece together a picture of prehistoric life based on the thousands of artifacts he found at Aztec. These helped to establish a time sequence for the ruin, which could be added to the growing number of site-specific time lines for the region. Eventually these chronologies helped Morris and the other archaeologists who attended the 1927 Pecos Conference to create the Pecos Classification.

Descriptive summary of data was alpha and omega of the work. Like most archaeologists who excavated at huge sites, and then were faced with overwhelming masses of artifacts and notes that had to be organized into comprehensive lists, Morris felt his work to be lacking. "In places the notes are meager," he commented, "in others, perhaps too voluminous. Some meet the writer's approval;

The restored interior of Kiva F at Aztec.

others fall far short; and always there is the haunting thought that the details which might have been of most significance escaped attention altogether."[39]

At Aztec, Morris concluded, an occupation of Chacoan people was followed after a period of abandonment by a migration of Mesa Verdeans. This later group appeared less sophisticated, judging from its architecture and pottery. Though they prospered for some time, eventually their numbers, and the quality of their arts, declined. Morris believed that a tremendous conflagration ended their occupation. He wrote:

> Upon this condition of cultural senility or disease came the fire of intentional origin which for an interval transformed all but the western side of the pueblo into a veritable furnace. Whether the remainder of the Mesa Verde people evacuated the place and then fired it, or whether an enemy was the incendiary, may never be known, but the burning thereof marked the close of human occupation of the Aztec Ruin.[40]

Subsequent excavations in the 1930s and after produced evidence that contradicted Morris's conclusions, which were published in 1928. It appeared that, for some time, the Mesa Verdeans and Chacoans had in fact occupied the Aztec Ruin simultaneously, and that final abandonment may not have coincided with the fire. Later archaeologists also conjectured that the fire might have been accidental rather than intentional. Excavations at the West Ruin and adjacent sites continued for decades, all of them adding more pieces to hypotheses about the vanished Chaco and Mesa Verde peoples of Aztec.

Morris was keenly interested in the relationship of the earlier Basketmaker people to the later Pueblo people. In 1922, after his excavations for the American Museum ended, Morris wrote to Director Clark Wissler:

> The outstanding problem now is to determine whether the Pottery Makers were directly descended from the Basket Makers who preceded them. The data to settle this point can be had only from cliff shelters where perishable materials such as baskets and textiles remain intact. I anticipate that somewhere in the recesses of the canyons there are sites where typical Basket Maker products will be found in association with the earliest types of pottery, this condition being representative of the transition between the two cultures.[41]

Morris pursued his fascination with Basketmaker sites in the years following the Aztec expedition. Accompanied by his wife Ann, and his faithful workmen Oley, Oscar, and Oscar's son, Omer, he dug at Canyon de Chelly National Monument in Arizona, in caves in the La Plata region of southwestern Colorado, and elsewhere in the Four Corners.

Morris's connection with Mayan archaeology, begun in his early days with Hewett, also continued. During the 1920s he excavated at Maya sites in the Yucatan, where he worked with Gustav Stromsvik, a Norwegian who followed Morris back to the United States and later assisted in reconstructing the Great Kiva at Aztec.

In 1953 his colleagues made Earl Morris the second recipient of the Alfred Vincent Kidder Award. Though he died just three years later, Morris's reports and collection of pottery have continued to influence archaeologists to the present day. Decades after Morris's death, Southwestern archaeologist Al Hayes said, "He was my hero. I think he was the best archaeologist the Southwest ever had." [42]

Interior of the church at Hawikuh, 1937.

CHAPTER 4

HAWIKUH

F. W. Hodge's Quest for Coronado's
Battle Site at Zuni

IN 1917, a year after Earl Morris's crews began wielding their shovels at Aztec Ruin, a middle-aged scholar named Frederick Webb Hodge began excavations at the prehistoric ruin of Hawikuh. There, on the Zuni Indian reservation in New Mexico near the Arizona border, the prominent East Coast ethnohistorian directed an expedition he had dreamed of for decades.

Hodge belonged to an earlier generation of archaeologists than Morris and his colleagues, who created the beginnings of scientific processes. Hodge's contemporaries, in contrast, were eclectic pioneers and explorers bent mostly on discovering new territory and peoples for study. In the decades after the Civil War they traversed the Southwest, supported by upper-class patrons interested in collecting Indian artifacts. These pioneer explorers were also aided by newly founded institutions that financed explorations into the Wild West, primarily to bring back "spoils" of Indian artifacts for museums.

Hodge's adventures in the Southwest began late in 1886, when he joined a group of Easterners exploring the Arizona desert as part of a major scientific quest for the origins of long-vanished Native Americans. Their goal was "to discover the identity of the ancestors of the Pueblo Indians."[1]

Known as the Hemenway South-Western Archaeological Expedition in honor of Mrs. Mary Hemenway, a wealthy Bostonian who funded the endeavor, the group traveled around Arizona and New Mexico from late 1886 through 1889, locating, surveying, and occasionally excavating the prehistoric ruins of the region. (The official dates usually given for the expedition are 1887–88.) The idea for the endeavor originated with anthropologist Frank Hamilton Cushing, best remembered today for pioneering the method of ethnological fieldwork now called "participant observation." In 1879, while on a mission to Zuni for the Smithsonian Institution, Cushing scandalized his traveling companions by going off to live with the Zunis, with whom he remained for more than four years. Cushing's methods of acquiring and recording his knowledge about the Indians, though controversial, were recognized for the meticulous detail of his thorough, if unsystematized, notes.

Other scientists arrived at Zuni before Cushing led the Hemenway Expedition on his next trip to the Southwest. Two brothers, Cosmos and Victor Mindeleff, visited Zuni in the early 1880s to make maps and architectural plans for display at the upcoming Columbian Exposition in Chicago and elsewhere. The Mindeleffs surveyed the inhabited pueblo and the surrounding ruins, including Hawikuh, an abandoned, prehistoric town fifteen miles southwest of the modern pueblo of Zuni. They also adopted the Hopi word *kiva* to designate the Indians' underground ceremonial chambers, instead of the Spanish terminology, *estufa,* that had been used by many early explorers.

In launching the Hemenway Expedition, Cushing began the search for the Pueblo peoples' ancestors, not at Zuni, but in the southern Arizona desert, where the tribe's legends indicated ancestral roots. The second year, the expedition moved to Zuni. Participants included historian and pioneering scholar of the Southwest Adolph F. Bandelier and ethnographer and archaeologist Jesse Walter Fewkes, who took over leadership of the expedition when Cushing's health failed.

The presence of young Frederick Webb Hodge linked the Hemenway endeavor to the next generation of Southwestern anthropologists and archaeologists. A shorthand stenographer for the U.S. Geological Survey and the Bureau of American Ethnology, the twenty-two-year-old Hodge had been recommended to Cushing by bureau head John Wesley Powell. Although he was born in England and educated in the college classrooms of Washington, D.C., Hodge soon became a Southwesterner at heart.

Hodge found the beginnings of his life's calling while serving as field secretary on the Hemenway Expedition. He also met the first of his three wives, Cushing's sister-in-law, expedition artist Margaret W. Magill. Hodge went on to become a scholarly editor, an ethnohistorian, an administrator, a self-taught archaeologist and excavator, and "an indefatigable worker ... [who] crowded 2

Left: Frank Hamilton Cushing wearing a studio costume, photographed in Washington, D.C., 1879. Right: Frederick Webb Hodge (left) with Edgar Lee Hewett.

days into one."[2] For nearly twenty years after his Hemenway experience, he worked for East Coast institutions that were lending crucial backing, credibility, and prestige to the new disciplines of archaeology and anthropology. As a respected editor, he developed a strong academic network.

Although he held no degree in anthropology or archaeology—in fact, no such credentials were available during his student days—after the Hemenway expedition Hodge became one of a number of scholars who helped to shape the newly formed Bureau of American Ethnology of the Smithsonian Institution. During his years at the Smithsonian, where he held the formidable, if somewhat catchall, title of "ethnologist-in-charge," Hodge completed several immense projects, including a monumental reference work, the *Handbook of American Indians,* published in 1910. He helped found the American Anthropological Association in 1902 and edited its publication, *American Anthropologist,* for years.

Self-taught, eclectic, versatile, and talented, Hodge became a recognized expert on Spanish colonial history as well as on Southwestern Indian tribes. One observer noted that it was an era when many professionals were fiercely competitive and "unrelenting antipathies were almost the rule rather than the exception in the pursuit of natural science in late nineteenth century America."[3] Yet Hodge became known for his ebullient generosity and good-heartedness.

After more than two decades at the Bureau of American Ethnology, Hodge

Standing walls of the mission church at Hawikuh in 1886.

developed a project based on his connection with two wealthy and influential men at the newly founded Museum of the American Indian, Heye Foundation, in New York: the museum's founder and director, George G. Heye, "an avid collector of archaeological and ethnological material,"[4] and one of the museum trustees, Harmon Washington Hendricks. Hodge interested them in the ruin of Hawikuh near Zuni, described years before by the Mindeleffs as well as the Hemenway group, and gained their support for a major archaeological expedition that he must have had in mind since the Hemenway Expedition.

Hodge believed that Hawikuh was the connecting point between the prehistoric and historic Southwest. From close study of the Spanish chronicles and his knowledge of the topography around Hawikuh, he concluded it was the town viewed in 1539 by the Spanish explorer Fray Marcos de Niza. Hodge believed it was at Hawikuh that Niza's guide Esteban was killed by angry Indians and that Hawikuh was the Zuni town attacked by Coronado's expedition in the summer of 1540. Coronado himself was injured in that battle.

These conclusions directly contradicted Bandelier's view that a prehistoric town called K'iakima was the focal point of Niza and Coronado's visits. Hodge asserted in an 1895 *American Anthropologist* article "that Hawikuh was the village first seen by Estévan, who there met death; that it was the 'city of Cibola' rising from the plain which Niza and his Piman guides viewed from the southern heights in 1539, and that it was the pueblo which Coronado stormed in the summer of the following year, seems indisputable."[5]

Like the mission church at Pecos Pueblo, then being excavated by Kidder, and the church at the prehistoric Hopi town of Awatovi, which would be explored two decades later by a Harvard Peabody Museum expedition, Hawikuh's Franciscan mission could provide datable historic artifacts and material that would shed new light on the Spanish chronicles.

Hodge's imaginative and entertaining stories of the Spanish explorations and the colorful history of Hawikuh intrigued Hendricks, the museum trustee. He supported the idea of an archaeological expedition to verify the site's significance and agreed to back the project financially. Heye provided the institutional support of the Museum of the American Indian, in hopes that Hodge would procure "specimens"[6] for that institution.

Hodge, then in his early fifties, was appointed expedition field director. This major midlife project was the kind of challenge that showed Hodge at his best; throughout his long life (he lived to almost ninety-two), he continued to initiate new, large-scale endeavors every few years. His drive seemed fueled more by enthusiasm, intellectual curiosity, and a dash of romance than by the fires of personal ambition. Although the Hawikuh project eventually became known as the "Hendricks-Hodge Expedition," Hodge himself preferred to refer to it as the "Hendricks-Heye Expedition."

The expedition took to the field in late May 1917, under joint sponsorship of the Museum of the American Indian and the Smithsonian, where Hodge was still employed during the expedition's first year. Hodge brought to the work a romantic approach to archaeology he had learned when, as a member of the Hemenway Expedition, he excavated in 1888 and 1889 at two prehistoric Zuni towns: Halona, located at present-day Zuni, and Heshotauthla, a big ruin east of the modern pueblo.

In the two years before Hodge arrived at Hawikuh in 1917 with his expedition crews, two young scientists had made breakthroughs at Zuni. Dr. Alfred L. Kroeber, professor of anthropology at the University of California, studied family life at the pueblo in 1915. During casual afternoon strolls, Kroeber gathered potsherds scattered on the ground. As he inspected them, he was inspired to develop a technique known as "seriation" for arranging pottery sherds in categories of oldest to most recent. Kroeber found that he could group, count, and then statistically plot the numbers of sherds gathered on the surface, creating a mathematical curve to identify the waxing and waning of styles of pottery. These findings could then be used in relative dating.

Archaeologist Watson Smith later called seriation "horizontal stratigraphy"[7] and referred to Kroeber's work as part of the "classificatory craze"[8] then sweeping through the discipline. Urging patience and precise scientific method, rather than hurried excavation, Kroeber wrote, "It is fatal for the investigator to exhume pottery in the morning, note architectural construction at noon, plot

Top: Excavated roomblock at Hawikuh. Bottom: Excavating the monastery, 1919.

rooms in the afternoon, and by evening become excited over a find of turquoise or amulets."[9]

Another scientist, Leslie Spier, came to Zuni in 1916 to help archaeologist Nels Nelson survey ruins in the nearby Ramah area for the American Museum of Natural History. Spier then carried out his own, much more extensive survey, using Kroeber's seriation system to begin dating the many prehistoric ruins around Zuni. His landmark paper, titled *An Outline for a Chronology of Zuni Ruins,* was published in 1917.

Archaeological historian Richard Woodbury wrote that "Kroeber and Spier represented a new generation of American archaeologists, relying on academic training rather than pursuing a romantic interest in archaeology that might result in digging with little method or system."[10] Hodge was not part of these breakthroughs, but he certainly intended to employ scientific methods in his archaeology at Hawikuh, especially stratigraphy, which he knew was being successfully used at Kidder's Pecos dig.

By keeping meticulous and accurate records, possibly an outgrowth of his professional lineage back to Powell and Cushing, and by using stratigraphy, Hodge aimed to make the excavations at Hawikuh as scientific as possible. He also hoped to find a connecting point between the historical chronicles of the early Spaniards and the archaeological record.

> Hodge's archaeological techniques were sophisticated for the time and encompassed stratigraphic excavation, systematic recording of rooms, features, artifacts, and in situ photographs. These techniques resulted in the recovery of thousands of artifacts of diverse types with relatively detailed documentation. … In addition, ethnographic photographs and films were made recording aspects of Zuni daily life and architecture and some contemporary material culture was collected since ethnographic analogy was of interest to Hodge in interpreting the archaeological record.[11]

When Hodge arrived in the summer of 1917, Hawikuh was a rock-strewn series of mounds. The ruins were in good condition. Unlike sites ravaged by pot-hunting explorers and homesteaders, Hawikuh, thanks to its relatively isolated location on Zuni land, showed few signs of vandalism.

The ruin stood at the end of a ridge rising sixty feet above the Ojo Caliente Valley, about two-and-a-half miles east of the Zuni River. In the distance rose Dowa Yalanne, sometimes known as Corn or Thunder Mountain, the mesa that provided the Zunis with refuge and defense in time of attack or jeopardy. In the 1880s Victor Mindeleff had admired the colorful cliffs of the nearby mesas and the forested Zuni Mountains in the distance, and described the ruin:

The village of Hawikuh, situated about 15 miles to the south of Zuni, consisted of irregular groups of densely clustered cells, occupying the point of a spur projecting from a low rounded hill. The houses are in such a ruined condition that few separate rooms can be traced, and these are much obscured by débris. This débris covers the entire area extending down the east slope of the hill to the site of the church. The large amount of débris and the comparative thinness of such walls as are found suggest that the dwellings had been densely clustered, and carried to the height of several stories. Much of the space between the village on the hill and the site of the Spanish church on the plain at its foot is covered with masonry débris, part of which has slid down from above.[12]

The silent, rocky mounds gave no sign that Hawikuh had been the scene of many colorful events and some violence. Early Spanish explorers thought that Hawikuh and several other nearby Zuni towns were among the Seven Cities of Cibola, where they expected to find fabulous golden riches.

Niza had contributed to this belief by giving an exaggerated, favorable description of the Zuni towns when he returned to Mexico. Why he delivered such an enthusiastic account of a masonry Indian village, which he had viewed only from a distance, remains a mystery. Jesse Nusbaum, who worked with Hodge at Hawikuh, later speculated, "Perhaps the sun shining on the houses laced with mica made them glitter like gold; perhaps the heat waves rising from the desert in a glorious mirage magnified the size of the town:... it was bigger than two Sevilles... the house walls of solid gold... there were game and wild cattle."[13]

When Coronado's expedition arrived in 1540, they were certainly disappointed by the absence of gold, or any other form of riches. And they were starving, so they attacked and took over the Zuni enclave. Subsequently there were sporadic visits to the Zuni villages by other Spanish expeditions, and in 1629 Spanish Franciscan missionaries established La Purisima Concepcion mission at Hawikuh. It was destroyed in the seventeenth century, and its ruins lay waiting when Hodge's expedition arrived.

HODGE WAS ASSISTED each year by five or six professionals. Among them were Samuel K. Lothrop; George Hubbard Pepper, who had worked at the turn of the century at Pueblo Bonito in Chaco Canyon; Jesse Nusbaum, later known for his archaeological work at Mesa Verde and leadership of Santa Fe's Laboratory of Anthropology; and the English archaeologist Louis C. G. Clarke, director of the University Museum of Archaeology and Ethnology of Cambridge University, England. Visitors to Hawikuh included the expedition's wealthy patron,

Top: The Zuni work crew in the mess tent at Hawikuh, c. 1917–23. Bottom: Frederick Webb Hodge ("Teluli"), seated at left, with A. V. Kidder at the Hawikuh field camp in 1920. Standing (left to right): Sylvanus G. Morley, Edwin F. Coffin, Jesse Nusbaum, Aileen O'Bryan, Eleanor Hope Johnson, Deric O'Bryan (child), Neil Judd, and Earl Morris.

Hendricks, and four peripatetic young archaeologists and friends—Earl Morris, Neil Judd, A. V. Kidder, and Sylvanus Morley—each of whom was making archaeological history on his own.

Work crews at the dig were staffed by Zuni Indians, among whom Hodge was apparently popular. Each season he employed about twenty Zunis, and the same men returned year after year to help. Though the Zunis had kept steadfastly to their traditional ways, they also had a long history of wise dealings with non-Indians. Hodge respected their cultural sophistication and political savvy as well as their tribal unity and pride. The Zunis took a serious interest in the excavations, and they considered some of the artifacts important enough that their medicine men came to see them.

Hodge visited Hawikuh in April 1917 and made preliminary arrangements for the work. Digging began in June and continued for six seasons, with one temporary shutdown in 1922. A fair amount of digging was also done at the neighboring prehistoric ruined pueblo of Kechipawan. Samuel Lothrop supervised those excavations, which were personally financed by Clarke.

Hodge's dig at Hawikuh was the largest excavation of a Southwestern prehistoric ruin ever undertaken up to that time. By the expedition's end, digging at the fifteen-acre site had uncovered approximately a thousand burials; 370 rooms in six room blocks; and the Spanish mission church and its friary. From Museum Director Heye's standpoint, the work was a success: over twelve hundred decorated pots and five hundred plain ones were shipped back to the museum, along with thousands of other artifacts.

At Hawikuh, as at Pecos, digging commenced in the trash heaps that enveloped the slopes around the town. Trash on the western slope stood considerably deeper than Hodge originally anticipated. Burials appeared at a depth of fifteen feet, where the excavators struck the foundations of prehistoric walls. Mysteriously, the bones of many of the earliest skeletons appeared to have been deliberately broken, while many others seemed to have been deliberately dismembered.

Among the burials Hodge found cremations, which he compared to those found decades earlier by Cushing and the Hemenway Expedition at prehistoric towns in the Salt River valley in Arizona. He wrote, "the Zuñis of Hawikuh also cremated some of their dead and deposited the incinerated bones in jars, which were buried with the usual vessels of food and water."[14]

In the third and fourth seasons of excavation, the expedition focused almost exclusively on uncovering room blocks, the tallest walls of which had probably risen to a height of three stories. The excavators found that the town was laid out in a series of house blocks.

Though he did not describe it as such because the concept had not yet emerged, Hodge was investigating Western Anasazi architecture, characterized by an expansive layout, room blocks linked around numerous plazas, and rectangular kivas. In contrast, at the Eastern Anasazi settlements such as Pecos, the architecture was "compact and cellular," and the kivas round.[15]

Hodge used stratigraphy in the excavations of trash and room blocks. Modeling his work on Kidder's, he recorded the levels at which artifacts occurred and also noted the frequency of pottery types, using a preliminary pottery time line, or "ceramic sequence," that he worked out. He also made a fine collection of whole vessels uncovered during the excavations.

Hodge took copious notes, filling ledger after ledger with closely written calligraphy detailing the excavations and finds. He made many sketches of room plans and had Nusbaum and another photographer take numerous photographs of artifacts and architecture, though only a few photos or drawings of burials were made.

Excavated room at Hawikuh, with examples of pottery in situ.

Top: The collapsed roof of a square kiva found beneath a plaza at Hawikuh. Bottom: The kiva's floor, firepit, and roof beams (with temporary supports placed by the excavators).

In the years after the Hawikuh excavation, a question arose concerning Hodge's handling of the pottery sherds from the dig. The general belief among archeologists was that he had discarded the potsherds after creating the ceramic sequence. More recently, however, a student who did some detective work on the subject made the following report:

> It has been published that Hodge did not save many sherds from the excavations. "Unfortunately, most of the sherds were not saved..." (Smith et al. 1966:5). However, the letters from Hodge to Heye in 1919 at the MAI [Museum of the American Indian] Archives indicate to the contrary: "I bagged every sherd from each room separately (that is, a bag to a room)"... (June 22), and "The house excavations keep me very busy, as every sherd is saved..."[16]

The account cites a Southwest Museum employee's statement that Hodge had once told him that George Heye had, in fact, shown no scientific interest in the sherds once they were received: "Hodge walked into the MAI to see Heye with a large pile of sherds in the middle of a table, all emptied from their bags and separated from their documentation."[17] The student summarized her findings by stating that the evidence was inconclusive, although the museum's records indicate the cataloging of a mere 3,592 potsherds.

Hodge differed from Kidder in neglecting to backfill once he completed his excavations. At Pecos, Kidder followed the standard procedure of refilling all excavated areas with dirt, an important step in protecting the site for the next generation of archaeologists. But Hodge left Hawikuh open to the ravages of the elements.

Because he was interested in Hawikuh at the time of and just after Spanish contact, a period later designated in the Pecos Classification as Pueblo V, Hodge focused mainly on the levels of occupation he termed "Recent," or "Hawikuh." Obvious earlier strata, which he designated "Ancient," or "pre-Hawikuh," he left unexplored. Later archaeologists who worked with Hodge's Hawikuh notes would conclude that he was correct, at least in identifying two successive building periods at the pueblo.[18] One wrote:

> Although Pueblo Indians had almost certainly lived at the site of Hawikuh for centuries before the arrival of the Spanish, it was not the purpose of the Expedition to investigate the earliest remains. Hodge was concerned only with the village as it existed at the time of discovery and thereafter until its destruction. The workmen repeatedly came upon walls and objects of the earlier occupancy beneath later ones, but these

were usually not further investigated. Hodge considered that they did not belong to Hawikuh, that they had been built by an earlier people unrelated to the builders of Hawikuh or to the Zuñis, and that they had been long abandoned before Hawikuh itself came into existence. Today we should classify them as Pueblo III and early Pueblo IV and regard them as directly ancestral to historic Hawikuh.[19]

I N 1923, the expedition's final season, Hodge dug a stratigraphic trench through the village plaza, "about 75 feet in length and 15 feet in maximum depth." He excavated this trench in layers about a foot deep and "classified and counted" sherds from each stratigraphic layer "in terms of the ceramic terminology that was developed . . . in the course of the work."[20]

Hodge uncovered, categorized, and placed in sequence several types of native ceramics, as well as some "foreign" ("intrusive") pottery. His notes contain references to early "black-on-white" and "black-on-red" types of ceramics, followed by numerous variations of "glaze" wares and "polychromes." Duly recording colors of slips and painted decorations, he worked out the development of eight native pottery types. He also found the corrugated and plain cooking wares that predominated at hearths at Hawikuh for centuries. As he did throughout the excavations, Hodge used the "pre-Hawikuh" designation for the earliest ceramics, writing: "Black-on-white and Black-on-red pottery was unquestionably of pre-Hawikuh origin, hence these types need not be more than alluded to."[21]

Hodge's perspective on the ceramics was influenced by his Hemenway Expedition experience, which had involved him in Cushing's search for the ancestors of the Zunis in the southern Arizona desert. During an interview with an Arizona archaeologist several decades after his dig at Hawikuh, Hodge mentioned that the "foreign" or intrusive pottery at the site included some "Hohokám" ceramics. This statement surprised many scholars, because it implied that Hodge had found evidence of a trade affiliation with the prehistoric Hohokam people. (It was not until 1931, some years after the Hawikuh dig, that the Hohokam culture was defined by archaeologists.)

The distinctive "Hohokám" pottery referred to by Hodge was not found in a subsequent search of the collections at the Museum of the American Indian; consequently, no definite conclusions about his statement were ever reached. Later archaeologists assumed that he was referring to pottery made by prehistoric groups now known as "Salado."[22]

Spanish artifacts, many of which were excavated in the vicinity of the mission church, provided benchmarks for the stratigraphic work with ceramics. Hodge later told a meeting of the American Ethnological Society that "considerable light was shed on the sequence of these pottery types by reason of their association or nonassociation with objects of European origin."[23]

Among the Spanish artifacts were remnants of manmade materials including metal, glass, porcelain, leather, and wood in the form of specific items such as "iron nails, a copper buckle, fragments of iron and copper, glass beads, bits of decorated porcelain, bottle-glass, and ... a Catholic metal or token. ... [Also found was] half of a pair of scissors."[24] The archaeologists also uncovered horseshoes and religious objects of various sorts. Though Hodge collected them, and shipped them back to the museum for permanent storage, the Spanish artifacts of Hawikuh were not formally analyzed and reported.

Hodge described his intent as the "restoration of the life of the inhabitants"[25] of Hawikuh. Like other prehistoric Indian towns, Hawikuh contained an immense assortment of objects that told much about the life ways and tastes of their vanished owners. For instance, the citizens of Hawikuh were apparently

An artist's reconstruction of the interior and altar of the Hawikuh mission church. Drawing by Ross Montgomery.

fond of ornaments; Hodge found beautiful wooden hair combs finely inlaid with turquoise and jet, and also inlaid earrings of a type Coronado had especially admired. Hodge wrote:

> Shell, stone and turquoise beads and pendants, a tortoise-shell pendant, and beads of juniper seeds, were among the personal ornaments found with skeletons, one necklace of seed beads consisting of many strands still in place. Finger rings made of a part of the seedpod of the Martynia were found ... and wrist-guards of slender bone tubes ... ; necklaces of smaller bone tubes were favorite ornaments of both sexes. A beautifully incised arm-band of thin bone was among the finest of the objects of this material recovered.[26]

Also recorded were fragments of woven cotton cloth, "probably procured by trade with the Hopi,"[27] and many thousands of wooden, stone, and bone objects. Bone items included awls, weaving tools, chisels, knives, needles and pins, flutes, whistles, bird calls, and spindle-whorls.

I N ALL, Hodge excavated six major room blocks at Hawikuh, which he designated House Groups A through F. The dwelling rooms were small, averaging well under one hundred square feet, and many were coated with thirty or forty layers of plaster, the inhabitants' way of refurbishing smoke-blackened walls. Hodge recorded other details, such as quality of masonry (which he described as unexceptional, sometimes even poor); locations and quantities of storage bins and fireplaces; size of roof beams; and locations and sizes of doorways, hatchways, and windows.

Skeletons of macaws, whose feathers were probably used in ceremonies, were found buried beneath the floors of the "Ancient" rooms. Some remains of turkeys, eagles, and dogs were also found.

Hodge was especially interested in "Recent" architectural features that he designated as "snake pens." These were quite small stone enclosures, about one-and-a-half feet square, and equally high, with tiny four-by-six-inch doorways. Based on an early account by Fray Estevan de Perea, Hodge believed that rattlesnakes were kept in these strange structures, possibly for use of their poison and/or in rituals. Two such features were found in Room 392 of House Group B; others were uncovered in the trash dump on the western side of the pueblo. Hodge had the pens carefully photographed and wrote a short paper on the subject after the excavations.

One of the most remarkable architectural features at Hawikuh was a passageway, designated as "Ancient":

One of the structures at Hawikuh that Hodge believed to be snake pens, c. 1917–25.

The purpose of the passageway was not clear, but Hodge was so much intrigued by it that in August, 1928, 5 years after the close of the final season in 1923, he did some further excavation at its easterly end in an attempt to clarify its structure and purpose. ... Hodge was doubtless impelled to return to the problem not only because of the puzzling nature of the passageway, but also because he had found an almost identical and unresolved situation at Heshotauthla when he excavated there for the Hemenway Expedition in 1889.[28]

Hodge found only one kiva at Hawikuh that he considered "Recent." It turned up in the course of trenching the village's central plaza. The kiva was square, as is typical of western Anasazi and Zuni kivas. Hodge's accounts also include descriptions of two "Ancient" or "pre-Hawikuh" round kivas "652 feet westwardly from the northwest corner of Hawikuh."[29]

Hodge's major work on Hawikuh, titled *The History of Hawikuh,* draws on early Spanish sources and includes information about the mission church. Built around 1629 of adobe bricks, which the Spanish friars preferred to the Indians' masonry, the mission was dissolving back into the earth by the time Hodge arrived. Victor Mindeleff had found some of the walls still standing in the 1880s:

The church in this village was constructed of adobe bricks, without the introduction of any stonework. The bricks appear to have been molded with an unusual degree of care. The massive angles of the northwest, or altar end of the structure, have survived the stonework of the adjoining village and stand to-day 13 feet high.[30]

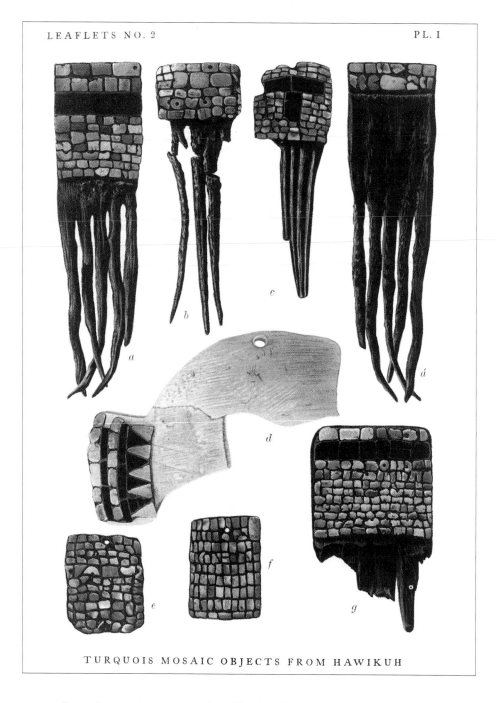

TURQUOIS MOSAIC OBJECTS FROM HAWIKUH

Turquoise mosaic ornaments from Hawikuh. Plate 1 in F. W. Hodge's "Turquoise Work at Hawikuh, New Mexico" (1921).

PLATE 26

a

b

c

d

e

f

g

Hawikuh Polychrome.

Examples of Hawikuh Polychrome pottery. Plate 26 from "The Excavation of Hawikuh by Frederick Webb Hodge: Report of the Hendricks-Hodge Expedition 1917–1923," by Watson Smith, Richard B. Woodbury, and Nathalie Woodbury (1966).

When Hodge began excavating, the walls of the church stood no more than ten feet high. The Franciscans who brought Christianity to the Pueblo Indians in New Mexico had built their mission churches according to standard specifications, which generally included a main sanctuary, main and side altars, a sacristy, a baptistery, a choir loft, bell towers, and an adjacent *camposanto* or cemetery, as well as a *convento* or friary, stables, kitchens, and other peripheral structures. All of these elements appeared during Hodge's excavations. He found nothing to tell him, however, precisely what the church had looked like, nor was he able to determine the exact sequence of its construction.

THE ZUNIS WHO WORKED AT HAWIKUH still lived according to the same cyclical religious calendar that the tribe was using when the Spanish arrived. Agricultural cycles played a major role in their daily lives, and rituals honoring seasonal changes remained an important responsibility of the tribe. Maintaining good relations with the Zunis was an important part of camp life at Hawikuh. On one occasion Hodge threw a huge party for "80 wagonloads of Indians" that was topped off by a fireworks display, which caused a "general stampede." [31]

Hodge's rapport with the tribe dated back to the time the Hemenway Expedition stayed at Zuni Pueblo. Three members of the tribe had then given Hodge a nickname that remained with him throughout his career in the Southwest: "Teluli," meaning "dig your cellar." The name came from one of Hodge's favorite Zuni folk tales. According to the story, a frightened mouse cried "Teluli! Teluli!" as it frantically dug its hole in the ground to escape a bird of prey circling overhead.

Hodge was famous for his practical jokes, a trait that the Zunis enjoyed. Both Hendricks and Nusbaum later recalled some of his humor, which included rigging a privy with bells to announce new arrivals, and placing dead field mice in inconvenient locations such as the toes of shoes. "A methodical individual and outwardly casual," wrote Neil Judd, "Hodge never permitted the seriousness of the day to interfere with a practical joke." [32]

Visitors to the camp found plenty of hospitality and ample food, mainly trucked in from Gallup, thirty miles away. Hodge and Nusbaum both enjoyed cooking, and teased each other for years after the expedition with anecdotes about their alleged culinary catastrophes.

LIKE THE LEADERS of many archaeological excavations, Hodge found digging easier than reporting. Though he did write the *History of Hawikuh* and several short papers on archaeological finds, he never completed the final report on the excavation. Finally, just a year before his death, he turned the project over to a younger archaeologist.

Watson Smith was a well-known figure in the reporting of Southwestern archaeology. He recalled enjoying a dinner at Hodge's home in Pasadena, California, where "Hodge liked to dress as a chef with a big white cap and make a salad."[33]

One day in 1955, Smith called on Hodge at the Southwest Museum, where Hodge, then in his nineties, was still director. Hodge asked his guest abruptly, "Would you like to write the report on Hawikuh?" Smith replied that he knew nothing about the site or its excavation decades before—but to no avail. Hodge took Smith to his home, where he led him to a cupboard and opened the double-doors, revealing piles of notebooks, maps, photographs, and room drawings from the Hawikuh excavation.

"It was all there," Smith remembered. "The maps, thousands of pages of notes in beautiful calligraphy, everything."[34] As usual, Hodge had his way. The reluctant Smith agreed to take on the project and called upon two respected archaeologists familiar with the Zuni vicinity, Richard and Nathalie Woodbury, to help him with the task of ceramic reporting. Within a year, in the fall of 1956, just a month before his ninety-second birthday, Hodge passed away at his newly purchased retirement home in Santa Fe.

Smith and the Woodburys intended to use Hodge's notes and room plans to organize and analyze the materials on Hawikuh's architecture and artifacts. After Hodge died, the project almost ground to a total halt when his widow received numerous offers from universities and museums wishing to purchase Hodge's papers, including the Hawikuh notes and other excavation materials. Nathalie Woodbury made a special trip to visit Mrs. Hodge and convinced her that the materials would go first to the writing team and then would be kept with the collections of artifacts from the dig.

Ross G. Montgomery, an expert on Spanish colonial architecture, wrote the chapter on the mission church using Hodge's notes and plans of the mission made after the excavation. Montgomery had helped J. O. Brew with the excavation of the mission at Awatovi in the 1930s; as would be expected, he found that the church at Hawikuh bore many similarities to the one at Awatovi.

In their work at Atsinna Ruin on top of El Morro in Zuni territory, the Woodburys had become familiar with the area's prehistoric ceramics. The drawings of the whole pots, and the vessels themselves, were of great importance to their research. Eventually the Woodburys created a modern ceramic sequence and typology for the site, based on the earlier one developed by Hodge.

Frederick Dockstader, director of the Museum of the American Indian, assured Smith and the Woodburys that the report would be published. Though according to Hodge the publication funds had vanished, Dockstader claimed that he found a special account, which had been there all along, earmarked for this purpose. The final document, titled *The Excavation of Hawikuh by Frederick Webb Hodge,* was published by the museum in 1966.

Hodge's findings at Hawikuh pertained primarily to data gathering. One colleague wrote of his work: "In general he was interested in presenting facts and raising problems rather than in dealing with theory."[35] This approach stemmed from his early years in the field, when data gathering was essential to the creation of the new sciences of archaeology and anthropology. At Hawikuh a great deal of information was collected, but few final conclusions drawn, though the Smith-Woodbury-Montgomery team was later able to make some interesting deductions based on Hodge's notes, maps, plans, and photographs. For example, expanding on Hodge's records pertaining to House Group C, they wrote:

> From these considerations, then, it seems a reasonable conclusion that family groups probably occupied single files of rooms (or occasionally two adjoining files) composed of from three to seven rooms each; that the back rooms were used normally for storage or sleeping, although, sometimes in the Recent period, they may have served other purposes as well; that most of the living, cooking, eating, and working took place in rooms of the second and especially of the third and fourth tiers. This is consistent with the situation in House Group A ... and at Pecos.[36]

Evidence as to whether or not Hawikuh was the scene of Coronado's battle with the Zuni has remained inconclusive. Hodge stuck to his original position that the location of the battle described in the Spanish documents matched definitely with the topography of the Hawikuh site. As he wrote in the *History of Hawikuh,* "Hawikuh was the only pueblo that could have been seen by Fray Marcos if he entered the Zuñi valley from the southwest, and the only one, according to the confirmatory accounts of the approach to it by Coronado, that could have been stormed and captured by him."[37]

Some of Hodge's conclusions seem obvious and unremarkable now. In the context of their time, however, they represented a major step toward a systematic examination of the chronological development of the town. Hodge reached some preliminary suppositions about relative chronology at different levels and parts of the ruin, writing, for example, that "it is certain that the eastern part of the pueblo is the oldest, or at least the eastern houses are older than the western, for before the latter tier of dwellings was constructed the area on which their foundations stand was the dump-ground for the eastern houses."[38]

Decades later, archaeologists would conclude that Zuni, like the Hopi towns and the pueblos along the Rio Grande, had developed its large prehistoric population sometime after the abandonment of Mesa Verde, which occurred by 1300.

Hawikuh proved typical of settlements built after that time, large pueblos of one thousand rooms or more, usually grouped around central plazas, as were the six major room blocks at Hawikuh. Glazed and polychrome pottery became prevalent at these enclaves. This sort of dissection of prehistoric patterns came long after Hodge's time. However, some of the architecture and artifacts uncovered at Hawikuh contributed to general knowledge that eventually supported this understanding.

Hodge's career underwent a dramatic shift as a result of his leadership of the Hawikuh expedition. Just a few months after the first field season, in February 1918, he resigned from his position at the Smithsonian and joined the Museum of the American Indian in New York, where he remained on staff until 1931. Then, at the age of sixty-eight, he became director of the Southwest Museum in Los Angeles, an institution founded by his old friend, journalist Charles Lummis. He held this position for twenty-five years, retiring in 1955, only a few months before his death.

To the last year of his life, Hodge's youthful spirit continued to amaze his fellow archaeologists. One member of the Harvard Peabody Museum Expedition to Awatovi recalled that the septuagenarian Hodge and his third wife, many years his junior, appeared at their isolated camp on the Hopi reservation one evening in the late 1930s. There Hodge entertained the assembled archaeologists by demonstrating one of the latest fads, an energetically choreographed number known as the Turkey Dance.[39]

Neil M. Judd's excavations at Pueblo
Bonito, 1922.

CHAPTER 5

PUEBLO BONITO

Neil Judd Takes On the Southwest's Greatest Archaeological Mystery

On a hot, dusty day in 1920, four young archaeologists arrived, via horse and wagon, at one of the most archaeologically rich but desolate wastelands in the Southwest: Chaco Canyon, New Mexico. The four men—Neil M. Judd, Sylvanus G. Morley, Alfred V. Kidder, and Earl H. Morris—had come to survey Chaco's immense prehistoric ruins in order to decide which site should become the focus of a large-scale excavation to be sponsored by the National Geographic Society. The question tested their knowledge and experience, for Chaco Canyon contained many of the most spectacular, mysterious ruins in the Southwest.

To this task the four archaeologists brought the expertise of substantial education and fieldwork. Both Kidder and Morley held Ph.D. degrees, while Judd and Morris had earned M.A.s, underscored by field training.

The impetus for their adventure had begun on April 1, 1920, when Morley proposed that the National Geographic Society sponsor an "archeological reconnaissance of the Chaco Canyon district, northwestern New Mexico."[1] The idea appealed to the ongoing public and institutional fascination with Southwestern archaeology, and the proposal was accepted. The society appointed thirty-two-year-old Neil Judd, curator of archaeology at the U.S. National Museum, a branch of the Smithsonian Institution, to make a preliminary exploration of the canyon. Judd first journeyed alone to the isolated site, and then returned accompanied by Morley and the others.

An important dig had already taken place at Chaco Canyon two-and-a-half decades before Judd and his friends arrived. Beginning in 1896, the Hyde Exploring Expeditions thoroughly combed a major portion of the large ruin called Pueblo Bonito in an all-out search for buried archaeological treasure. The Hyde Expeditions were directed by a talented Harvard graduate student, George Hubbard Pepper, under the guidance of Frederic Ward Putnam. One of the founding fathers of American anthropology and archaeology, Putnam was then curator of anthropology at the American Museum of Natural History, the official institutional sponsor of the expeditions. Since he visited Chaco only twice during the expeditions, oversight of the endeavor rested with young Pepper and his foreman, Richard Wetherill, a veteran of more than a decade of Southwestern archaeological explorations at Mesa Verde, Grand Gulch, and many other sites. That early dig at Bonito, like virtually all fieldwork around the turn of the century, took place with minimal use of scientific methods.

The Hyde Expedition to Chaco had been Richard Wetherill's idea, and he paid close attention to its daily progress. Under his watchful eyes, crews of about a hundred Navajo and Zuni workmen uncovered some of the most spectacular finds in the history of Southwestern archaeology.

The artifacts from the pueblo were said to have been those expected among a sedentary people who had reached a high level of development. Perishable items, such as ceremonial sticks, wooden arrows, fragments of cloth, pieces of buckskin, and sandals and cordage of fiber were remarkably preserved in the dry debris of deeply filled rooms. The aesthetic attainment of the pueblo's occupants was reflected in the color designs found on wooden tablets and the encrusted and mosaic work on exceptional pieces such as inlaid scrapers, a mosaic-covered basket, and animal effigies. The use of turquoise in beads, pendants, and inlays, Pepper believed, exceeded that of any other Southwestern site.[2]

The artifacts were hauled for more than sixty miles, on a road that the expedition improved,[3] from Chaco Canyon to the Santa Fe Railroad siding at what is now Thoreau, New Mexico. From there they were shipped by the boxcar-load back East to the expedition's wealthy benefactors, Talbot and Fred Hyde, heirs to the Babbitt Soap Company fortune. Fred Hyde often visited the excavations, and he and his brother eventually donated the archaeological bounty to the American Museum. Though he never wrote a final report, Pepper left copious field notes eventually published as an anthropological paper of the American Museum.

Top: Fetishes uncovered at Chaco Canyon c. 1900. These pieces were once part of
B. Talbot Hyde's personal collection. Bottom: Pottery in room 28 at Pueblo
Bonito, c. 1896.

The Hyde Expeditions were halted officially in 1901, though their work slowed before that, because of government investigations resulting from local protests about the wholesale removal of artifacts from Pueblo Bonito. In the long run, the expedition had a salutary effect. It inspired pioneer archaeologist Edgar Lee Hewett and others to lobby for passage of the 1906 Antiquities Act, which protected archaeological sites on federal land from rampant digging.

Navajo members of the Hyde Expedition in room 62, Pueblo Bonito, c. 1900.

Hyde Expedition members searching for turquoise in a dirt pile at Pueblo Bonito, c. 1900. Left to right: Navajo crew member, Orian Buck, George Pepper, and Richard Wetherill.

Empowered by the Act, President Theodore Roosevelt proclaimed Chaco Canyon a national monument in 1907. By then the Hyde excavation teams had scattered. A few years later, in the summer of 1910, Chaco's early archaeological phase came to a violent end when Richard Wetherill, the last Anglo member of the Hyde Expeditions remaining in the canyon, was shot and killed by an angry Navajo near the trading post he founded at Chaco in 1898. In 1916 Chaco Canyon came under the aegis of the newly created National Park Service.

Indians and eighteenth-century Spanish explorers gave the ruins at Chaco Canyon melodious names—Chetro Ketl, Pueblo del Arroyo, Una Vida, Hungo Pavi, Casa Rinconada, Kin Kletso, Peñasco Blanco. These names were adopted by nineteenth-century Anglo military men and pioneers, who translated one of the simplest and most descriptive names, "Pueblo Bonito," to mean "pretty town" or, as Judd later poetically phrased it, "the City Beautiful."[4]

One of the geologic and geographical expeditions of the 1870s, the Hayden Survey, passed through Chaco in May of 1877. With the survey expedition traveled two of Judd's "life-long companions"[5] and mentors—his boss at the National Museum, explorer and pioneer archaeologist William Henry Holmes, and his friend, William Henry Jackson, the photographer of the West, who led the expedition's trip into the canyon.

During that venture Jackson endured one of the major photographic misfortunes of the early West: he lost four hundred images of the Chaco ruins because his "films"—a newfangled invention soon to replace glass plates—failed him. Victor Mindeleff had better luck ten years later, when he spent several winter weeks surveying and successfully making photographs for a study of Pueblo architecture he was preparing with his brother Cosmos. Mindeleff's photographs revealed holes knocked in walls and other signs of pothunting in Bonito and nearby Pueblo del Arroyo.

Scott Morris, father of Judd's colleague, New Mexico archaeologist Earl Morris, dug an exploratory trench through one of Pueblo Bonito's trash deposits in 1893. He was perplexed, as were all those who came after him, by the scarcity of burials. Richard Wetherill, whose interest in Chaco inspired the Hyde Expeditions, visited in 1895 with his future wife Marietta and her family.

The peripatetic pioneer of Southwestern stratigraphy, Nels C. Nelson of the American Museum of Natural History, spent two weeks at Pueblo Bonito in July 1916. With his assistant, Earl Morris, Nelson made stratigraphic tests in the ruin's trash deposits but noted that because of the unusual composition of the refuse, "the results were thoroughly disappointing."[6]

N EIL JUDD'S EARLY CAREER was intertwined with the lives of his friends Kidder, Morley, and Morris, who became the hub of a group of archaeologists working in the Southwest at that time. The young scientists formed firm personal and professional bonds, and pursued interrelated research interests at several major sites. Of particular importance were Mesa Verde and Chaco Canyon, both of which they identified as the center of an Anasazi culture area.

Pueblo Bonito, 1901.

Judd's actual professional training began in 1907, when he made his first summer field trip to explore archaeological sites in the Four Corners region with his uncle, Dr. ("Dean") Byron Cummings. At the time, Cummings was a classics professor at the University of Utah, where Judd studied Greek and Latin under him.

Like his colleague and rival Hewett, Cummings became a leader in the development of Southwestern archaeology. Both men helped shape the progress of the discipline, partly through their own work, but mainly through the careers of their many students.

In 1907, Judd went with Cummings to Bluff City, a town in southeastern Utah that was a meeting point for the expedition. "Our task for the summer of 1907 was the examination of local cliff-dwellings and like remains and, more important, a survey of three natural bridges in White and Armstrong Canyons," Judd wrote.[7] Hewett also participated in this expedition,[8] as did his promising young student, Ted Kidder.

In 1908, under Cummings's direction, Judd and Kidder took part in some of the earliest explorations at Alkali Ridge, later the scene of significant scientific breakthroughs by John Otis Brew. That year Judd met Jesse L. Nusbaum, then the photographer of the School of American Archaeology. Judd remembered Nusbaum as an energetic individual who had grown "deep sideburns... just to annoy the Director [Hewett]."[9] Nusbaum later served as superintendent of Mesa Verde National Park and director of the Laboratory of Anthropology in Santa Fe. "Vay" Morley, another of Hewett's students, "may have happened along that same summer, or perhaps the year before, his shortsightedness leading him repeatedly into unsuspected obstacles—sandstone ledges, cactuses, and protruding branches."[10]

In 1909 Judd explored Tsegi Canyon in the Rainbow Bridge–Monument Valley country as

a member of the Cummings-Douglass expedition, which included among its achievements the first recorded viewing by white men of Rainbow Natural Bridge on August 14, 1909. He considered this one of the high points of his life and had strong convictions as to which of the two expedition leaders (Cummings) was first to set eyes on the great sandstone arch.[11]

On that trip Judd also visited the spectacular ruin called Betatakin, a site that he partially excavated, repaired, and stabilized in 1917.

By the time they made their reconnaissance in Chaco in 1920, Judd, Morley, Kidder, and Morris were all seasoned veterans of more than a decade of explorations and fieldwork. In a memoir Judd described their entrance into the canyon behind a "team of magnificent bays ... [that] pulled ... [a] wagon, water barrels on each side.... Diverse stories, some disparaging and some true, grew out of that exploration-by-wagon, but it was a memorable trip, scarcity of water and edibles notwithstanding."[12]

They found the canyon sparsely inhabited by a few Navajos. The ruins stood in empty, eerie silence at an elevation of just over six thousand feet. Chaco's average rainfall of less than ten inches a year produced a barren, dry terrain, and the canyon's extreme temperatures could reach below zero in winter and over one hundred degrees Fahrenheit in summer. Without the protection of trees or large vegetation, the canyon floor stretched flat, parched, and vacant. Only in some of the side canyons did greenery offer relief from the brown expanse.

A few sounds occasionally broke the silence: cries of cliff-nesting swallows, hoots of burrowing owls, coyote howls, and the scratching of dry wind in sagebrush, greasewood, and wild grasses. Kidder reported finding Chaco's silence and isolation uninviting, describing the canyon as "little better than a desert ... many parts of it, indeed, are absolutely barren wastes of sand and rock."[13] Judd, in contrast, liked the place and called it "a favorite refuge of mine."[14]

Through the center of the canyon sliced the dry Chaco Wash, "sometimes called the Chaco River by courtesy of its length, but always an ephemeral stream."[15] It opened a sandy gash through the narrow river valley, barely a mile across at its widest point. Presiding over the canyon stood Fajada Butte, looming

Neil M. Judd in his student days. Alkali Ridge, 1908.

starkly at the southeast end, while Chacra Mesa bordered the canyon on the south. Directly across from the ruin of Pueblo Bonito stood a break between Chacra and South Mesas called "The Gap," or sometimes "South Gap."

Here and there *tinajas,* or water holes, pocked the sandstone surfaces around the canyon cliffs and mesa tops. Tucked away in the *rincons,* or small side canyons, were unexpected smaller ruins and specimens of ancient rock art. The rincons flowed with runoff during heavy rains; some later archaeologists believed that the prehistoric Chacoans used them to channel irrigation water.

Around Chaco, prehistoric seas had created a "country of sandstones and shales."[16] From the tops of the canyon's cliff walls, which rose two to four hundred feet on either side, the Chacoans quarried a strata of the finely layered, dense rock, called Mesaverde sandstone, which they used to build their elaborate towns.

More than a dozen large masonry pueblos and uncounted smaller ones filled the fifteen-mile-long canyon cut by the Chaco River. Within the canyon's thirty-two square miles, the largest ruins were Bonito and its neighbor Chetro Ketl, which stood in friendly proximity on the north side of the canyon. Each was laid out systematically in a D-shaped arrangement of rooms around central courts, a pattern characteristic of the Chacoan pueblos, many of which had D- or E-shaped designs.

Just across the wash stood Casa Rinconada, with its enormous Great Kiva, the largest excavated kiva in the canyon. Nearby stood a line of small ruins, later called "Bc sites" (a term from an early site numbering system). Vestiges of smaller, simpler communities were found along the canyon's southern cliff bases.

BY NOVEMBER OF 1920 Judd had returned from Chaco to recommend that the National Geographic Society send its expedition to Pueblo Bonito, which appeared to have the longest architectural history of any ruin in the canyon. The Hyde Exploring Expedition of 1896–1901 had proved that the enormous ruin, the largest at Chaco, contained fabulous artifacts. As part of the National Geographic team's work, nearby Pueblo del Arroyo would also be excavated.

At Pueblo Bonito Judd hoped to find evidence that would help explain the development of the so-called Chaco Culture, one of the main goals of the Society's Committee on Research.[17] The term "high Chaco Culture" referred to the emerging belief among many archaeologists that the prehistoric towns of Chaco Canyon had been the center of "perhaps the most extraordinary pre-Columbian settlement north of Mexico."[18]

The National Geographic Society approved Judd's proposal to dig at Pueblo Bonito, and the National Museum granted him a leave of absence of four months a year to work at Chaco. Beginning in 1921, Judd spent seven field seasons in the canyon.

Pueblo Bonito stood massive and enigmatic when Judd arrived. "The famous old ruin covers more than three acres in ground area ... [and] razed walls and village debris lie twelve feet beneath the surface," he wrote.[19] Its walls had been naturally preserved when the top walls of the upper stories had collapsed and fallen over lower ones, in effect stabilizing them. However, the ruin had deteriorated over centuries of abandonment, and had been ransacked by many nineteenth- and twentieth-century treasure seekers.

Four hundred feet to the southwest of Pueblo Bonito lay Pueblo del Arroyo, right at the edge of Chaco Wash. Judd later concluded that this pueblo may have been a sort of suburb of the larger site. Like Bonito it had a D-shaped floorplan.

Above Bonito loomed Threatening Rock, a huge vertical slab that was gradually cracking away from the main cliff and would someday topple onto the pueblo. Concerned prehistoric builders had engineered a contraption of timbers, mud, and stones to prop it up. Nelson had noted "the shored-up cliff block"[20] on his 1916 visit, and the ancient jerryrigging was still there when Judd arrived. Despite Park Service attempts to prevent its collapse, Threatening Rock finally crashed down onto Pueblo Bonito in 1941.

Threatening Rock, Pueblo Bonito, c. 1920.

Neil Judd operated with a bare-bones staff at Chaco. Each season two or three field assistants, usually graduate students from various institutions, came to work with him. He also employed a surveyor and men to perform tasks such as camp work, cooking, and photography.

Judd's professional staff included Karl Ruppert; H. B. Collins, Jr.; Frans Blom; L. C. Hammond; Monroe Amsden; Frank H. H. Roberts, Jr.; and Henry B. Roberts. Visiting experts ran a battery of tests at the site—hydrology, sedimentation, and soil analysis—all related to the environmental part of Judd's research plan. Dr. Kirk Bryan, then with the U.S. Geological Survey, prepared a geologic profile of Chaco.

Beginning in 1922, the internationally known astronomer A. E. Douglass also participated. At the time, Douglass was creating the science of tree-ring dating—dendrochronology—and the National Geographic Society provided $7,500 for a three-year project to ascertain the ages of Pueblo Bonito and Pueblo del Arroyo.[21]

In his memoirs, Judd acknowledged the services of his secretary and a number of "men met along the trail":

Pueblo Bonito viewed from the cliff top.

Among others, there was Jack Martin, a former freighter for the Hyde Expeditions and my sometime teamster; and there was Joe Lovelady, a lonely cowboy at Smith's ranch who married a mail-order bride from Kansas City and regretted the choice almost immediately. The bride arrived on schedule, equipped with red hair and all else that seemed necessary, but when she saw her future home, a one-room board shack overlooking the watering troughs and the corrals, she insisted upon instant return to Thoreau.[22]

Another equally dependable member of my Chaco Canyon staff was O. C. "Pete" Havens ... a stenographer and bookkeeper. ... He was that rare individual in an archaeological camp — a "man-of-all-trades."[23]

Havens took many of the excellent photographs used in *National Geographic* coverage of the expedition and also in Judd's 1964 final report on architecture of Pueblo Bonito.

Judd hired more than two dozen Navajo and Zuni Indians as excavation laborers. Although he was warned that this intertribal approach would result in disastrous feuding, he reported that the Zunis and Navajos worked peaceably side by side at the Chaco excavations.

The Zunis traveled from their reservation and camped at the dig; the Navajos generally walked or rode to work each day from their hogans. On Sunday nights the Zunis entertained themselves around the campfire with traditional songs and dances while the Navajos sat on their ponies in the shadows beyond the firelight and watched. "Only the scarcity of firewood limited the entertainment to a single night [each week]."[24]

The expedition camp lay just south of Pueblo Bonito,

on the edge of a long, cellarlike excavation that had been the Hyde Expedition's storeroom for wool and Navaho blankets. ... We dug our well, on a sand bar at one side of the main watercourse. ... Water for camp purposes was pumped into a tank elevated above the tents; gravity carried it down into the kitchen, at the east end of the old cellar, and to a mud box near the ruin.[25]

Creature comforts were definitely lacking at Judd's camp. In spite of the well, water shortages plagued the expedition. Food and other supplies had to be hauled from Gallup, about a hundred miles away — a seven-hour trip in dry weather. In wet weather, roads turned to impassable mires. Firewood came from locations at least twenty miles distant. Besides the intense solitude, lack of water, and summer heat, incessant wind and blowing sand frequently made conditions

Top: Navajo excavation crew and photographer William Henry Jackson (in profile, right) at Chaco Canyon, 1925. Bottom: Symposium at Pueblo Bonito, 1925. Left to right: Monroe Amsden, L. C. Hammond, Kirk Bryan, Frank H. H. Roberts, Jr., W. H. Jackson, Karl Ruppert, Frank A. Thackery, Neil M. Judd, C. S. Scofield.

Chaco Canyon visitors, 1920. Seated (left to right): unknown, Mrs. Edgar Lee Hewett, Sylvanus G. Morley, Earl H. Morris. Standing: Neil Judd, unknown, Wesley Bradfield, Edgar Lee Hewett, A. V. Kidder, Jack Martin (freighter).

miserable. A series of five cooks served the expedition. As Judd commented, "That only one cook returned for a second season is ample evidence...that Chaco Canyon has its limitations as a summer resort."[26]

During the field seasons of 1921, 1922, and 1925, Judd convened informal scientific symposia in the isolated canyon, to which he invited fellow archaeologists and "a chosen company of friends and colleagues skilled in Southwestern geology, physiology, Indian agriculture, and related subjects."[27] Judd's beloved friend, photographer William Henry Jackson, attended the 1925 gathering at the age of eighty-two and, to the consternation of his friends, "insisted upon climbing" one of the ancient stairways he had explored nearly fifty years earlier.[28]

These Chaco symposia may be considered the forerunners of the Pecos Conference:

> In Kidder's invitation to Morris in March 1927 he mentioned a preliminary discussion in Neil Judd's office at the U.S. National Museum in the autumn of 1926. Kidder and Judd were close friends, and in view of the fact that Judd had held a series of what he called "symposia" at his Chaco Canyon field headquarters, it may have been his suggestion to continue the meetings, in at least modified form, at Pecos (the work at Chaco having come to an end).[29]

Judd remembered the problems of holding a meeting at Chaco: "We found that distance from the railroad and the limitations of our facilities were too great. Then, in 1927, Kidder inaugurated his famous Pecos Conference, and we were content to end ours."[30]

JUDD'S ORIGINAL PLAN was to dig at Bonito for five years, but the immense task stretched into two additional seasons. To investigate Chaco's mysteries, he planned to study not only the pueblo itself but also "everything identifiable with the life of these two prehistoric communities. Their domestic water supply, their sources of food and fuel, their entire subsistence problem — all lay within the scope of our inquiry." [31]

> The agricultural possibilities of the valley in prehistoric times, its then sources of water and fuel, and the location and extent of the ancient forests that had furnished timbers for the roofs of Pueblo Bonito and neighboring communities likewise were subjects for inquiry.[32]

Eager for any information on the site, Judd pored over a prepublication copy of Pepper's notes on Pueblo Bonito. The Hyde Exploring Expeditions had backfilled the Bonitian rooms after excavation. Using Pepper's descriptions, Judd was able to avoid the 198 rooms of the ancient town already explored and to concentrate on uncovering the unexcavated "half" of the pueblo.

Each season, Judd directed several additional projects besides the main excavations. His workmen pioneered the stabilizing of Bonito and repaired damage inflicted by early pothunters. Judd also oversaw excavations at several smaller Pueblo and Basketmaker ruins in the canyon and at promising trash middens. The expedition conducted some stratigraphic testing at the sites of Peñasco Blanco and Pueblo Alto, and Judd directed surface collections of sherds and other artifacts around the canyon.

Pueblo Bonito became the scene of much earth-moving. According to a *National Geographic* article, "One hundred thousand tons of earth, stone, and blown sand have been carted from the ruins of Pueblo Bonito. . . . When conditions are favorable, thirty-five or more Indians, ten white men, and eight or nine horses are busy in the ruins." [33]

One of Judd's first projects, in the spring of 1921, was to "trench" the West Mound with a five-foot-wide cut

> through a previously undisturbed section. . . . A stratigraphic column, 3 feet square, at the end of that trench reached clean sand at a depth of 19 feet 5 inches. . . . From 23 unequal layers floored by ash, variously colored sand, or otherwise, we collected 2,119 potsherds. . . .
>
> That sherd collection disclosed a puzzling mixture of pre-Pueblo and later pottery types, top to bottom.[34]

The reverse chronology clearly shown by the pottery sherds, with oldest on top and newest beneath, remained a mystery for the next three seasons, though

Clearing debris from the outer south wall of Pueblo Bonito, 1924.

Judd repeatedly made stratigraphic tests. By the end of the 1924 season, many of the settlement's older rooms, as well as newer sections and the entire area known as the West Court, had been cleared. Then, in 1925, the stratigraphic puzzle of the West Mound was solved when a ten-foot-deep trench revealed a Great Kiva, whose foundations had been created after both prehistoric digging in early refuse and also some ancient Bonitian remodeling. Judd conjectured that rubbish from the Bonitians' Great Kiva building project, "nearly 2000 tons of it, may well have started the West Mound — the mound we had profiled 4 times, 1921–1924." [35] The baffling, topsy-turvy stratigraphy resulted from all these ancient construction activities in one spot.

In 1925 Judd put his assistant Frank H. H. Roberts, a promising young Harvard graduate student in anthropology who went on to become a giant in the field, in charge of the stratigraphy of Bonito. Roberts successfully profiled an undisturbed, and less unique, section of the ruin, and finally the archaeologists could begin relative dating with a correct stratigraphic progression of pottery types.

After 1925 Roberts, assisted by Monroe Amsden, processed a mountain of distinctive Bonitian pottery. Using a workshop in the southwest corner of the ruin, the men "sorted, counted at least twice, and classified an estimated 2,000,000 potsherds. After eliminating all recognizable duplicates there remained some 203,188 fragments [sherds] for tabulation." [36]

The potters at Pueblo Bonito had developed their art to a fine level, much admired by the archaeologists who explored their remains. "Beginning with Kidder (1924)," Judd wrote, "archaeologists have extolled the exceptional whiteness of its surface slip, the variety and the perfection of its hachured designs, the blackness of its paint."[37]

Beneath the eight-foot level, the pottery from Roberts's stratigraphic tests fell into the categories that would be defined at the 1927 Pecos Conference as Pueblo I and Pueblo II. Judd referred to the makers of this pottery as "Old Bonitian." Based on Roberts's findings, Judd described the evolution of Chaco pottery designs in this early period: "Squiggled hachure [cross-hatching] began early and so did stepped triangles, waved lines, and free-standing figures. There were transient preferences for designs composed of broad solid lines, for hachured figures with solid tips, and others balanced by opposing elements."[38]

Above eight feet, the pottery changed and the design element most commonly associated with Chaco — straight-line hachure — appeared,[39] as did "a hybrid variety of domestic pottery" called the Chaco–San Juan.[40] Judd concluded that "makers of a different pottery complex came to dwell at Pueblo Bonito after Old Bonitian household waste had accumulated to a depth of 8 feet or more."[41]

This second group, whom Judd termed "Late Bonitians," exhibited Pueblo III characteristics. Judd believed that the Old Bonitians and Late Bonitians lived at the pueblo contemporaneously for a time.

The interior of a kiva at Pueblo Bonito.

Window and masonry
detail, Pueblo Bonito,
1920.

Pueblo Bonito's ruin presented the excavators with an elaborate, compli-cated puzzle whose elements included many kinds of masonry, with numer-ous subvarieties of each major type; a huge maze of collapsed rooms, kivas, and Great Kivas; and a central plaza bisected by a single row of rooms and one Great Kiva. Judd slowly developed an overview of the town's gradually sprawling growth from the original northern core of rooms to its complex and heavily remodeled final floor plan.

Like the other monumental Chacoan ruins, Pueblo Bonito had grown from humble beginnings to a multistoried apartment house, with tiers of rooms stair-stepping up in solar-heated, south-facing layers. The thick sandstone and mud walls held heat during winter and provided interior coolness in summer. Though at its peak the pueblo may have included roughly eight hundred rooms, prob-ably no more than six hundred were in use at any one time. Judd estimated that Bonito had housed "in its heyday, no less than 1,200 individuals." [42]

He concluded that Pueblo Bonito's walls were evidence of a progression of four distinct building periods. The earliest walls, in the north and northwest sections, were of relatively crude construction, made of "single-coursed, wall-wide slabs of sandstone bedded in a near-surplus of adobe mud" with some interior walls of "upright slabs ... or posts with mud and rocks between." [43] Later, tree-ring analysis indicated the earliest rooms were built shortly after AD 900. Roberts's stratigraphic pottery analyses correlated this building period with the Pueblo I and II people whom Judd called Old Bonitian.

The less sophisticated construction was superseded by the core and veneer masonry characteristic of most of Pueblo Bonito. Judd believed this shift to more sophisticated construction indicated the arrival of a new group of people, the Late Bonitians. These later people created three successive styles of masonry, all made with sandstone, adobe mortar, and fine veneers of alternating bands of small and large stones, which "faced" the wall's rubble core.

The Late Bonitian builders planned for a multistoried design, and their tapered walls reveal their architectural skill. The ground-floor rooms had very thick walls and high ceilings while the walls of upper-story rooms, which did not bear as much weight, were narrower.

In a very few Old Bonitian rooms, but in many Late Bonitian parts of the ruin, inexplicable construction details appeared, such as T-shaped doorways, a design for which no functional explanation has yet been found. These doors often lead out to kiva courts. Corner windows, which obviously required much preconstruction planning, were another oddity.

Particularly interesting was the presence of thousands of immense wooden ceiling beams, or *vigas.* These were covered with a criss-crossing of wooden poles, or *latillas,* overlaid with a mat of reeds to create a ceiling. The reeds, in turn, were covered with a hard-packed coating of adobe, which formed the floor of the next story. Neither Judd nor later archaeologists could say definitely where the ancient woodcutters, with their stone axes, had found their supply of timber.

Another oddity was the lack of fireplaces. Judd found only sixty-nine hearths in the ruin, almost all in ground-floor rooms. Yet fires for cooking and winter warmth would have been crucial at most Anasazi settlements, where hearths were the centers of domestic life. Judd did, however, find firepits in the Bonitian plazas.

Excavation revealed evidence of much remodeling. Windows and doors frequently were plugged to make solid walls for new rooms, and ground-floor rooms filled with trash served as foundations for the next story. Sometimes rooms were razed to make space for one of the pueblo's nearly three dozen kivas. Twice, additions had been made by merging new walls with old so cleverly that it was difficult to detect any difference. Northeast of the pueblo were foundations for a third addition, which was never built.

Judd hoped to uncover the same amounts and quality of artifacts as Pepper had in the late 1890s. But though he obtained plentiful remains of the Bonitian material culture, including a few phenomenal finds, his discoveries did not rival those of the Hyde Expeditions.

At Pueblo Bonito, as elsewhere in Chaco Canyon, turquoise was abundant, in sharp contrast to Mesa Verde, where little turquoise turned up. The most famous artifact of Judd's excavation was a turquoise necklace, much touted in the press. In 1925 Judd described its workmanship in *National Geographic:*

The reader can scarcely know that an unbelievable amount of labor went into fabrication of this prehistoric jewel; that the rough, unworked stone was obtained only at the cost of great human effort; that the 2,500 beads composing the string were made individually by rubbing small disks of matrix back and forth across sandstone tablets; that each tiny piece was drilled separately with a sharpened flint or some still more pointed instrument.[44]

The copious finds of turquoise, as well as discoveries of exotic items such as parrot feathers, copper bells, obsidian, and ocean shells, led Judd and others to speculate about widespread Chacoan trade and possible connections with Mexico. In fact, at Bonito and other Chaco sites, much nonlocal pottery surfaced, including pieces from Mesa Verde, Kayenta, Mimbres, and other places, as well as some that may have come from Mexico.

Remnants of everyday Anasazi life found at Bonito included housewives' manos and metates, cooking stones, baskets (some of distinctive conical shapes), stone axes and other tools, hunting paraphernalia, tanned skins, rabbit-fur blankets, fragments of cotton cloth, and yucca sandals. Also found were oddments such as caches of red clay that Judd speculated contained women's rouge. "Our Zuni [workmen] begged every fragment we came upon in the excavation and laughingly streaked their faces with it," he wrote.[45] He reported finding children's toys—"rude, miniature ladles and pitchers bearing the imprint of baby fingers"; cottonwood and bark dolls; and other playthings.[46]

Most items became the property of the institutions sponsoring the dig. The bulk went to the U.S. National Museum (the Smithsonian), while the National Geographic Society retained some of the most spectacular items.

THE EXISTENCE OF SO MANY RUINS in the canyon posed a tantalizing mystery. How did the presumably large, ancient population survive in their harsh surroundings? Why did the Chacoans choose such a forbidding environment in which to build a major urban center in the first place?

Besides the ruins themselves, Chaco presented other enigmas. Local Navajos, as well as photographer Jackson, the Wetherills, and Judd, had all noted vestiges of prehistoric stairways in the cliffs behind Pueblo Bonito and other ruins. During his seven years there, Judd explored remnants of broad pathways that led from the wilderness to the stairways. He commented, "The Navaho refer to these pathways as 'roads' and my guess is no better."[47] Decades later, archaeologists would theorize that these ancient thoroughfares were part of a regional system of nearly a hundred settlements now known as "Chaco outlyers," a concept that Judd began researching during his years at Chaco.

The scarcity of burials is perhaps Chaco's best-known archaeological mystery. Despite evidence that a large number of people had lived there, relatively few burials were found before Judd's arrival. Judd and all the generations of archaeologists who followed explored the vicinity for graves, such as those uncovered at Pecos, Hawikuh, and Aztec. Yet Judd found only a few dozen, and his successors no more than a few hundred, a very small amount considering the number and size of the ruins.

In the decades since Judd worked in the canyon, various theories have addressed the riddle of Pueblo Bonito and the other so-called Great Houses, as well as the vast network of prehistoric roads that connect Chaco to outlying settlements. As scientists from many disciplines accumulate more data, the puzzle

The Jackson Staircase (named for explorer-photographer William Henry Jackson) on the north wall of Chaco Canyon near Chetro Ketl.

becomes even more mysterious. One contemporary archaeologist wrote that Chaco "should be a flag alerting us to prehistoric weirdness. When Judd excavated Pueblo Bonito and Hewett dug Chetro Ketl, both were automatically seen as prehistoric Pueblos, just like Zuni. Today, we are not even sure that anybody really lived in those buildings."[48]

Perhaps, some archaeologists now conjecture, a vast ceremonial center once comprised Bonito and the other monumental Chaco buildings. Anasazi farmers from outlying settlements might have traveled over the great roads, bringing foodstuffs for storage and redistribution, and staying for a time in the canyon to attend rituals.

Other archaeologists suggest that the Great Houses could have been palaces for an elite priesthood, while commoners lived in the more humble homes that are scattered along the south canyon wall and elsewhere in the canyon. Or, suggest others, the Great Houses may have been part of a farflung empire centered in Mexico, and the roads may have been built for colonial armies and trade caravans. While archaeologists have developed scientific theories, many Pueblo Indians regard Chaco as an intrinsic part of their cultural heritage. To them, the Great Houses are their ancestral homes.

ONE OF THE MOST INTERESTING environmental studies at Chaco was done by geologist Kirk Bryan, who related the geology of Chaco Canyon to the archaeological stratigraphic record by demonstrating how the erosion and deterioration of farm lands might have affected the Chacoans. Especially significant to Bryan's work was the phenomenon of arroyo cutting.

Judd later summed up Bryan's exploration in the arroyo:

> He examined minutely the banks of the present arroyo, of post-1850 origin. ... He discovered dead campfires and bits of broken pottery 20 feet and more below the surface; he noted that relics of Pueblo III peoples, the builders of Pueblo Bonito and its kind, occurred in the upper 4 feet only and those of earlier peoples below that level.[49]

> Below that level every potsherd was a product of Early Pueblo (PI) or Basket Maker peoples.[50]

Bryan's findings of Basketmaker materials correlated with Judd's discoveries of similar remains, including some beneath Pueblo Bonito. Frank Roberts made archaeological history with his study of a Basketmaker III enclave at the edge of Chacra Mesa, a now well-known site called Shabik'eshchee Village, which he discovered in 1926 and excavated in 1927 for the Smithsonian.

From the environmental studies performed by Bryan and other scientists, Judd got the idea that Chaco had enjoyed "a wetter climate 800 or more years ago." He concluded that "Chaco Canyon was greener when Pueblo Bonito was inhabited and pine trees, cottonwoods, willows, and rushes grew close at hand."[51] One indication of an abundance of trees in prehistoric times was Judd's discovery that a pine tree had actually stood in Pueblo Bonito's West Court, "alive and green, when Pueblo Bonito was inhabited."[52] Judd wrote that "altogether, our observations indicate the former existence of a pine forest in close proximity to Pueblo Bonito, principally on the south [Chacra] mesa but with fringes reaching down into the rincons and even out upon the valley floor."[53]

Judd surmised from the environmental studies that the Bonitians failed to remain in balance with their environment. Although they also hunted and gathered, he believed that they relied heavily on their crops and maintained them through a floodwater irrigation system. Several early visitors and archaeologists had noted what they inferred to be vestiges of an irrigation system, the existence and nature of which became the subject of a vigorous, ongoing archaeological and geological argument.

Though he advanced several possible causes of the eventual abandonment of Pueblo Bonito, Judd suspected that environmental factors were the most likely, beginning with deforestation, which lead to "soil erosion, arroyo cutting, a lowered water table, poorer crops, and eventually abandonment."[54] Most archaeologists today question Judd's notion of the existence of nearby forests, and the source of wood used in Pueblo Bonito's construction remains a mystery.

Without an absolute dating system to work from while he was excavating at Pueblo Bonito, Judd relied on Roberts's stratigraphy to mark the changes over time in pottery and architecture. Later he described the contributions of other archaeologists:

> The color of pottery from prehistoric ruins became a clue that narrowed the search, and here, because of their knowledge of such pottery, Harold S. Colton, director of the Museum of Northern Arizona, and two of his assistants, Lyndon L. Hargrave and Emil W. Haury, contributed materially to the success of our effort to determine the age of Pueblo Bonito.[55]

Judd, like his friend Earl Morris, recognized the tremendous potential value of astronomer A. E. Douglass's work in tree-ring dating. Beginning in 1918, Douglass had worked with specimens Earl Morris procured for him at Aztec. In 1922 Judd sent Douglass the first of more than ninety specimens from Pueblo Bonito that the scientist eventually dated for the National Geographic Society investigations.

Mouthpieces of effigy vessels found at Pueblo Bonito. Figure 55 in "The Material Culture of Pueblo Bonito" by Neil M. Judd (1954).

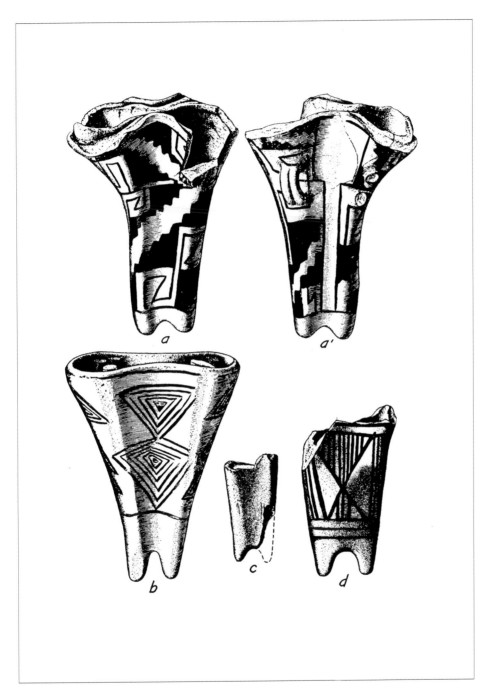

Earthenware effigies of bifurcated baskets excavated by Judd at Pueblo Bonito.
Figure 100 in "The Material Culture of Pueblo Bonito" by Neil M. Judd (1954).

In his research, Douglass used not only whole beams but also charred wood fragments. However, though he examined numerous specimens throughout the 1920s, he was able to create only a "floating" chronology, that is, a sequence of tree-rings that could be used to date specimens up through the present but that was not joined to the prehistoric continuum. Douglass had obtained tree-ring sequences that extended from modern times back to AD 1280 and had developed an earlier prehistoric sequence that was 580 years long. He needed a wood specimen that would provide the necessary "missing link" by connecting the two sequences.

The National Geographic Society's Beam Expeditions of 1923, 1928, and 1929 searched for such a specimen to close the gap. Because of his involvement with Douglass's research, Judd became a leader of the 1923 and 1929 Beam Expeditions. On the third expedition in 1929, the missing link was found by Lyndon Hargrave and Emil Haury. A sequence extending from 1929 back to AD 700 was made possible by this piece of prehistoric wood, numbered HH-39.

> Douglass completed the study of HH-39 during the summer of 1929, and quickly moved on to further work. He used additional specimens … to bolster those parts of the chronology with defective or unconvincing sections. All the new specimens confirmed the results from HH-39. Douglass now confidently began assigning absolute dates to pueblo ruins. He reported to Neil M. Judd in the fall that cutting dates from the Pueblo Bonito timbers ranged from 919 to 1130; most beams had been cut between 1033 and 1092, indicating the height of Bonito activity.[56]

Elated, Douglass wrote in an article for *National Geographic*: "We can now date nearly forty prehistoric ruins in the Southwest and reconstruct there a succession of major events through which Indian settlements rose, passed their heyday, and disappeared."[57]

After Douglass's discovery, Judd was finally able to date the Chaco ruins. He concluded that Pueblo Bonito, a small settlement in the 900s, had undergone two hundred years of intermittent construction to reach its final size of about eight hundred rooms.

It is now believed that most of Pueblo Bonito was built between AD 850 and 1140, and that the biggest burst of construction took place between 1075 and 1115. So much activity indicates a possible immigration of a new group of people. However, contemporary archaeologists have moved away from Judd's early hypotheses about settlement by two distinct and chronologically overlapping groups.

During the course of the excavation Judd wrote several *National Geographic* articles, all published in the 1920s. Partly as a result of these accounts, Pueblo Bonito became a popular symbol of the flowering of Anasazi culture at Chaco Canyon.

Judd completed his scientific reporting tasks much more slowly than his writings for the general public. In 1927, when he returned from his last season at Chaco, Judd intended to begin his final reports on the excavation, planning optimistically to finish them the following year. He finally completed this task more than three decades later, while some additional smaller reports he had hoped to author remained forever unwritten. Probably the major obstacle to completing the final reports was Judd's curatorial work at the National Museum, which took up most of his time and energy.

Waldo Wedel described his friend Judd's meticulous writing process:

> Neil habitually wrote in long hand, with pencil; I never saw him composing on a typewriter. In my first few years at the museum, when I came to the division office for research after hours and on weekends the waste basket beside his desk not infrequently held masses of yellow legal-size paper covered with his running script, heavily marked up with red or blue pencil, and then, after frequent revisions, discarded for a fresh start next week. Some of these sheafs consisted of 20–30 pages, and undoubtedly represented several weeks of patient writing, all scrapped when they failed to measure up to his standards.[58]

Judd originally wanted to publish his results in the same sequence that the discoveries were made. However, in the end, Douglass's 1935 work "Dating Pueblo Bonito and Other Ruins of the Southwest" became the first official publication of the expedition. The second was Bryan's report on the geology of Chaco Canyon. Next to appear were Judd's *Material Culture of Pueblo Bonito*, published in 1954, and *Pueblo del Arroyo, Chaco Canyon, New Mexico*, published in 1959. Judd's other final report, *The Architecture of Pueblo Bonito*, appeared years later, in 1964.

Judd paid for his slowness in reporting, enduring pressure and criticism from his colleagues, the Smithsonian brass, and his National Geographic Society sponsors. In the early 1950s, when his final report on Bonito's material culture was approaching readiness for publication, the Smithsonian balked at the lateness and cost of the project.

Gilbert Grosvenor, president of the National Geographic Society, wrote in the preface of the 1954 report: "After his completed manuscript was submitted to the National Geographic Society, its Board of Trustees, acting upon the recommendation of the Research Committee, placed the material at the disposal of the Smithsonian Institution and provided for its publication."[59] The title page of the report was inscribed, "Published under a Grant from the National Geographic Society."

Though his reports came out years after the expedition, Judd deserves credit for completing the massive documents. Some Southwestern archaeologists, including Hewett, his successor at Chaco Canyon, who excavated Chetro Ketl in the late 1920s and 1930s, never did write final reports on their digs.

Judd's final reports traced developments from Basketmaker III times through Pueblo Bonito's abandonment in the 1100s. He used the terminology of the 1927 Pecos Classification instead of his earlier "Old" and "Late Bonitian" nomenclature:

> Pueblo Bonito began as a wide-spreading crescent of Pueblo II houses with storerooms at the rear, several subterranean kivas out in front, and the village trash pile beyond. After that trash had accumulated to a depth of 8 feet or more, after 5 feet of sand had settled against the old P. II houses, another people came to join the original settlers—a Pueblo III people with a more advanced architecture and a different pottery complex. Together, the houses these P. III people built and the pottery they made are now widely accepted as earmarks of a distinct social development, "The Chaco Culture"....
>
> I am of the opinion that the P. II and P. III peoples who formerly dwelt there had come independently from beyond the San Juan River, but I can only guess at their destination after leaving Chaco Canyon.[60]

Judd believed that the High Chaco culture, the origins of which were sought by the National Geographic Society, was brought to the canyon by the Pueblo III people when it was "just short of full bloom."[61] He saw evidence of the spread of this Chaco culture to settlements such as Aztec Pueblo and Lowry Ruin near Mesa Verde. He also believed that after its initial abandonment, Pueblo Bonito was resettled for a time by Mesa Verde people, a pattern seen at other Southwestern ruins.

Later generations would question and debate many of Judd's conclusions, and some would criticize his reports as being hard to read and to use in subsequent fieldwork. Still, his work was undeniably monumental. In 1985, researcher Joan Mathien wrote: "Many of the data and inferences made as a result of the Expedition's work provided a strong basis for future debate, reexamination, and additional research."[62]

Judd retired from the National Museum in 1949. Once his reporting on Chaco was finished, he found time to write an entertaining institutional history, *The Bureau of American Ethnology* (1967). The following year his enjoyable memoir, *Men Met Along the Trail: Adventures in Archaeology* (1968) appeared. Judd's affection for his colleagues, his appreciation of the foibles of his fellow human beings, and his mellow sense of humor emerge clearly in these little volumes.

In 1965, Judd received the A. V. Kidder award. Just a few years earlier, surveying the changes he had seen during his long career, he wrote:

> Archaeology has come of age. . . . Fieldwork is more thorough today; members of the profession are better prepared. And, in general, they are softer. Autos and hard-top roads, bridges, telephones, and can openers have erased the rugged individualism of 50 years ago. Pack mules are obsolete. And so's the diamond-hitch. Few, if any, archaeologists can stir up a batch of baking powder biscuits in the top of a flour sack today; few can crush a pound of Arbuckle's coffee in the corner of a bedtarp; few, if any, would try to sleep under a sweaty saddle blanket. But, as in every other activity, richer rewards came in the wake of the pioneers.[63]

Excavations of Hohokam houses of the
Sacaton phase at the Snaketown II dig,
1964–65.

CHAPTER 6

SNAKETOWN

Emil W. Haury's Discoveries in the
Land of the Hohokam

IN THE EARLY 1930S a major scientific discovery was made at a cluster of barren, sun-baked mounds in the Arizona desert, a place inhabited only by a small group of Pima Indians and some healthy rattlesnake colonies. Archaeologists digging there uncovered the remains of a sophisticated, prehistoric farming culture that had once spread across the upper Sonoran desert, with influences extending as far north as present-day Flagstaff.

"Snaketown," as the site was called, lay south of today's sprawling megalopolis of Phoenix. Once a thriving agricultural and urban center, it had flourished in its inhospitable desert environment far longer than has Phoenix.

The ancient people of Snaketown and their many neighbors, whose settlements and irrigation canals crisscrossed the desert, disappeared inexplicably sometime before the first Spanish explorers arrived. Sixteenth- and seventeenth-century Spanish accounts mention Indians of the tribes now called O'odham (Pima and Papago) living near Snaketown. But the Europeans saw no living evidence of the prehistoric desert farmers; the only remains of those ancient people were their abandoned towns, which had by then disintegrated into sandy mounds.

In the late 1800s and around the turn of the century, some exploratory excavations had been conducted in the Phoenix area at sites in the

Salt-Gila River drainages. Frank Hamilton Cushing led the Hemenway Expedition, via horse and wagon, into southern Arizona in the late 1880s. At the ruin of La Ciudad de los Los Muertos, some ten miles north of Snaketown, Cushing performed excavations that were systematic for his day. He noted unusual finds, including cremated burials and remnants of ancient irrigation systems.

Peripatetic anthropologist, historian, linguist, and ethnologist Adolph Bandelier had visited the area before Cushing, in the early 1880s. He returned in 1888 with the Hemenway party to observe its excavations at Los Muertos and also to visit the mysterious, four-story-high adobe ruin known as Casa Grande, thirty miles southeast of Snaketown. In 1891 Cosmos Mindeleff visited Casa Grande ruin and wrote about its unique architecture in a Bureau of American Ethnology report published in 1896. Walter Hough passed through the area with the Museum-Gates Expedition just after the turn of the century.

Jesse Walter Fewkes, of the Bureau of American Ethnology, had excavated at Casa Grande by 1910. Fewkes called the ancient desert dwellers *Hohokam,* a Pima term meaning "those who have vanished" or, more literally, "all used up."[1] Though not the first to use this term for the prehistoric desert people, Fewkes introduced it to the scholarly world. He did not distinguish the desert farmers culturally from the prehistoric people whose stone and adobe pueblos and other remains had been found to the north and east.

Fewkes, Cushing, and others of their era adhered to the widespread belief that a single culture had inhabited the entire American Southwest and possibly extended into Mexico. They "regarded culture change as indicative of the migration of a single people through differing environments."[2]

Some years after Fewkes's dig, archaeologist Arthur Woodward excavated another ruin known as the Grewe site, just east of the Casa Grande ruin. Later archaeologists would refer to Woodward's 1931 report on his systematic excavations as they tried to develop a chronology for the desert farming culture.

These early explorers obtained a sketchy overview of the desert sites, which consisted mainly of mounds rising only a few feet above the desert floor. Most archaeologists then turned their attention to the Anasazi remains to the north, particularly to the spectacular masonry ruins such as those at Mesa Verde and Chaco—sites where impressive architecture piqued curiosity and stirred hopes of exciting finds.

Consequently, it was not until the Depression years of 1934 and 1935 that a young archaeologist, Emil W. Haury, made scientific history in the Arizona desert. The twenty-nine-year-old Harvard Ph.D. went to Snaketown in the fall of 1934 under the auspices of a research organization called Gila Pueblo. His boss and financial backer at the Snaketown dig was Harold Sterling Gladwin, a hard-driving, eccentric, amateur archaeologist who left an indelible mark on

Harold Gladwin at Gila
Pueblo, 1930s.

Southwestern archaeology. Gladwin founded Gila Pueblo and used it to carry
out some remarkable archaeological enterprises for two decades, beginning in
the late 1920s.

After making a fortune as a Wall Street tycoon, in 1922 Gladwin sold his
seat on the Stock Exchange and moved to California. A personal friendship
he developed with Alfred Vincent Kidder stimulated Gladwin's interest in becoming an amateur archaeologist. Kidder suggested that Gladwin look at sites
in the southern deserts, which the astute archaeologist believed needed more
attention.

Though both Kidder and Alfred Kroeber of the University of California
recognized the possible significance of Arizona's desert farmers to the unfolding
prehistory of the Southwest, it was Gladwin who had the time and the money
to make the mounds in the desert his main focus. Under the auspices of the
Southwest Museum in Los Angeles, the financier-turned-archaeologist was soon
excavating there.

Gladwin's archaeological interests were also strongly influenced by Frank
("The Boss") Pinkley, the chief administrator of the National Park Service's
Southwestern Monuments, headquartered at Casa Grande National Monument.
Pinkley, whose self-styled leadership made him a Park Service legend, was also
the custodian of the monument.

An old hand at Arizona archaeology, he had dug with Fewkes at Casa Grande. In 1919 Pinkley was considering stratigraphic excavations at a prehistoric trash deposit near Casa Grande, likely inspired by reports of archaeologist Nels Nelson's work in the Galisteo Basin and Kidder's use of stratigraphy at Pecos. In a letter to his Park Service boss, Pinkley wrote of his plans for a stratigraphic excavation: "So far as I know this experiment has never been tried in the trash mounds in this valley."[3] Pinkley shared his interest in the project with Gladwin, who subsequently dug in the midden of Compound B at the ruins of Casa Grande, and also at a site at nearby Adamsville, in 1926.

In 1927, while exploring in Six Shooter Canyon on the outskirts of Globe, Arizona, Gladwin found pottery sherds, similar to "intrusive" ones he had noticed at Casa Grande, scattered at the site of an abandoned fourteenth-century pueblo. "I ... was delighted," he wrote, "to find that the ruin was a large mound covered with the same kind of black, white, and red polychrome which we had found at Casa Grande, ... [which] was the only kind of [local decorated] pottery made by the people who had once lived there [near present-day Globe]."[4]

That discovery set in motion Gladwin's greatest contribution to archaeology. He decided to build a research center at the site of his pottery find. The idea for this endeavor had developed earlier, on a trip Gladwin made to Acoma, New Mexico, with the Kidders. In the winter of 1927–28, Gladwin, his future wife, Winifred Jones MacCurdy, and their secretary began to make his idea a reality. As part of the project they started to reconstruct the ancient pueblo.

Gladwin tried to recreate the appearance of the old pueblo, though he soon gave up attempts to duplicate the exact floor plan. For building materials, the work crews used reinforced concrete and cobblestones rather than adobe. The final product, completed in 1934, was a rambling, three-story, pueblo-style building of charm and grace, surrounded by gardens and trees. This research center, which the Gladwins named Gila Pueblo, became their home, workplace, and headquarters for the Gila Pueblo Archaeological Foundation, which they established to sponsor exploration and scholarship in the Southwest.

Other institutions for archaeological research were springing up around this time, such as the Laboratory of Anthropology in Santa Fe, the Museum of Northern Arizona at Flagstaff, and the Amerind Foundation at Dragoon in southern Arizona. Each strengthened the discipline by coordinating and focusing some phase of regional research. Their existence provided a regional network that lessened Southwestern scholars' dependence on more distant institutions.

By 1934 Gila Pueblo had supported a number of archaeological projects. The Gladwins also oversaw a landmark series of reports covering their explorations. These they published under the series title of the Medallion Papers—a name inspired by a design on one of the prehistoric pots found at ancient Gila Pueblo. The organization's archaeologists, including Harold Gladwin himself, reported their work promptly under the Medallion imprint. This commitment to timely reporting and publication was another of Gladwin's major contributions.

Archaeologist Watson Smith visited Gila Pueblo in its heyday, and later wrote:

> Mr. Gladwin was a monomaniac on the subject of archaeology. He had an intense mind, an active mind, which was never quiet, and having established Gila Pueblo to unravel the problems of the archaeology of the Southwest, he never let that subject rest. During mealtimes at Gila Pueblo it was discussed, mostly by him in terms of a monologue, and at least once a week, a staff meeting was held in the big living room at the Pueblo, presided over by Mr. Gladwin and often attended by visiting dignitaries like Dr. Kidder or Paul Martin or whomever. These were seriously ... planned discussions of archaeological theory and practice.[5]

Besides the influence he wielded as head of Gila Pueblo, Gladwin used his idiosyncratic intellectual approach to goad the research of Southwestern archaeologists, many of whom regarded him as a gadfly.[6] More than one archaeologist was forced to take to the field and/or research laboratory in order to prove a point to Gladwin. Archaeologist Katharine Bartlett, colleague of and assistant to Dr. Harold Colton, founder of the Museum of Northern Arizona, remembered how Gladwin's statements about Colton's hypotheses on the Sinagua people had annoyed Colton. "Dr. Colton was quite upset by it," she recalled, "and he did start very soon on a book to prove Gladwin was wrong."[7]

There was no doubt that Gladwin enjoyed arguing with those whom he referred to as "my Ph.D. friends." Archaeologist J. O. Brew wrote, "With Gladwin ... one really should work in conversation. He moves too fast for publication."[8] In the preface to one of the volumes of his Medallion series, Gladwin made a typical challenge: "Those theories which are not now acceptable may be charged to my account, but this should be regarded as a warning that I intend, someday, to prove them all, provided that I do not change my mind; a possibility which these men will recognize."[9]

His jabs could be cruel, and he lost many friends to ideological battles. Kidder was among those estranged. In his 1947 cartoon-illustrated book, *Men Out of Asia*, Gladwin created a character named Dr. Phuderick Duddy,[10] whom Kidder took be a caricature of himself. On the dedication page of the book, Gladwin wrote, "The apparent resemblance of any character in this book to any living person is purely intentional."

Though his manner was irritating, Gladwin made a vital contribution to archaeological exploration: money. During the Great Depression, his solid financial status and unflagging interest and support provided needed backing for the still-young profession at a time when the nation lingered in financial doldrums.

G LADWIN HAD AN INSATIABLE CURIOSITY about the origin of man in the Americas. He believed it could be traced back to Asiatic migrations, and he disagreed with the then-prevailing one-culture hypothesis of Southwestern prehistory. He wanted to find out more about the prehistoric origins of man in the Southwest, and particularly the mysterious people whose ruins were scattered abundantly in the Salt-Gila River basins. Accordingly, in 1927 Gladwin launched a region-wide archaeological survey sponsored by Gila Pueblo.

Young Emil W. Haury, whom Gladwin recognized as an intellectually gifted scientist and indefatigable worker, was invited to participate in and help direct the survey. Gila Pueblo teams visited well over ten thousand sites, from the Mississippi River to the California Coast and from Utah to Mexico. A huge map was kept at Gila Pueblo for recording discovered sites. Pottery sherds brought back from the surveyors' travels were mounted on large boards for convenient inspection.

Though Gladwin began the survey with the idea of learning more about the people who built Casa Grande and Los Muertos, the explorations uncovered traces of other cultures, including one group in the highlands of eastern Arizona and western New Mexico that later became known as *Mogollon*. The ongoing survey continued throughout Gladwin's career at Gila Pueblo. Of all the mysterious desert sites it located, none proved more intriguing than those in the Gila-Salt River vicinity, especially the site called Snaketown.

After considering many places, Gladwin and his team of archaeologists decided to take a closer look at the Snaketown mounds, which they had located in 1927. The site appeared to be in the "core area"[11] of the ancient desert farming culture—the Gila-Salt River basins. It lay on Pima land some twelve miles southwest of the farming community of Chandler, at an elevation of about 1,175 feet.

When Haury and his colleagues arrived, Snaketown was a Pima settlement of "about fifteen houses with a population of about fifty persons."[12] Some of the Pimas elected to work on the excavation crews.

The vandals who had ravaged so many other mounds near Phoenix had missed Snaketown, perhaps because of its obscure location and, possibly, the watchfulness of the Pimas. Gladwin described it as "a site which we all believe is probably the only unspoiled one of its kind to be found."[13]

The days when anyone who cared to could excavate wherever he or she pleased were over, and Gladwin was required to apply to the U.S. Department of the Interior for a permit to dig at the site. While the archaeologists waited for offi-

cial permission, "Stephen Knox, a Pima, ... patrolled the site daily throughout the summer [of 1934] to prevent the plundering of pot-hunters."[14]

Snaketown comprised sixty mounds,[15] spread over an area about three-quarters of a mile long and half a mile wide. The mounds varied in height from one to three meters and measured ten to sixty meters wide.[16] Over and around the mounds were scattered bits of red, plain, and red-on-buff pottery, the ceramic trademark of the ancient desert farming people.

At such a large site the archaeologists hoped to find vestiges of public architecture, which would help unravel the complexities of the vanished society. They also suspected that because Snaketown quite likely had been inhabited for centuries by a large number of people, the farmers must have practiced sophisticated agricultural methods in order to produce enough food for the entire population.

The ruins of Snaketown proper were surrounded by bare, cracked, sandy soil containing deposits of a lime-rich substance known as *caliche,* used by the ancient Indians as a kind of natural cement. The sparse desert vegetation—cacti,

Aerial view of the Snaketown II excavations, 1964–65. More than sixty Hohokam house floors are visible.

mesquite, palo verde, and creosote and salt bushes—offered little greenery or shade from summer's blazing heat.

A little less than a mile from Snaketown lay the usually dry bed of the Gila River, which in ancient times had flowed perennially between banks fringed with cottonwoods and willows, offering a haven for birds and game. The Snaketown settlement extended for about a square kilometer across a flat, fertile river valley on the upper terrace of the Gila River. On this higher area, and also on the lower terrace just above the river's floodplain, the ancient Indians irrigated their crops of maize, beans, and cotton. Though the fertile river valley soil worked in their favor, the hot, arid climate did not.

Moisture came to the desert farmers biannually, during summer thunderstorms and winter rains. Though it might fall in torrents, overall annual precipitation was very light, only ten inches or so a year. At the peaks of wet weather, the level of the mountain-fed Gila River would rise, providing extra water for the farmers' elaborate canal system.

In the distance the ragged tops of barren volcanic mountains fringed the horizon. To the southeast jutted rugged Gila Butte, and to the southwest stood Pima Butte. The jagged silhouette of the Sierra Estrella rose to the west.

The Pima Indians called the spot "Place of the Snakes" because of the large colonies of rattlesnakes that hunted rodents from their burrows in the soft fill of the mounds. Haury later commented that during the excavation anxiety about the snakes helped sharpen everyone's powers of observation.

Besides snakes and burrowing rodents, the area was home to many small, hardy creatures, such as coyotes, jack rabbits, cottontails, quail, and hawks. "There were many coyotes around Snaketown because the Pimas did not harm them. As many as six or eight would come through the job site, right past us all," remembered one of the crew.[17]

The archaeologists living at Snaketown developed an almost mystical appreciation for the subtle beauty of the Sonoran desert. Haury wrote:

> Beyond the dry statistics of the physical setting, the Hohokam habitat had an ethos peculiar unto itself, a quality best experienced to understand it. Perhaps it is the combination of many things that establishes in a resident the feeling of peace and tranquility and an honest appreciation of the contrasts between the searing heat of the day and the bone-rattling chill of the night; the powder-dry land one minute, a quagmire the next; the unbelievable mirages in the morning and the crystal-clear night sky; the dust devils, the dimensionless vistas ending in a ragged mountain backdrop that reminds one of pasteboard cutouts, and the smell of the desert after a rain. . . . It is easy to convince oneself

that these environmental influences were felt by the Hohokam in the tenth century as well.[18]

Haury's esteem extended also to the desert farmers' enduring way of life: "Obviously in archaeology we must draft a different set of guidelines to judge the toughness of a people," Haury wrote, "but the endurance of a society...is a quality we should try to measure, for it might say something to us about our own survival."[19]

THE SON of a Kansas college professor, Haury was introduced to Native Americans by stories in *National Geographic, American Boy,* and other magazines. He was fascinated by the ancient potsherds in his father's curio cabinet, gathered by his parents on a visit to Walnut Canyon near Flagstaff, Arizona. From his boyhood he hoped for a career in archaeology.

Through a "lucky break" at the age of twenty-one,[20] he met Dr. Byron Cummings, who in 1925 sponsored his participation at a dig at Cuicuilco, near Mexico City, and subsequently helped him enter the University of Arizona's archaeology program. In 1929 Haury worked for Dr. A. E. Douglass, creator of the tree-ring dating technique. The next year he took up his role as Gladwin's assistant director of Gila Pueblo.

Four years later, Gladwin appointed him director of the Snaketown dig. In the interim, Haury worked prodigiously, excavating at a central Arizona site known as Roosevelt 9:6 and obtaining his doctorate from Harvard. He wrote his thesis on Cushing's excavations at La Cuidad de los Muertos.

Haury's humor and good manners softened the somewhat austere impression created by his intellectual intensity and physical stamina. Colleagues found a good friend behind his dignified reserve. One archaeologist commented that Haury could also be "a stubborn Dutchman" when it came to defending his intellectual concepts.[21] According to his biographer, J. Jefferson Reid, Emil Haury agreed to work with Gladwin, known to Southwestern archaeologists as an eccentric, "because Gladwin promised fieldwork and publication opportunities and support for doctoral studies."[22]

With his academic credentials and personal integrity, Haury legitimized Gladwin's program. His presence at Gila Pueblo deflected the criticism of some local civic leaders, who viewed the wealthy amateur as a pot hunter.[23] Haury's dignified demeanor helped to balance the effects of Gladwin's flamboyant and outspoken personality.

Though Gladwin was important to his career, Haury particularly appreciated the influence of his earlier mentor, A. E. Douglass. "I value the year I had to work with him," Haury later said, "because it taught me the discipline I

Left: The staff of the Gila Pueblo excavations at Snaketown, 1935: (left to right) Emil Haury, Julian Hayden, Evelyn Dennis, Irwin Hayden, E. B. Sayles, Nancy Pinkley, Erik K. Reed, and J. C. Fisher Motz. Right: Astronomer A. E. Douglass, inventor of the tree-ring dating technique, obtaining a core sample near Forestdale Ruin, Arizona, 1928.

needed, which Cummings had not, being a social scientist — they look at things differently. . . . Douglass did a lot to instill the principles of scientific procedures in me."[24]

On June 22, 1929, while working for Douglass, student archaeologists Haury and Lyndon Hargrave discovered HH-39, the prehistoric wood sample that provided the tree-rings needed to complete the sequence from modern back through prehistoric times. "That was the single most exciting moment in my archaeological career," Haury remembered.[25]

The discovery of that specimen, which later archaeologists termed "the 'Rosetta log' of Southwestern tree-ring dating,"[26] meant that, as Haury pointed out, "we have been able to speak of the ages of Pueblo Bonito, the Mesa Verde Ruins, Aztec, Betatakin, Keet Seel, and others with confidence, in terms of absolute dates."[27]

Haury saw the tree-ring discovery as the result of years of meticulous scientific work. In a 1988 interview he commented,

> In archaeology it's seldom that you make a great discovery . . . in the course of a day or two. . . . The finds don't come that way. What we learn about the lifestyle of a people — their cultural behavior, their relationships — is the product of many years' work. Instant discoveries don't happen. But HH-39 is one that did. However, you have to put it into the context of what Douglass had done, how many years he had been working on the tree-rings to set the stage for that.[28]

Before that, while under Cummings's tutelage in 1926, Haury participated in a vital discovery at Whitewater Draw in southeastern Arizona. At a place known to archaeologists as the "Double Adobe site," mammoth bones were found in association with remains of the so-called Cochise culture. The find showed that these people inhabited the vicinity of present-day southern Arizona as early as 8000 BC. Like another discovery that year, a find of early man's artifacts at the "kill site" of a Pleistocene bison at Folsom, New Mexico, the Whitewater Draw remains extended the "time-depth" of Southwestern prehistory. Some archaeologists concluded that the Cochise people were the ancestors of the desert farmers of Snaketown and other ruins. This idea proved controversial, and after a second Snaketown excavation, Haury rejected it.

THE CUMULATIVE EXPERIENCE of the Snaketown team was impressive, and some of the archaeologists later became well-known for their important contributions to the field. E. B. ("Ted") Sayles served as Haury's chief assistant at Snaketown. He had also participated in the Gila Pueblo survey of prehistoric sites in California and Chihuahua, Mexico.

Two other crew members, already familiar with southern Arizona sites, were Irwin Hayden and his son, Julian. The Haydens had excavated for the Los Angeles Museum, and Irwin held a degree in anthropology from Harvard. A lively intellect with a natural bent for anthropology, Julian provided the Snaketown team with a mix of construction skills that came in handy around the dig.

Another archaeologist on the Snaketown staff was Erik K. Reed, who had worked with Haury the year before at prehistoric Mimbres sites in western New Mexico. "Boss" Pinkley's daughter, Margaret, acted as the Snaketown expedition's field secretary.

Haury provided incisive leadership, demanding hard work and disciplined reliance on scientific procedures. He contributed not only a sharp intellect but also physical strength. Standing 6 feet, 3 inches, his lean figure had earned him the Navajo nickname of "Tall Slim Guy"[29] during a summer when he worked for Cummings on Four Corners archaeology.

Strong camaraderie developed among the archaeologists, who all lived at the site. "That's the kind of nice camp it was," remembered Julian Hayden. "We could all joke, we all got along."[30] The Gladwins visited from time to time. Other visitors included Kidder, Sylvanus Morley, John Otis Brew, and Harold Colton.

Some twenty-five Pima (O'odham) Indians worked each year for Haury as excavators. Gladwin wrote:

We place the Pima in a class by themselves; they work harder, are more careful, have a greater interest in their work, than any other people we have used. We regard many of them as personal friends, and it was a great pleasure to find most of our old workmen waiting for us when we returned to the site in the autumn of 1935.[31]

"The Pimas were delightful to work with … a cheerful lot," Haury recalled.[32] Occasionally Haury asked the Pimas to tell him their myths and legends, which hinted intriguingly at prehistoric events, though generally such lore would not be included in the scientific work. For some of the archaeological features at Snaketown, the Pimas had their own stories and names; for example, they called the large depression that later proved to be a ballcourt "Bat Man's Dancing Place." Woven into some of their tribal legends were tales of calamities, including a major flood; later tree-ring dating indicated that rainfall during some prehistoric years could indeed have caused severe flooding. Such catastrophes were sometimes suggested as reasons for the disappearance of the ancient farmers of the desert.

Summer temperatures of well over a hundred degrees Fahrenheit made excavating at Snaketown impossible during the hottest months. Digging proceeded from late September through May for two consecutive seasons, 1934 and 1935. Gladwin wrote,

> Our permit was granted, and camp was established in late September, 1934; board floors were laid for the tents; we cleaned out one of the Pima shallow wells and piped water over to a tank near the mess tent. This gave us ample water for domestic use and for washing sherds, although

Excavation of House II, grid 6G, at Snaketown in February 1935.

analysis showed the presence of typhus and other bacteria, making it necessary for us to haul our drinking water from Chandler.[33]

The Pima crews spent many hours tediously hand-digging trenches and test pits at the one-kilometer-square dig, which the archaeologists carefully gridded: "Our first step was to divide the site into blocks, each sixty meters square, each block indicated, west to east, by a letter of the alphabet, and north to south by a numeral."[34]

The archaeologists' field method focused first on creating a "horizontal stratigraphy" for the numbered blocks at the site:

The first step in testing a block was to put down a series of pits until solid caliche was reached. These pits were two meters apart and Hayden rigged up a long lath frame so that his holes would all be symmetrical. As a general rule, caliche was found at about half a meter, but often, without any warning, deep pits were found which ran down to two meters or more. Regardless of the depth, all sherds from each test hole were sacked and marked. These were then taken up to Gila Pueblo, classified, and counted.[35]

Haury assigned each archaeologist to manage a work crew:

Sayles, Reed, and Irwin Hayden were each given four or five Pimas, and they then chose where they would begin their tests. Hayden began in the northwest corner in blocks 3 C and 3 D; Sayles, with an uncanny sense of hidden treasure, took 6 G; and Reed began in 9 E and 9 F.

Haury took Julian Hayden and his gang of Pimas and cut a trench through Mound 11, in the northwest quarter of the site.[36]

Later Haury worked on the deep trash deposit of Mound 29, which he chose to explore "because of its size, being the highest above desert level in the village, therefore offering the greatest possibility of a long sequence."[37] Broad stratigraphic trenches were dug through the trash middens, and the central trench at Mound 29 reached a depth of fifteen feet. Haury described the work:

The decision was reached to remove an entire cross section of the mound under conditions of absolute control. This would then enable the study of the material from all contiguous parts of the mound in conjunction with observation of the stratification. . . .

The chief consideration was that the trench should pass through the crest of the mound so as to test the rubbish at its maximum depth.[38]

Mound 29 at Snaketown, trenched during the first Snaketown excavations to provide Haury with stratigraphic data used in his chronology of the site.

Digging in the soft fill of the mounds proved treacherous. The trenches were dug sufficiently broad that if the towering sides caved in, the dirt would have plenty of space to spread out, and the workers would have room to duck away from the collapsing walls. Haury himself was half-buried one day during a cave-in.

Julian Hayden, who worked at "facing," or smoothing the sides of the stratigraphic cuts in Mound 29, remembered his anxiety about working beneath the sheer trench walls. He recalled having "nightmares about being down there" with sides towering ten or fifteen feet above him. One morning after a particularly nervous night, he returned to the trench to find "the whole thing had caved in." [39]

A FTER THE GILA PUEBLO SURVEY, Gladwin wrote reports on the "Red-on-buff culture," a term referring to the distinctive pottery of the desert farmers. When the Gila Pueblo archaeologists began reporting on the Snaketown excavation, however, they used the term *Hohokam* for the vanished Indians.

Hohokam architecture became Sayles's specialty, while Haury focused on ceramics. Their work conclusively distinguished the Hohokam buildings and pottery from those of the Anasazi.

The Anasazi Indians built their pottery by coiling thin ropes of wet clay and then smoothing the walls by scraping with a piece of gourd or other smooth-edged implement. The Hohokam also coiled their pots, but used an anvil (usually a river cobble) to support the wet clay walls while smoothing the surface with a wooden paddle.

The Snaketown artisans made pots of desert clay containing shiny bits of mica, often covering them with geometric designs or animal or human figures painted in red. Frequently they used lively curvilinear motifs. Another favorite design showed flat-footed figures, dancing with arms outstretched and hands waving extended fingers.

The usually buff-colored Hohokam vessels included large storage jars with capacities of up to thirty gallons; shallow, flat-bottomed dishes; jars with narrow openings flaring to bowl-shaped bodies; scoops, beakers, and vases; effigy vessels; and legged containers such as incense burners.

Excavations showed that the shapes and designs of Snaketown pottery evolved gradually. Haury grouped the pottery into ceramic types and then used the sequence of ceramic development, indicated by stratigraphy, to create a relative chronology.

Haury noted the questions he asked himself during this process:

> Since the chief material used in defining horizons was pottery, the story it tells may, or may not, also confirm the stratified arrangement. That is, do the changes in form and design of pottery follow through logically when arranged in chronological order? Are the transitions from type to type smooth and the style changes rational?[40]

Gladwin later challenged Haury's time periods, which were based on the stratigraphy of Mound 29, partly because of the arbitrary two-century-long intervals into which the chronology was divided. As a result, Haury eventually returned to Snaketown to reexamine both stratigraphy and chronology.

Sayles's report on Snaketown's architecture helped develop a picture of the prehistoric Southwest as divided into roughly two architectural provinces, Anasazi and Hohokam. Unlike Pueblo structures of rock, mud, and timber, Hohokam dwellings were built on a framework of poles, brush, and reeds, to which mud, fortified with caliche, was applied.

The Hohokam built their oval or rectangular huts over very shallow pits. Their single-story, probably single-family, homes included entryways, living areas with basin-shaped firepits, and storage spaces. They also built outdoor shade structures, or *ramadas*.

Late in the Hohokam era, after about AD 1200, the desert farmers started building the large adobe structures that archaeologists call "Big Houses." The monumental, multistoried ruin at Casa Grande dates from the fourteenth century. Snaketown proper was not inhabited then, though adjacent settlements just to the west were.

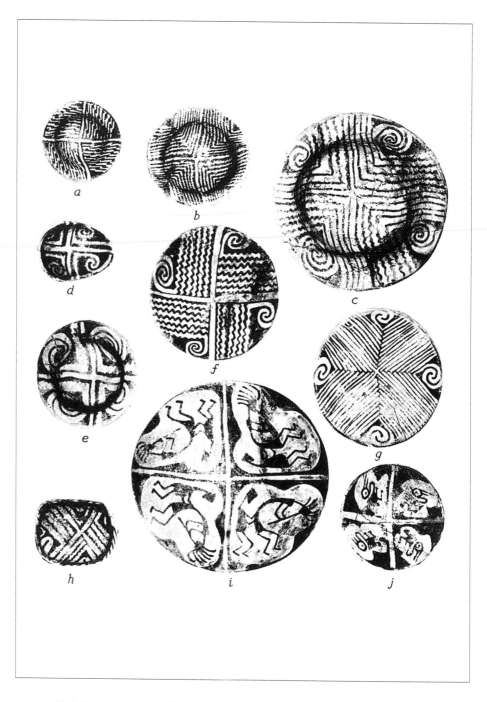

Hohokam pottery classified as "Santa Cruz red-on-buff." Plate 158 from "Excavations at Snaketown: Material Culture," by Harold S. Gladwin, Emil W. Haury, E. B. Sales, and Nora Gladwin (1937).

PLATE CI

Hohokam palettes found during the Snaketown I dig. The use of these artifacts is still unknown. Plate 101 from "Excavations at Snaketown: Material Culture," by Harold S. Gladwin, Emil W. Haury, E. B. Sales, and Nora Gladwin (1937).

Floor plans of Hohokam dwellings, drawn from E. B. Sayles's postulated reconstructions. Figure 36 in "Excavations at Snaketown: Material Culture," by Harold S. Gladwin, Emil W. Haury, E. B. Sales, and Nora Gladwin (1937).

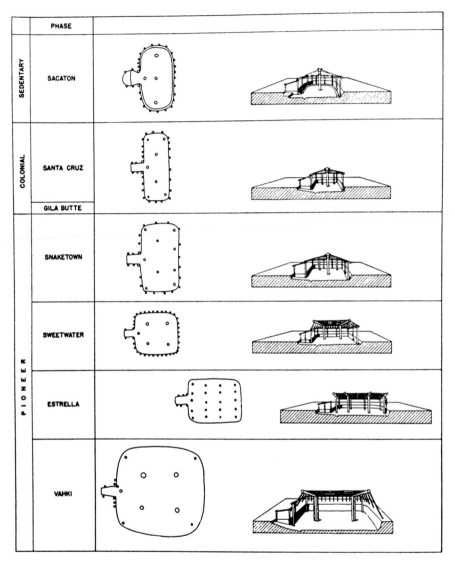

Some of the brush and mud houses at Snaketown had floors covering as many as forty square meters. These large, relatively flimsy dwellings were much less permanent than the solidly constructed Anasazi pueblos, however, and the Hohokam walls must have collapsed shortly after the inhabitants ceased to maintain them.

Excavating Snaketown meant searching for remnants of Hohokam floors, the only remaining vestiges of their homes. This delicate task required clearing fill to find a hard-packed floor level, then gingerly scraping away debris to reveal the outlines of the dwelling. Seen from above, the Snaketown excavation looked like an irregular patchwork, outlined by the holes that once held poles supporting the houses' outer walls and ceilings. As with Anasazi architecture, newer houses were built on top of older ones. This superposition of structures made excavating all the more difficult, but it also enabled the crews to uncover many centuries of architecture on one block of ground.

NINETEENTH-CENTURY SETTLERS in the Phoenix area had noted "ribbons of brown soil mounded between the [prehistoric] towns."[41] These were vestiges of a widespread prehistoric Hohokam canal system created with no technology other than stone tools, sharpened sticks, and carrying baskets. In 1930 Neil Judd described a Smithsonian-sponsored project to map the ancient waterways, using aerial survey and photography to locate canal remnants.[42]

Haury pointed out that the Hohokam culture depended upon the canals. He also wrote that "an appreciation of the Indians' accomplishments came first through the recognition of their canal systems, for the white settlers busy in

Trench in bed of Snaketown canal, excavated by the Gila Pueblo archaeologists, 1934–35.

constructing their own irrigating systems were spared many hours of labor in some cases by clearing out the ancient ditches."[43]

Many of the old waterways were as much as two meters deep and three meters across; some, such as those behind the Pueblo Grande ruin, were even wider:

> The canals at Pueblo Grande were marked by two pairs of conspicuous ridges, the remains of the banks which several centuries of erosion had not yet leveled. ...
>
> One of the most impressive revelations of [the excavation] trench was the size of the original canals, about 10 and 6 m. wide at the former ground level, and about 26 and 18 m. wide from crest to crest of the banks.[44]

The water system at Snaketown included both wells and canals. For domestic use, the people probably relied on water from shallow wells, drawing on a near-to-the-surface aquifer beneath their settlement. The river water in the canals would have been used mainly for irrigation.

Based on the 1934–35 excavations, Haury reported on vestiges of three canals at Snaketown, all associated with later stages of the settlement's development. One archaeologist commented:

> The only thorough excavation of a Hohokam canal that has been reported [as of 1960] is the cross sectioning at Snaketown in 1935 ... which provided clear association between the stages of construction and use of the canal and the ceramic sequence being worked out at the site. On this basis it was possible to assign the beginning of the Snaketown canal to about AD 800 and suggest that it was in use for about 500 years.[45]

Ceramic evidence indicated that the Snaketown canals had been constructed several hundred years after the town's founding. For Haury, the questions remained: How did the first Snaketown residents water their crops? Where were their early canals?

Haury also investigated the diet of the people of Snaketown, based on the organic remains in the trash deposits. Initially he felt certain that the Indians ate mainly cultivated foods, but he did not find abundant evidence of domesticated plants in the diet. Bones and other refuse indicated that the Indians not only farmed but also hunted and gathered; their diet included the flesh of wild animals as well as cactus fruit, seeds, and other native plants. Apparently, they also took some fish and shellfish from the river. In a later study of the Snaketown diet, conducted at a second excavation, Haury was able to verify the Snaketown residents' heavy reliance on domestic plant foods.

The prehistoric Snaketown farmers cultivated a warm weather plant—cotton—which flourished in their irrigated fields. Perhaps, some scientists thought, ancient peoples in Mexico developed crops and farming techniques, as well as pottery making methods, which then spread to the Hohokam settlements to the north. The questions of how these "traits" reached the Hohokam, and the origins of the first Hohokam settlers, became subjects of intense debate.

Architectural features that were common at Anasazi sites, such as kivas, were absent from Snaketown. Instead, excavators found structures peculiar to the Hohokam such as the major system of irrigation canals, and ballcourts that apparently had been used in some sort of spectator sport. These structures suggested a well-organized society with time for nonutilitarian construction projects and games. In contrast to the pithouse-to-pueblo-and-kiva architectural sequence of the Anasazi, at Snaketown there was no evidence that the ballcourts had evolved from simpler, earlier architectural features.

Mayan archaeologist Sylvanus Morley visited the Snaketown excavation in the 1930s to examine a mysterious, east-west oriented, 120-by-33-meter oval depression that some thought resembled the unexcavated ballcourts found at

Excavated ballcourt from Snaketown I.

Hohokam etched shell; human effigy vessels.

Maya sites. A smaller, north-south oriented structure was found near Snaketown's eastern edge. Morley "helped us confirm that those ... were ballcourts," remembered Haury.[46] Earlier archaeologists had speculated that such depressions, found at many Hohokam sites, served every purpose from reservoirs to threshing pits.

The Snaketown dig turned up artifacts one would expect to find at any prehistoric site: tools and implements of stone and bone, and baskets of various materials. The archaeologists also discovered thousands of other kinds of artifacts, many of which were unique to the Hohokam: animal and human figurines made from various materials, etched shells, many kinds of stone and shell carvings, stone effigy vessels, stone palettes and mosaic plaques, Mexican copper bells (similar to those found at Pueblo Bonito and Aztec), and cotton textiles.

The uses of some of these objects, such as the stone palettes, remain a mystery. For others, the archaeologists could identify a function. For example, they knew that figurines and certain ceramics accompanied the ashes of the Hohokam dead. Cremation was the prevalent burial practice in Hohokam civilization: The deceased were burned in shallow pits, and their ashes placed either in jars or beneath the pits themselves.

Jewelry, some of it painted, was apparently popular among the Hohokam, and many of their beads, pendants, rings, bracelets, and earrings indicated trade or travel. Seashells were the favorite jewelry material of these landlocked people of the desert. Prehistoric artisans worked them with stone carving tools. Sturdy ocean shells were preferred over softer, more fragile fresh-water and land shells. The inventive Hohokam jewelry makers also created remarkable seashell etchings, using a waxy resist and an acid made from fermented cactus juice. They favored frog and snake motifs, as well as other animal designs. Archaeologists found about three dozen types of seashells at Snaketown, almost all from the Gulf of California and the Pacific Coast. Haury wrote, "This western source for the Snaketown shell material conforms with the findings at Los Muertos where all species came from the west, except one which came from the Gulf of Mexico."[47] Besides shell, the Hohokam used jet and turquoise, also not found in the Snaketown vicinity.

IN 1931, at a scholars' meeting known as the Gila Pueblo Conference, the concept of Hohokam as a distinct prehistoric culture began to emerge. Gladwin and archaeologists at the conference postulated developmental periods for the Hohokam people based on the gradual evolution of desert farmer architecture, ceramics, and other remains. They also outlined a tentative dating system for the Southwest that Gladwin felt was better adapted to the evolution of the desert farmer culture than was the Pecos Classification. The Gila Pueblo Conference came about, in fact, because Gladwin and archaeologists working in the Arizona deserts wanted a time-ordering scheme better tailored to their discoveries.

Gladwin's system categorized prehistoric sites according to a new time-measuring method that divided ancient cultures according to "roots," "stems," "branches," and "phases." Gladwin postulated that the Hohokam culture (a root) passed through periods that he called "Colonial," "Sedentary," and "Classic." These periods were further broken down into developmental phases.[48]

Gladwin published his chronological system in 1934. Like everything he did, it became the focus of controversy. Archaeologist J. O. Brew commented, "As with all his theories, Gladwin quite properly states it as an assumption and allows that it may be questioned."[49] In fact, Hohokam time became the subject of a debate that continues to the present day.

Haury's stratigraphy of Mound 29 provided the only means of dating Snaketown's remains in the 1930s. Archaeologists had to content themselves with a relative system because no trees grew in the region, although later some tree-ring dates for Snaketown were obtained from a few timbers apparently transported to the site by the Hohokam. Since Hohokam pottery was so distinctive, the archaeologists could easily identify "intrusive" sherds from the Anasazi. The black-and-white Anasazi pieces had been accurately dated through tree-rings, and were used for cross-dating at Snaketown.

The stratigraphy of Mound 29 indicated an amazingly long chronology. Haury estimated that people first settled Snaketown around 300 BC and continued an unbroken habitation until well after the end of the first millennium AD. This sequence became the subject of constant debate; but even when it was revised and shortened by Haury's critics, there was still evidence of a remarkably long human occupation in the harsh desert. It appeared that Snaketown had been continuously inhabited considerably longer than any of the Anasazi sites of the Southwest. The Hohokam, clearly, were unlike the cliff dwellers of Mesa Verde and the builders of Chaco's so-called Great Houses, who stayed a century or two and then moved on.

As LATE AS 1947, Gladwin was still writing vigorously and sponsoring archaeological activities. But the heyday of his work came to an end shortly after World War II. In 1948, after unsuccessfully offering Gila Pueblo to Harvard and the University of California, the Gladwins donated the research center's archaeological collections to the University of Arizona and left the Southwest. The extensive Gila Pueblo collections became part of the Arizona State Museum, and the land and buildings were sold to a local real estate company. The National Park Service eventually bought Gila Pueblo, and it later became a campus of Eastern Arizona College.

By the time his mentor departed the Southwest, Haury held a prestigious post as head of the anthropology department at the University of Arizona and was also director of the Arizona State Museum. He had become influential in defining the Mogollon culture, which appeared to share origins with the Hohokam. The Mogollon people had inhabited the highlands to the northeast on the New Mexico–Arizona border.

The Hohokam way of life could be identified by several characteristic traits that revealed much about the desert farmers' culture. Awareness of culture as a society's unique way of adapting to environmental, social, and other factors had become an integral part of archaeologists' thinking by this time. Identification and understanding of prehistoric cultural traits and their changes over time were, in fact, the joining point of the disciplines of anthropology and archaeology.

The unique Hohokam traits included oval or rectangular pithouse-type architecture; a sophisticated system of irrigated agriculture, which included the crop of cotton; buff-colored pottery painted with red or maroon designs; cremation of the dead; ballcourts; and several distinctive artifacts, including slate palettes and carved shells.

The theory of distinctive Hohokam and Mogollon cultures, separate from the Anasazi one, drew critics' objections. In his book on the history of the Pecos Conference, Richard Woodbury describes an encounter that took place at the 1931 conference and was one of Haury's favorite anecdotes:

Emil Haury ... recalled that there were, however, still skeptics: "I have a most vivid recollection about the general conservative attitude on the part of the conferees toward the new names being bandied about, Mogollon and Hohokam. ... I was sitting next to Frank Roberts around the big table in the Laboratory of Anthropology when I reported on Roosevelt 9:6 and had occasion to use the word 'Hohokam.' He turned to me and said quietly, 'That's a lot of hokum.'"[50]

During his long career Haury also investigated other groups—the Salado in the Gila Pueblo vicinity and the Mimbres people in southeastern New Mexico. At excavations at Ventana Cave, some fifty miles south of Snaketown, he traced Southwestern prehistory back more than eleven thousand years. His wide-ranging work made substantial, innovative contributions to an increasingly diverse prehistoric picture of the Southwest.

Controversies about Hohokam culture, origins, and chronology continued for decades after the Snaketown dig. Haury commented that he preferred to "side-step"[51] controversy unless it might lead to new knowledge. In archaeology, however, controversy seemed to go with the territory.

E MIL HAURY LEFT GILA PUEBLO in 1937 to become the head of the department of archaeology at the University of Arizona. He broadened the department's scope, renaming it the department of anthropology. A decade later his work at Snaketown engendered yet another controversy stirred up by Gladwin.

As time passed, Gladwin challenged the conclusions of the Snaketown archaeologists. In 1942, and again in 1948, he published Medallion papers in which he disputed many of Haury's findings, especially the very long strati-graphic chronology of Mound 29, which Gladwin argued overestimated the age of Snaketown.

Haury was surprised and disturbed by Gladwin's pointed comments and decided to return to the site to excavate again and reexamine his earlier con-clusions. Twenty years later, during the winter seasons of 1964–65, with a sab-batical leave and funding from the National Science Foundation, he finally was able to return to Snaketown to conduct an excavation now known as "Snake-town II." Noting one colleague's comment—"He's returning to the scene of the crime!"[52]—Haury himself explained in a 1988 interview: "These great argu-ments that we have about chronology and various aspects of the archaeological picture can only be argued in the field, by getting more dirt under your finger-nails. You can sit at your desk and dream up all kinds of philosophical notions but that doesn't answer it. You've got to get more data."[53]

The Snaketown II team relied on the grid system originally created under Haury's direction for the Snaketown I excavation. Using it, they could be "fully coordinated with the earlier findings." [54] To improve their data on Snaketown's age and chronology, the archaeologists used high-technology innovations including archaeomagnetic, radiocarbon, obsidian hydration, and alpha-recoil track dating methods.

Another modern addition—a controversial practice even today—was the use of a backhoe and front-end loader to dig exploratory trenches and haul away backdirt. Julian Hayden, who returned to work with Haury at the second dig, recalled the laborious hand digging of exploratory trenches at Snaketown I. "But at Snaketown II," he remembered, "if I wanted a trench, I'd just call the backhoe driver and say, 'Hey, Fred, *alla.*' " [55]

Haury chose Al Lancaster, seasoned and respected field director of many digs in Anasazi territory, to assist him with fieldwork. [56] The two men were totally different—Haury professorial, dignified, and reserved; Lancaster self-taught, remarkably sharp-eyed, and endowed with backwoods grit, humor, and common sense. While Haury might spend hours analyzing data, Lancaster in his spare time treated Julian Hayden and other crew members to lessons in dowsing for water in the desert.

Although most of Haury's time was devoted to directing and managing the operation, he also joined Lancaster in uncovering one of the numerous caches of Hohokam figurines, carved stone, and other artifacts found during the Snaketown II excavation. "One of the caches, a round hole that was full of all sorts of cultural material, I helped Al Lancaster dig ... because I wanted to see for myself just how these things occurred." [57]

After Snaketown II, Haury reworked his Hohokam chronology, generally sticking with his original delineations of periods, each of which included several developmental phases. He defined them as the Pioneer period, 300 BC to AD 550; the Colonial, AD 550 to 900 (contemporary with the Anasazi Basketmaker III/Pueblo I period); and the Sedentary, AD 900 to 1100. The late sites adjacent to and west of Snaketown proper came within the Hohokam Classic period, AD 1100 to 1450.

One Hohokam archaeologist wrote in 1991 that "chronology has been an overriding concern of desert archaeology." [58] As the debate over Hohokam time continued during the next decades, archaeologists recognized the "integrity of Haury's phases." [59] They continued to question, however, the dates when various periods and their developmental phases began—and their durations—as well as the possibility that some of the phases occurred simultaneously. The Pioneer and early Colonial periods, the oldest periods of the Snaketown chronology, have proved especially tough to fix in time.

During the second Snaketown dig, evidence of structures called platform mounds, a relatively late Hohokam development, appeared. Similar flat-topped pyramidal structures, made of earth and stone and sometimes reached by a flight

Top: Al Lancaster (left) and Watson Smith at the Snaketown II excavation in 1965. Bottom: The field crew at Snaketown II, 1964–65. Top row (left to right): Roger Pedro, Leroy James, Fred Marietta, Jr., Larry Porter, Iver Sunna, Fred Marietta, Sr., Leonard Marud, Joseph O. Marietta. Middle row: Clinton Lewis, Everette "Moon" Howard, Eldridge Cross, David Moore, Jones Williams, Delbert Lewis, Job Hayes, George Kyyitan, Raymond Cawker. Front row: Eddy Harrison, Rupert Hall, Leonard Stone, Dennis Williams, Justin Miller, Larry Lewis.

of stairs, appear at ruins in Mexico and elsewhere to the south. Their function at Snaketown remains an enigma.

At Snaketown II, Haury refined his thinking about the much-debated topic of the origins of the Hohokam: "Based on reexcavations at the important Hohokam site of Snaketown, Haury (1976) concluded that the Hohokam represent a migration of people from Mexico who were not related to the indigenous Cochise."[60]

Another goal at Snaketown II was a closer look at the site's irrigation system. On the first excavation, puzzled by the lack of very early canals, Haury wondered how the first residents of Snaketown could have survived without irrigation. He aimed to answer this lingering question.

Excavating the ancient, hand-dug waterways around the site, the teams searched for older canals by following more recent ones. They watched carefully for a change in color of the dirt in the canal sides, which would indicate the branching of another canal. This time, Haury said, they found vestiges of much older canals "that then explained the ability of the Hohokam to settle in that arid country and make a go of it because they had irrigation from the moment they arrived."[61]

After restudying the canals and architecture, Haury drew conclusions about Snaketown's founding and early period:

> Based on his work at Snaketown, Haury interprets the development of Hohokam irrigation as a rather gradual process in which irrigation systems were slowly expanded and elaborated. His view is that construction of the Pioneer period canal at Snaketown did not require a greatly coordinated labor force and the work could have been accomplished by the informal cooperation of as few as 50 men. Further, Haury estimates that the founding population of Snaketown was relatively small, based on the number of Pioneer period houses excavated.[62]

The second excavation made it clear that Snaketown was the largest Hohokam settlement known. In fact, because of its size and the remarkable length of time it was inhabited, some archaeologists considered it an atypical Hohokam settlement. In light of these factors, Haury commented, "I tend to look upon it as a likely candidate for the original and parent Hohokam village."[63]

THE SECOND SNAKETOWN DIG took place in a new era of Southwestern archaeology. "The 1960s, when Snaketown was being restudied, was a decade of searching for values, a quest for the 'relevancy' of what archaeologists do to the complex social problems of the times," Haury wrote.[64]

Haury's method remained firmly based on fieldwork, extensive data gathering, and inductive analysis. This approach was viewed as passé by archaeologists who structured their work around specific hypotheses and research problems. Critics denounced much of what Haury had done as being an outmoded approach characterized by "*mere* collection, description, and chronology." [65]

Despite such criticism, Haury remained a highly respected exponent of the inductive approach to archaeology, in which the person who knows the field data most thoroughly is the one who makes the authoritative statement about the excavation's findings. Yet, although he emphasized reliance on scientific fieldwork and data analysis, Haury viewed the discipline as "humanistic... 90 percent art and 10 percent science." [66]

Although Haury witnessed the fading of his approach, he also saw acceptance of two prehistoric Southwestern cultures that he had played a strong role in defining—the Hohokam and Mogollon. He taught at the university during a time of nationwide growth in departments of anthropology, which in turn gave birth to many archaeological field schools around the Southwest. Haury himself took charge of an ongoing field school program, first at Forestdale Valley and then, from 1946 until 1960, at Point of Pines in Arizona.

Vociferous critics and constant debate notwithstanding, by the end of his career Haury had become a legend among archaeologists. In 1986 the University of Arizona Press published *Emil Haury's Prehistory of the American Southwest*, an anthology edited by J. Jefferson Reid and David E. Doyel. Reviewer Watson Smith wrote: "Practically everyone should read this book.... It is essentially a drama in which the prehistoric American Southwest is cast as protagonist.... What is important is the elucidation of the mental climate of one man, who has been the epitome of 'Old Man Southwest' in the folklore of our time." [67]

As his career drew to a close, Haury bequeathed to the discipline a legion of devoted students. One prominent archaeologist who worked under Haury commented, "If you look beyond Haury's bibliography to his students, that's a significant part of his contribution." [68]

Excavating a square kiva at Awatovi.

CHAPTER 7

AWATOVI

J. O. Brew Excavates in the
Realm of Hopi Legend

Hopi Indian accounts tell of a tribal tragedy that took place on a winter night many centuries ago. Warriors from several Hopi villages perpetrated a brutal massacre at Awatovi, a Hopi town on Antelope Mesa about a dozen miles southeast of the First Mesa settlement of Walpi in what is now northeastern Arizona. In a surprise raid staged during an Awatovian ceremonial celebration, the attackers burned all the men of the town to death in their kivas, killed some of the women and children, and abducted the rest. The raid left Awatovi a smoking, deserted ruin, never to be inhabited again. Historians have established the probable date of this legendary catastrophe as the winter of 1700–01.

The massacre probably resulted from tribal political tensions, possibly exacerbated by pressures from the Catholic Church. Awatovi had been receptive to Christianity, providing early seventeenth-century Spanish missionaries with a foothold in Hopi country before the Pueblo Revolt of 1680 ousted them from the Indian towns. After the Spanish Reconquest, beginning in 1692, some of Awatovi's citizens were sympathetic toward both Christianity and the Franciscan friars, who wished to return to the mission established there in 1629. Other Hopi villages, however, steadfastly resisted efforts to reestablish the Christian religion, preferring to keep to their ancient ceremonial ways.

The Peabody Museum of American Archaeology and Ethnology of Harvard University launched an archaeological expedition beginning in 1935 to explore the demolished village. The Southwestern adventures of an imaginative teenager sparked the idea for the museum's endeavor.

In 1912, nineteen-year-old William Henry Claflin, future business tycoon and treasurer of Harvard, traveled extensively in Hopi land and became fascinated with the numerous prehistoric ruins he visited in the region of Jeddito Valley, a vast, barren plain rimmed by mesas. One of the mesatop ruins was Awatovi, whose grim history Claflin had heard from Hopis. He never forgot his Southwestern experience, or Awatovi, and over the years he kept in touch with his Hopi friends.

Claflin was not the only visitor intrigued by the ruin. The Mindeleff brothers, who had surveyed, photographed, sketched, and mapped Hawikuh in Zuni country and other Indian ruins in the 1880s, also visited and documented the Antelope Mesa ruins. In 1892 Jesse Walter Fewkes, of the Smithsonian Institution's Bureau of American Ethnology, excavated a kiva at Awatovi. He reported that his Hopi crews, horrified by the human remains they were uncovering, showed such anxiety that Fewkes stopped digging.[1]

Just after the turn of the century, Walter Hough carried out excavations at the neighboring ruin of Kawaika'a for the U.S. National Museum as part of the National Museum–Gates Expedition. Hough reported finding painted murals at Kawaika'a, a discovery that put the Peabody expedition on the lookout for similar paintings. The Antelope Mesa ruins were also visited in the 1920s by archaeologist Earl Morris, who made notes and maps of Kawaika'a; his report is on file at the University of Colorado Museum.

In 1934 three men of considerable archaeological influence journeyed to Awatovi: Harold S. Gladwin, retired financier and head of the archaeological research center of Gila Pueblo in Globe, Arizona; Alfred V. Kidder, of the Carnegie Institution, former director of excavations of Pecos Pueblo, New Mexico; and Donald K. Scott, director of the Peabody Museum. After seeing the ruin, the three decided it was worth excavating.

Like Pecos and Hawikuh, Awatovi displayed the signs of an important site—extensive ruin mounds strewn with pottery sherds that indicated centuries-long prehistoric occupation. Kidder had seen the site some years before he looked it over with Scott and Gladwin. "Just going over the mounds at Awatobi [sic] you could see that everything was there, just as ... at Pecos," Kidder remembered.[2] Complementing its large mounds and abundant ceramics, Awatovi's mission church was proof that the town was still occupied by the Indians when the Spanish came, an important benchmark in time.

After his visit to Awatovi, Scott decided that the Peabody Museum would sponsor an archaeological expedition to explore the site. Claflin fulfilled his long-held dream when he became one of the dig's financial backers.

One of Harvard's most promising archaeologists, 29-year-old John Otis ("Jo") Brew, then a graduate student, was chosen to head the expedition. The gifted, ambitious, and industrious son of a working-class, Boston-Irish family, Brew was intuitive and intellectually adroit, sociable, and humorous—and a natural diplomat to boot. He was also known affectionately to his many friends as a "confirmed romanticist" and a "good raconteur."[3]

As a member of an archaeological survey known as the Emerson-Claflin Expedition to Utah in 1931, young Brew had already experienced the Southwest's archaeological potential. He had also impressed Peabody Museum director Scott, who traveled with the group, with the courage and grit he exhibited in his greenhorn determination to learn the art of horseback riding, "even if it killed him."[4] The upshot was that Brew had become Scott's informal protégé.

Brew had directed excavations at Alkali Ridge in southeastern Utah from late 1931 through 1933, and during the Awatovi expedition he worked on his doctoral dissertation on the Alkali Ridge project. Published in 1946, it was a scholarly masterpiece clarifying the development of Pueblo I settlements.

John Otis ("Jo") Brew.

Antelope Mesa and the Jeddito Valley from the air. The long, fingerlike feature extending across the center of the photograph is Antelope Mesa. Awatovi is located on the far side of the mesa, beyond the sand dunes at left of center. In the distance are the Hopi Buttes.

THE AWATOVI SITE lay on the Hopi reservation overlooking Jeddito Valley, about seven miles southwest of Keams Canyon, Arizona. The ruins stood at a precipitous cliff edge near the tip of Antelope Mesa, which was dotted with numerous prehistoric towns. Spectacular views extended to the San Francisco Peaks near present-day Flagstaff, seventy miles to the west. Tawny plains stretched southward toward the valley cut by the Little Colorado River. To the southeast lay the wild mesas, mountains, and pine and juniper forests of Zuni country.

In prehistoric and historic times, Antelope Mesa was a stopping point on ancient Indian trails. One path ran between the Hopi settlements on First, Second, and Third Mesas, and the Zuni towns, including Hawikuh, whose mission was contemporaneous with Awatovi's.

Awatovi had been the most extensive of the prehistoric Antelope Mesa pueblos. Eventually the expedition archaeologists found that the Awatovi site spread over nearly twenty-five acres, though the entire area was never occupied all at one time. The ruin stretched over a third of a mile along the cliff edge, with mounds up to thirty feet.

To the north lay Tallahogan Canyon, where modern Hopis from First and Second Mesas tilled fields of corn, beans, and squash, much as the people of

Awatovi must have done. Some of them belonged to clans claiming ownership of the Awatovi site. Eventually their claims would affect the fate of the Awatovi expedition.

The professional crew at Awatovi represented a flowering of Eastern anthropological and archaeological talent. No longer was archaeology a discipline without a professional foundation. Brew was attended by a squadron of graduate students from colleges and universities offering degrees in anthropology and archaeology, as well as by members of other scientific disciplines.

Among the expedition's archaeologists and students were Richard Wheeler, Edward T. "Ned" Hall, Erik K. Reed, and George W. Brainerd. Visiting researchers, such as ceramic analyst Anna O. Shepard, worked at the dig on special projects. During the 1938 and 1939 seasons one student on the expedition, Richard Woodbury, took charge of Awatovi's massive stone and bone artifact finds.

As director of the Peabody Museum, Donald Scott wielded great influence over the excavation, though he and his wife visited only occasionally. Burt Cosgrove, research associate of the Peabody Museum, and his wife Harriet ("Hattie"), museum research assistant, became the expedition's two oldest members. Former hardware-store owners from Silver City, New Mexico, the Cosgroves had become Kidder's protégés after the famous archaeologist saw their remarkably well-executed amateur digs in the Mimbres prehistoric culture area of southwestern New Mexico.

Brew selected veteran field archaeologist James Allen ("Al") Lancaster to serve as assistant director. He had worked for Brew at Alkali Ridge, and Brew considered Lancaster's abilities vital. Another member of the expedition was Charles Amsden, a Farmington native who had worked as a boy on Kidder's 1914 explorations in the dry caves in northeastern Arizona. At the time of the Awatovi expedition, Amsden worked at the Southwest Museum in Los Angeles and volunteered his annual vacations at the dig. Two other volunteers were Ross G. Montgomery, a Southern California architect and an expert on colonial Spanish missions, and Watson Smith, a wealthy former lawyer and veteran of Paul Martin's expedition at Lowry Ruin near Mesa Verde.

A Cuban visiting the United States on a Guggenheim Fellowship serendipitously joined the Awatovi team after visiting the dig. In a 1949 report on findings at Awatovi, Brew listed him as "Professor Carlos García-Robiou, University of Havana, photographer." García-Robiou did, in fact, make many of the best large-format photos taken at Awatovi.

Geologist John T. Hack added his expertise to this interdisciplinary expedition. Hack's work included studies of the geology of Hopi country, its water supply, and prehistoric agriculture. He investigated prehistoric coal mines along the southern edge of Black Mesa, a subject that had piqued the interest of earlier archaeologists. Fewkes and Hough had noted coal ash in refuse deposits and rooms during excavations, as did Brew once he began digging.

Another interdisciplinary member of the team was Volney Jones, an ethnobotanist from the University of Michigan. He used a new technique known as "water flotation" to obtain seeds, stalks, peach stones, and other plant remains from adobe bricks of the mission, in efforts to learn more about prehistoric agriculture.

Lindsay C. ("Lin") Thompson, a Southwesterner and a veteran of Utah digs, served as camp cook. Several team members later recalled Thompson's gourmet meals as the high points of camp life. Five decades after their Awatovi experience, they still remembered the taste of Thompson's fragrant hot cakes, cinnamon rolls, angel food cake, and fresh fruit pies.

The excavation crews included about thirty Hopis, who returned to their homes over the weekends, "running all the way there—and back on Mondays."[5] To avoid intervillage rivalries, Brew hired equal numbers from First and Second Mesas. The villages on Third Mesa were too far away.

The Indians became highly skilled archaeological fieldworkers. Like Lancaster, they occasionally took time to teach beginners how to excavate. Brew's wife, Evelyn, remembered one of the Hopi diggers showing her how to lift out the potsherds that paved the floor of the mission church at Awatovi. "They enjoyed the work and were glad to have it," she remembered, "and they had a wonderful sense of humor."[6]

Brew's diplomatic skills smoothed crosscultural relations with the Hopis. Hattie Cosgrove, Al Lancaster, and Donald Scott also enjoyed good rapport with the workmen. Lancaster, especially, helped keep peace between the First and Second Mesa contingents and became a confidante of many of the Hopis, who seemed to respect his modesty and sense of humor. He delighted them with practical jokes and self-mocking slapstick performances of Indian dances.

Despite the apparent harmony, however, the very ownership of the land on which Awatovi stood was disputed by various Hopi clans. This quarrel held the seeds of the premature end of the Harvard Peabody Expedition to Awatovi.

B REW SUMMARIZED THE ARCHAEOLOGISTS' TASKS during the hot, windy, early fall days of the first season in 1935: "We visited Awatovi ... walked over its many mounds, sat on its protruding walls and thought about how to attack that stupendous ruin, the largest any of us had ever seen."[7]

As he sat on the crumbling sandstone cliff and watched cloud shadows scudding over the vast plains below, Brew must have pondered several Awatovi mysteries. Like Hawikuh, Awatovi belonged to the territory of the prehistoric Western Anasazi. One unsolved puzzle concerned the connections between the

Top: The Hopi excavators at Awatovi. From left: Hoppy Dennis, Chester Dennis (Talashoywema), Jake Coochnyama, Emory Dennis (Coochwikvia), Arthur Masaytewa, Alec Dennis (Siwinmtewa), Leland Dennis (Naquahitewa), Sylvan Nash (rear), Evans Poleahla, Patrick Coochnyama, Gibson Namoki. Bottom: The 1938 staff at the Awatovi excavation. Top row (left to right): Jay Hooton, Watson Smith, Charles ("Happy") Foote, Hattie Cosgrove, Carlos García-Robiou, John Hack, Kirk Bryan, Harold P. Winchester, Edward T. Hall, Alden Stevens. Front row: Richard Woodbury, Evelyn Nimmo (later Brew), Al Lancaster, J. O. Brew, Marian Stevens, Helen Claflin.

Western Anasazi, Awatovi's prehistoric and historic citizens, and the modern Hopis. In his memoirs, Watson Smith summarized the question:

> The heavy occupation of the Marsh Pass and Kayenta country just to the north of Black Mesa came to an end around the year 1300. ... Thus ... a plausible hypothesis [was] that maybe the people from Kayenta came south to the Jeddito Valley, and added their numbers to Awatovi and some of the adjoining pueblos. Excavation would determine this. Furthermore, there was evidence from surface finds of pottery that Awatovi and its environs had also been the scene of ... interchange with areas to the south and particularly to the southeast in the Little Colorado Valley. Excavation of the site, therefore, could shed a good deal of light upon the movements of peoples in the western Pueblo country prior to ... historic times.[8]

Another question that expedition participants wanted to answer was which Hopi village Coronado's lieutenant, Don Pedro de Tovar, first encountered on his sortie from Hawikuh into Hopi country in 1540. One hypothesis suggested that Tovar stopped at Kawaika'a, a few miles northeast of Awatovi. Others believed that Tovar stopped first at Awatovi. Later the Coronado expedition's Don García López de Cárdenas led a group toward the Colorado River and subsequently discovered the Grand Canyon. Cárdenas's guides may have been citizens of Awatovi.

Besides questions of prehistory, history, and excavation strategy, Brew also had to think about money. Because of the Depression the threat of budget shortages was ever-present. William Claflin's support of the expedition became vital. Other contributors included Raymond Emerson, Henry S. Morgan, and Philip R. Allen. Even with wealthy patrons, Brew later said that he felt pressed to do the job at Awatovi as economically as possible. Depression prices and wages helped keep costs down. For instance, the Hopi crews worked for 40 cents an hour ($2.80 a day) on a 35-hour-a-week schedule.

Lancaster and Brew forged a successful partnership, often holding Sunday morning conferences sitting side by side on a mound or wall overlooking the dig. While Lancaster was strong and athletic, Brew was rotund and scholarly; and their working styles were as different as their looks.

Lancaster supervised the fieldwork, making the necessary, on-the-spot decisions. Brew focused on intellectual direction, observing the digging with clipboard and pipe in hand. He also dealt with a huge load of paperwork, including the accounts, and oversaw all team members' archaeological field notes.

At the start of the first season, no one knew the size and dimensions of the site, so the Peabody Awatovi expedition commenced in 1935 with what Brew de-

Excavations at Awatovi, with the floor of the mission church partially exposed.

scribed as "an extensive reconnaissance trip."[9] Accompanied only by a skeleton crew, for six weeks Brew explored the surrounding area, locating sixty-one sites in a twelve-mile stretch on the north side of Jeddito Valley. Cartographer Alden Stevens surveyed and gridded the entire Awatovi site. Brew wrote, "Within a few days of our arrival at Jeddito we began the excavation of a very nice small Pueblo I–Pueblo II site on the mesa top above the trading post, later known as Site 4."[10]

The archaeologists also dug a two-meter-wide, north-south stratigraphic trench extending about 233 meters (255 yards) across the center of the site, uncovering 106 rooms and 5 kivas.[11] Brew obtained wood samples for tree-ring dating—the first of many—which yielded early sixteenth-century dates, though some rooms appeared to have been occupied a hundred years earlier. Sheep bones found in some of the kivas signified the arrival of the Spaniards.

The 1936 season geared up with a full contingent of professionals and digging crews. The excavators worked through the ruin known as the Western Mound in search of older architecture and artifacts. The mound, a beehive-like protuberance, stood about twenty-five feet high near the southwestern corner of the site. Digging in approximately 120 rooms resulted in the uncovering of about 350 "stratigraphic blocks."[12] These revealed three ceramic periods, the earliest extending back into Pueblo III times. "By mid-season 80,000 potsherds had been tabulated," wrote Brew, "and at times during the third month more than 5000 a day went over the classifying tables."[13] That season, the crews also dug nineteen test pits spaced at regular intervals around the site so that the archaeologists could date the periods of occupation in each part of the town.

Work on the mission church began in 1937, and Brew optimistically hoped it would be completed that year. The job turned out to be bigger and more complicated than expected, however, and concealed several dramatic surprises. As had happened at Pecos, Aztec, and other large Southwestern excavations, the archaeologists' plans were disrupted by unforeseen, intriguing discoveries in prehistoric parts of the ruin as well.

In 1936 Al Lancaster's sharp eyes spotted bits of painted adobe plaster in debris of the Western Mound. Before long, diggers had uncovered an early fifteenth-century painted mural hidden beneath several layers of plain adobe plaster on the walls of one of the prehistoric kivas. It was the first of a remarkable group of pre- and post-historic kiva murals that were found at Awatovi and Kawaika'a and soon became internationally renowned.

Each season, new kiva paintings came to light on the ceremonial chambers' adobe- and clay-plastered sandstone walls. In all, the Awatovi expedition excavated over two hundred kiva paintings. When the first one was discovered, Brew appointed Watson Smith, newly arrived at Awatovi, to direct the kiva mural excavation team. Under Smith's enthusiastic and determined leadership, the excavators successfully recovered many of the crumbling, cracked, and broken — but still stunningly beautiful — works of art.

Lancaster and Smith had both worked at Lowry Ruin, where kiva wall paintings were uncovered, in the early 1930s. Murals also had been found at Mesa Verde, Alkali Ridge, Kuaua, and other Southwestern sites. Still, the kiva murals at Awatovi proved exceptional for their beauty and revelations of prehistoric ceremonial life. Smith devoted much time, during the excavations and for decades thereafter, to studying Hopi cultural material to help him interpret the paintings.

The murals danced with complex ceremonial iconography — geometric shapes; human figures, sometimes dressed in ceremonial kilts and sashes; and religious symbols such as kachina figures, both masked and plain, and prayer sticks. Parading across the walls were animal and natural motifs: birds, tadpoles and frogs, lizards, snakes, clouds, lightning, feathers, and plants. Some forms resembled designs on Hopi pottery; others the excavators had never seen before.

The paintings' colorful earth-toned hues lit up the ancient plaster. "Black, white, reds, and yellows are most common," wrote Brew, "but shades of pink,

Top: Preparing to remove a kiva mural from a wall at Awatovi. Bottom: Mural from Awatovi in situ.

orange, green, and blue also occur."[14] The mural artists used mineral pigments derived from iron-oxides, colored clays, red ochre, charcoal, manganese, azurite, malachite, and kaolin.

Over the centuries, Awatovi's citizens had painted the murals for ceremonial occasions; then, when each ceremony was over, they replastered the walls with a plain coating, which was in turn repainted with vivid colored designs for the next ceremony. In one kiva, excavators discovered more than a hundred layers of plaster, twenty-seven with painted designs.[15]

Excavating and preserving these remarkable paintings involved many delicate tasks: first scraping away the blank plaster layers one by one to uncover the painted ones; then photographing the designs and making painstaking, color-coded scale drawings of them. These techniques had been pioneered at Kuaua by teams working for the University of New Mexico.

Armed with color dictionaries and pen knives, Smith's crews—which often included visitors to the dig—worked for hundreds of hours on these tedious tasks. "You couldn't be heavy handed at all, the plaster coats were thin—maybe an eighth of an inch. But it wasn't difficult if you took it easy," recalled Penny Davis Worman, who worked as an artist and excavator in the kivas. "To me every single painting was just a miracle. Some of them were very big—sixteen feet long. You just couldn't wait to see what the picture was—when you started uncovering a line, you'd wonder, 'Is this an animal, or a bird's wing? What *is* it?' "[16]

Once they had uncovered and recorded the murals, crews used liquid adhesive and muslin to strip some of the best-preserved paintings from the walls. They were then transported to the Peabody Museum. Many were also reproduced at the museum, painted with materials imported from the Awatovi site.

AWATOVI HAD RECEIVED THE SPANIARDS early. In 1629, the same year that a mission was established at the Zuni town of Hawikuh, the Franciscans built a church, San Bernardo de Aguatubi, and a convent at the cliff edge on the east side of Awatovi. Wherever the friars went in the New World, they built for future large congregations, regardless of how small the number of original parishioners. They laid out each structure according to master plans that all Franciscans used in establishing missions in the New World.

The Peabody team lacked experience in church excavation and felt stymied by the mysterious Spanish ruins at Awatovi. Then in 1936, at the recommendation of Charles Amsden, Brew invited ecclesiastical architecture expert Ross Gordon Montgomery of California to visit Awatovi. Brew wrote that after Montgomery's arrival, "The feeling of working completely in the dark disappeared."[17]

With Montgomery's assistance, the excavators thoroughly explored and uncovered the Spanish mission. They found that it stood on top of beehive-shaped

Artist's reconstruction of the San Bernardo de Aguatubi mission church at Awatovi. Figure 35 in "Franciscan Awatovi," by Ross Gordon Montgomery, Watson Smith, and John Otis Brew (1949). Drawing by Ross Montgomery.

mounds of older Hopi remains. The mission included a friary built around a traditional sacred garden; offices and schoolrooms; workshops and storerooms, some attached to the church, others separate buildings; and foundations for a barracks-stable.

The archaeologists assumed that the Spanish had built one church at Awatovi. To their amazement, they discovered an elaborate grouping of buildings, including what appeared to be the remains of several churches. By the end of the excavations, they had uncovered the foundations of a large, cruciform, unfinished structure, which Brew dubbed "Church 1," and remains of two completed churches, which the archaeologists called "Church 2" — or "the main church" — and a later "Church 3."

Because some rooms of Church 2 overlay Church 1's foundations, Brew deduced that the first church had been abandoned in favor of the smaller Church 2. The location and lesser size of the second church may have been considered more practical by the padres. During most of the five decades when the Spanish mission was active at Awatovi, the friars and Indians used Church 2, with its east-facing facade, two bell towers, and basilica. On the walls of this church were many layers of painted murals, reminiscent in technique of those found in the kivas. The designs of the church wall paintings, however, were European, and included floral patterns and motifs found on Spanish tiles.

One visitor to the dig, archaeologist Katharine Bartlett of the Museum of Northern Arizona, was vividly impressed by a tour of the church excavations. "It was the most realistic thing I ever saw at an archaeological dig. They took us in the 'front' door," she recalled, "The doors had been fastened on poles. You could see where the doors had dragged on the floors." [18]

During the excavations of Church 2, Montgomery was able to predict, based on his knowledge of the Franciscan master plans, exactly where each feature of

Bowls and a ladle of Awatovi Black-on-yellow pottery. Figure 267 in "Painted Ceramics of the Western Mound at Awatovi," by Watson Smith (1971).

the mission would be found. His expertise made possible a more precise dissection of the church than had been done at Pecos or Hawikuh. Of Montgomery's predictions about Church 2, and the superposition of the new religion's altar upon the old, Brew recalled:

> He told us where we should find the baptistery and there we found it, with the baptismal font still in place; he told us that there would be a kiva ... under the main altar and there we found it, intact, filled with clean sand just as the priests had prepared it to demonstrate the dominance of the new religion over the old.[19]

Excavations confirmed the few extant references in Spanish historical accounts indicating that the Indians destroyed Church 2 during the Rebellion of 1680 and then converted the remains of the mission for their own use. When the Spanish priests returned in the 1690s, they built "a small, long, and narrow church, obviously a make-shift."[20] The archaeologists found this structure, Church 3, on the east side of the friary.

Though few burials were found in prehistoric Awatovi, more than a hundred presumably Christian Hopi graves lay in the yard in front of Church 2 and inside the building. Besides burials under the floors, one grave was found under the altar—the bones of a young male. Excavators thought at first that these were the remains of Father Porras, the most charismatic of the original Spanish missionaries at Awatovi. This idea later proved groundless.

During the Awatovi expedition hundreds of sites were surveyed and many of these were checked for pottery sherds and other surface artifacts. In all, twenty-one small sites were excavated in addition to Awatovi, some of them highly significant because they provided evidence of occupation back to Basketmaker III times, commencing shortly after AD 500.

Preliminary surveys and exploratory digging helped determine which sites might be worth excavating, and which contained little information. For example, after investigating Site 101 during the expedition's last season, Brew wrote that although the surface had looked "very promising ... it was merely a very shallow coating of site material on top of an undisturbed sand dune."[21]

Awatovi's mounds yielded a rich harvest of artifacts, which required meticulous staff attention. Richard Woodbury handled the demanding and tedious task of cataloging some 11,700 objects of stone and bone. He seriated and dated them by relative chronology, according to their association with stratigraphically classified pottery sherds. In the pottery tent Hattie Cosgrove and her assistants washed and recorded a staggering number of ceramic fragments—some 243,871 potsherds in 1938 alone. The excavation resulted in the cataloging of some 8,500 whole ceramics and hundreds of thousands of sherds.

Awatovi also produced some perishable artifacts such as bits of baskets and cloth. Surprisingly few Spanish artifacts turned up, though the excavators found some items such as iron nails, bits of china, and religious medals, as well as remains of European-imported domestic animals. Still, the total number of Spanish artifacts was much smaller than that found at Hawikuh, although the two towns shared similar histories under Spanish missionaries.

Prehistoric Awatovi provided pottery samples beginning in the Pueblo III times of the early thirteenth century, through 1700. Brew described the array:

> The black-on-whites of Pueblo III give way to a black-on-orange, which is the first of the so-called Hopi colored wares. The designs in this black-on-orange and general treatment suggest that it arose from the combination of influences from both the Kayenta region to the north and Little Colorado to the south, meeting on the Hopi mesas. After the black-on-orange comes the first true yellow, still geometric in design and varying little from the black-on-orange except in color. This style lasted but a short time and was superseded before the beginning of the 15th century by the famous Jeddito Black-on-yellow ware with beautiful designs of highly conventionalized bird and animal figures. This fashion culminated during the decades preceding the Spanish invasion in pottery generally described as the most beautiful in the Southwest, Sikyatki Polychrome.[22]

Stratigraphy indicated that the oldest part of the town was, as originally suspected, the Western Mound. From there the settlement grew towards the east and north, with the last century of occupation mainly at the eastern end. Changes in the sandstone masonry of the walls, combined with differences in pottery, indicated a cultural change, possibly an influx of new inhabitants, which at least one archaeologist placed at the beginning of the fifteenth century. Smith wrote that the architectural changes probably did not mean a "great cultural change" but rather "a new period of growth incident to a rather sudden inflow of new people who were already closely related to the old residents."[23]

The expedition crew set up camp a mile east of the prehistoric ruin in a depression amid the constantly moving sand dunes covering Antelope Mesa. They called their enclave of wooden-floored, walled tents, set around a central plaza, "New Awatovi," and it was probably one of the driest, windiest, sandiest spots on earth. The shifting sands of the campsite were stabilized by scrubby juniper and piñon. Eventually the archaeologists created a cactus garden in camp, a monument to the hardy vegetation that clutched at the slippery mesatop dunes.

Army squad tents housed the Hopi workmen from First and Second Mesas, who slept and ate in two separate groups, according to their custom. There were

Antelope Mesa. The expedition camp, "New Awatovi," is in the foreground; Old Awatovi appears as a mound on the horizon just to right of center.

cartography, pottery, and storage tents, and Lin Thompson presided over a clapboard kitchen and dining room. The camp had its own electric generator. Al Lancaster built the cement-lined cistern behind the mess tent, and water was hauled in milk cans from nearby Tallahogan Canyon.

Before dark there might be games of horseshoes, at which Brew excelled. Nightly pinochle games sometimes reached peaks of hilarity and excitement so great that Brew recorded the results in his journal. Singing and storytelling also helped to pass time around the evening campfire. From the neighboring Hopi fire drifted the rhythms of old tribal songs, perhaps once sung by Awatovi's prehistoric citizens.

Hattie Cosgrove became the expedition's ex-officio social coordinator. "She was a born hostess," remembered Evelyn Brew.[24] She also became a champion at a unique, very physical sport akin to sledding known as "dune sliding" or "dune skiing."

When she was not overseeing operations in the pottery tent, Mrs. Cosgrove took photographs of the dig and its crew and provided tours for the constant stream of visitors. Drawn by the mystique of archaeology and rumors of Thompson's delicious food, as well as Brew's hospitable invitations, several hundred visitors made the adventurous journey to Awatovi. They included numerous museum directors and archaeologists, Franciscan priests, and miscellaneous acquaintances and relatives of the archaeologists. "Jo urged people to come by," remembered Richard Woodbury, "and he picked their brains while they were there."[25]

Hopi visitors—families and friends of the crew, and tribal leaders—also came to Awatovi. They arrived by car, in borrowed school buses, or by wagon.

Smith remembered, "Almost without exception they displayed a great interest in and a very considerable understanding of what we were doing."[26] Hopi potters scrutinized the prehistoric designs on the expedition's pottery collections, as the famous potter Nampeyo had done with sherds from Fewkes's excavations.

Brew enjoyed music, and since Carlos García-Robiou played superbly, a piano was hauled to camp for him. It was installed in the pottery tent, where it provided music for the June 11, 1939, wedding of Brew and his secretary, Evelyn Nimmo.[27]

Sorrow as well as joy was shared at the camp. Catastrophe struck on October 25, 1936, when Burt Cosgrove was taken suddenly ill and died after being rushed to the BIA hospital at Keams Canyon. In spite of the tragedy, Hattie Cosgrove remained with the expedition.

Thanks to their Hopi friends, the Awatovi group attended many Indian ceremonies and dances. Brew's journal also records ethnographic information that he and other crew members collected on Hopi customs and ceremonies.

Several motor vehicles were used at Awatovi, including Smith's car, the Cosgrove's Dodge truck (provided by the Peabody), and later a new Plymouth. The weekly shopping trips to Keams Canyon, Indian Wells, or Jeddito—or further away to Winslow or Holbrook (a day's round-trip drive)—entailed slipping and sliding vehicles across the sand dunes to get to the narrow reservation roads. Not surprisingly, auto maintenance became a valuable skill. The expedition's most famous vehicle was "Pecos Black," named after the location of its first tour of duty. Smith recalled, "Pecos went to Awatovi in 1935 and served there through 1939, roaring down the steep sand-dune behind Jeddito, Jo at the wheel with the aplomb of an Arab camel driver."[28]

The Awatovi Expedition ended with the 1939 season. Ongoing objections of some Hopis toward the archaeological work played a part in the project's demise. But the *coup de grace* came when the Hopi Tribal Council refused to support the expedition's presence on Indian land, a complicated political maneuver resulting from rivalry over ownership of Awatovi among different Hopi clans. The Hopi Council's action reflected empowerment of the tribe's leaders stemming from the Indian Reorganization Act, passed by Congress in 1934.[29] As a result, the Department of the Interior did not renew the Peabody Museum's permit to excavate.

Knowing that the expedition's five-year permit would expire in 1939, Brew worked hard for two seasons to prevent this situation; but even his adroit diplomatic talents failed. Brew found himself stymied by complex tribal politics. "Jo was all over the mesa," remembered Evelyn Brew, "going to see this old man and that old man."[30] Earlier in the summer Brew had written in his journal:

This is a highly involved political situation, and, if we don't get the permit renewed, the general statement is going to be that the Hopis did not want us to work. This, of course, is not so. The actual ruin and the excavation of it appear less and less important as negotiations go on. The really important point lies in the various claims [of the clans] for control of the surrounding farm lands. ... These disputes probably go back hundreds of years, and I imagine played an important part in the sacking of Awatovi.[31]

That last season, some members of the archaeology team stayed on into September, packing and shipping artifacts and equipment. Most of the expedition's scientific participants returned to Cambridge. Equipment, lumber, tents, and even Pecos Black, were presented to the Hopi crews and their families as farewell gifts. The parting, remembered one participant, caused much sadness and good-byes were sometimes tearful. The expedition's premature end left much work unfinished. For example, "they [the Awatovi teams] were going to work out ... the sequence of [prehistoric] rooms," remembered Watson Smith years later.[32]

Soon the expedition members were engulfed in the cataclysm of World War II. The interruption made reporting the work all the more complicated.

The expedition's work on the Franciscan mission at Awatovi was the most thorough uncovering of Spanish colonial church architecture anywhere in the Southwest up to that time. Brew and his colleagues reported on the mission first, telling the story of the long sequence of Spanish activity and describing the remains of the three churches.

As part of the major 1949 volume *Franciscan Awatovi: The Excavation and Conjectural Reconstruction of a 17th-Century Spanish Mission Establishment at a Hopi Indian Town in Northeastern Arizona,* which he co-authored with Montgomery and Smith, Brew summarized the history of Awatovi and described the excavations of the Franciscan buildings.

Ross Montgomery wrote and illustrated the volume's fascinating, monumental description of the architecture of Awatovi's churches. He fleshed out the account with many details about the daily lives of the Franciscans, with whom he felt a strong bond. Watson Smith reported on the church murals, describing four European-style types of designs, paint pigments, and other technicalities about the mission wall paintings, and giving comparative details about similar ones in Mexico and Spain.

Some Ph.D. dissertations were done on the Awatovi work. Richard Woodbury published his as an exhaustive report on stone implements from the dig, complete with meticulous chronological tables and appendices. Other archaeologists contributed reports on artifacts and wrote short papers for journals.

Crosses and other Spanish artifacts from the Awatovi mission church. Figure 31 in "Franciscan Awatovi," by Ross Gordon Montgomery, Watson Smith, and John Otis Brew (1949).

Reconstruction of mural decorations in the mission church at Awatovi.
Figure 55 in "Franciscan Awatovi," by Ross Gordon Montgomery, Watson
Smith, and John Otis Brew (1949).

Eleanor Roosevelt with Hopi painter Fred Kabotie in front of a replica of an Awatovi kiva mural, at the 1941 exhibition "Indian Art of the United States," produced by the Museum of Modern Art in New York.

As the years passed, Brew's concern with reporting on Awatovi apparently was overshadowed by his new duties as director of the Peabody Museum, where he took the helm in 1948, superseding Donald Scott. Smith accepted the task of writing several volumes about Awatovi, a process that continued for decades, into the 1970s. His best-known work was the comprehensive description of the painted kivas titled *Kiva Mural Decorations at Awatovi and Kawaika-a: With a Survey of Other Wall Paintings in the Pueblo Southwest.* This 1952 volume, the fifth in the series on the Awatovi Expedition published by the Peabody Museum, was embellished with color plates. It fueled increasing public fascination with the murals, which were displayed in numerous museum exhibitions, including one at New York's Museum of Modern Art, and praised in articles in *The New York Times* and other newspapers.

In the early 1950s, when Watson Smith moved to Tucson, barrels of potsherds followed him to the home that Brew suggested be called the "Peabody Museum West of the Pecos." In fact, Smith's home did become an official Harvard field office. There he wrote a thorough, much-needed pottery report, *Painted Ceramics of the Western Mound at Awatovi* (no. 8 in the Awatovi series), published in 1971. Unfortunately, it covered only a small portion of the pottery actually found at the dig, and many of the later period ceramics went unreported.

By 1978, eleven major reports on Awatovi had come out, but there was still no "final" report summarizing the expedition's findings.[33] Prehistoric architecture and most of the pottery data—of vital interest to later archaeologists—went unpublished, as did much information on the smaller sites, Volney Jones's ethnobotanical work, and some of the other interdisciplinary studies. Such gaps led later archaeologists to question the value of large-scale excavations that, too often, were not adequately reported. What was the point of all the excavating, many wondered, if the data remained unanalyzed and the results went unpublished?

In a brief description of Awatovi written decades later, Brew commented, "Actually, except for the Franciscan buildings, which we excavated completely, the final results of our five years of digging at Awatovi may best be described as extensive testing."[34] He was probably overly modest. Actually, the expedition had excavated approximately 1,300 of Awatovi's estimated five thousand rooms, spanning an occupation period from the 1200s to 1700, or Pueblo III through Pueblo V times.

The expedition's extensive surveys had located some 296 sites, including historic Hopi and Navajo ones. With the material gathered at smaller prehistoric sites, the archaeologists could account for a time span extending from AD 500 in the early Basketmaker III period to Awatovi's destruction in the Pueblo V era—twelve centuries of human occupation at more than twenty excavated sites.

Brew concluded, from examination of the historical documents and excavation findings, that by the seventeenth century, at least, the people at Awatovi were Hopis. Using data compiled by Smith in the 1971 pottery report, he traced Awatovi's connection to abandoned prehistoric towns in the Kayenta region, in the upper Little Colorado Valley, and in the area near present-day Flagstaff. Of the probable migration of the prehistoric Western Anasazi from those places to Awatovi he wrote, "This study proves conclusively, to my satisfaction, where some of them [the migrating Anasazi] went."[35] The finding of many small, early sites and fewer large, later ones substantiated a changing pattern observed by other archaeologists—from a "large number of very small settlements to a few towns with populations in the hundreds."[36]

Efforts to obtain archaeological evidence to augment historic documents did not get far, in part because only scanty historic documentation existed and little more came to light. Describing the historic record on Awatovi, Brew wrote, "We have found *no document* which we know to have originated there and the few references in contemporary record, as will be seen, are very meager indeed."[37] In the end, the expedition participants found no evidence that enabled them to say definitely whether or not Awatovi was the first town visited by Tovar.

Regarding the legends of Awatovi's violent demise Brew wrote, "These accounts are effectively substantiated by our archaeological evidence."[38] An

Awatovi kiva in Test 31, Room 1 revealed scattered human bones; charred reeds, grass, and beams; and heat-discolored plaster and stones. In a 1972 report Watson Smith wrote that this may have been the kiva that Fewkes had begun excavating in 1892, until his workmen's distress at the burning, death, and desecration they were uncovering caused him to stop.[39]

EXPLORATION OF THE AWATOVI VICINITY did not end with the departure of the Peabody expedition. In the 1960s, archaeologists surveying sites in the area found additional evidence to support the stories of the destruction of Awatovi. Skeletal remains were uncovered in a mass grave at the edge of Polacca Wash, ten miles south of the Hopi villages. Summarizing their finds, Christy Turner and Nancy Morris wrote,

> Thirty Hopi Indians of both sexes and all ages were killed, crudely dismembered, violently mutilated, and probably cannibalized about 370 years ago. ... The location of, dismemberment of bodies in, and radiocarbon age of this mass burial suggest the bodies were once the few live villagers, taken captive by other Hopi warriors, referred to in the legendary account of the destruction of Awatobi [sic] pueblo that occurred ten to twelve generations ago.[40]

Watson Smith (right) with his friend and colleague Robert Burgh, in front of Smith's Tucson home, the "Peabody Museum West of the Pecos," in 1958.

Fewkes had reported that Indian accounts told of dismemberment and mutilation of captives from Awatovi. Turner and Morris concluded, "Southwestern archaeological evidence fitting legendary events has seldom been better."[41] The article raised strong controversy among Indians and non-Indians about possible anti-Native American biases in anthropological reporting. It also indicated that Awatovi's legend would not be forgotten.

The Hopi tribe has kept close watch over the ruin ever since the Peabody expedition. In retirement, Brew, Lancaster, Smith, and others followed with interest any news of archaeology relating to Awatovi. But in spite of more recent excavations, the question of the town's final chapter has remained unsolved, and probably always will be an enigma.

Rainbow Bridge–Monument Valley
Expedition pack train at Kiet Siel, 1934.
Milton Wetherill at right.

CHAPTER 8

THE RAINBOW BRIDGE—
MONUMENT VALLEY EXPEDITION

The End of the Great Romance

O N A HOT JUNE DAY IN 1933, a small group of men accompanied by a pack train of burros trudged over a faint trail on the banks of Laguna Creek in northeastern Arizona. The narrow track wound through Tsegi Canyon on the Navajo Reservation, crossing from one side of the streambed to the other. Men and animals splashed back and forth across the shallow water and over the damp beaches, which were dotted with jello-like patches of quicksand.

Amid the spectacular scenery of the Rainbow Bridge–Monument Valley region, these men were launching a scientific expedition. Dozens of scholars and students traveled to the Navajo Reservation each summer during the Depression years of 1933–38 to participate in an endeavor that changed many of their lives. During some of the same years when the Awatovi expedition was exploring prehistoric ruins on the south side of Black Mesa, these scientists and students were working on the mesa's other side, seventy miles due north of the Awatovi camp, as part of the Rainbow Bridge–Monument Valley (often abbreviated "RBMV") Expedition. It was one of the last of the grand, nineteenth-century-style scientific expeditions, and it combined the traditional approach of bringing generalists, amateurs, and artists into the field with a twentieth-century innovation: an interdisciplinary group of specialized scientists. Besides archaeologists, the RBMV

Expedition included experts in geology, biology, ecology, paleontology, and paleoecology. These scientists introduced techniques such as aerial photography and fossil pollen analysis that enriched the archaeologists' fieldwork.

The expedition's goal was to explore and excavate the prehistoric ruins of the Western Anasazi people, known to archaeologists as the "Kayenta Anasazi," who inhabited the region until AD 1300. The plan was to survey three thousand square miles of isolated, relatively unknown, and spottily mapped wilderness on the Navajo Reservation and public lands. This immense study area was bounded roughly by Black Mesa on the south, the San Juan River on the north, Monument Valley on the east, and the Colorado River on the west. A remote world of deserts and arid mesas laced with oases of verdant canyons and pine-forested mountains, it encompassed some of the most superb scenery in North America.

The RBMV Expedition was the brainchild of Ansel Franklin Hall, who in 1933 held the title of chief of the Division of Education and Forestry of the National Park Service. Hall was an energetic, successful administrator and a visionary educator dedicated to introducing young people to the wilderness. He was also, in the words of one archaeologist, "an unlikely combination of shrewd promoter and romantic idealist." [1]

Hall used his position with the National Park Service to engineer the RBMV Expedition, a private endeavor originally created to support the development of a national park in the Rainbow Bridge–Monument Valley area. He envisioned a privately funded expedition to study the proposed park and report on its natural history, resources, and recreation potential, as well as to recommend boundaries. Hall's efforts to create an expedition to northeastern Arizona got results, although politics squelched the idea for a national park.

During that first 1933 season, seventy-four RBMV Expedition members participated in "extensive reconnaissance, by motor where practicable, but for the most part afoot and by pack train, augmented by boat transportation in the deep and inaccessible canyons of the San Juan and Colorado rivers." [2] Far-reaching though they were, these preliminary surveys were only the beginning of the RBMV Expedition's ambitious endeavors. Hall had charged his teams of explorers with many-faceted and complicated tasks.

He engaged the family of John Wetherill, the well-known Navajo trader, Southwestern explorer, and self-taught archaeologist, to outfit and guide the expedition. Although the Wetherills and some of their clients had made hundreds of trips in the area, much exploration — not to mention the task of mapping many of the area's archaeological, geological, and topographical features — remained to be done.

A legacy of archaeological and scientific reports formed a foundation for the RBMV Expedition's initial investigations. Early explorers in the region had reported the existence of well-preserved Indian ruins, some of which had been visited by archaeologists including Jesse Walter Fewkes, Byron Cummings, Neil Judd, Earl Morris, A. V. Kidder, and Samuel Guernsey.

Beginning in 1909 scientists such as Cummings, William B. Douglass, and Herbert E. Gregory made wide-ranging examinations of the Navajo region, recording landmarks and geological features. On one trip Cummings and W. B. Douglass, guided by John Wetherill, "discovered" the Rainbow Bridge, a stunning landmark known for centuries to the Navajos:

> Orthodox history has it that Rainbow Bridge, the world's largest natural stone span, was first seen by literate whites on August 14, 1909, on an expedition consisting of the rival but combined parties of University of Utah archaeologist Byron Cummings and U.S. government surveyor William Boone Douglass. After a difficult journey to discover the bridge, the Cummings group and Douglass each claimed the credit, and the controversy as to "who was first" has continued to the present. . . . [There is] evidence that neither Cummings nor Douglass was "first," that in fact the Wetherills had visited Rainbow Bridge months previous but had kept the trip a secret in order to let Cummings think he was the first white ever to see this natural wonder. There also is reason to believe that Rainbow Bridge had been seen (but not formally reported) decades earlier by prospectors, cowboys, and perhaps others.[3]

In their reports Gregory and Douglass noted only major topographic and hydrographic features such as the amazing sandstone arch of the Rainbow Bridge. Unexplored and unrecorded were the region's complex geology—including its many volcanic features—and the details of its natural history and its unique and varied flora and fauna.

Archaeologist Earl Morris, outfitted by Wetherill, accompanied wealthy businessman Charles L. Bernheimer to the Rainbow Bridge early in the 1920s. Late in that decade the archaeologists of the Gila Pueblo research center in Arizona surveyed some sites in the vicinity of Marsh Pass and Tsegi Canyon.

The RBMV Expedition crews aimed to expand on these earlier explorations and surveys by filling in gaps in geological and environmental information and locating the most significant prehistoric sites. They also planned to excavate some of the ruins in the hope of learning more about the prehistoric sequence of cultural changes, from Basketmaker through Pueblo times, before the area was abandoned at the end of the Pueblo III era.

Early archaeological investigations in the RBMV country had focused on its most spectacular ruins, Betatakin and Kiet Siel, and on especially well-preserved materials in caves and rock shelters. A vast array of smaller, less conspicuous sites remained undocumented. Archaeologists were beginning to realize that

Top: Rainbow Bridge from the west side, looking toward Navajo Mountain, 1933.
Bottom: Aerial view of Tsegi Canyon, 1937.

intriguing details about the everyday lives of prehistoric people could sometimes be found at excavations of such small settlements.

Like many of their predecessors in the region, most of the RBMV Expedition participants were not native Southwesterners. The beauty and romance of the Navajo country captivated them as it had so many others, from author Zane Grey to U.S. president and international explorer Theodore Roosevelt.

Monument Valley exerted an especially powerful allure. In his memoirs archaeologist Neil Judd expressed the feelings of numerous early visitors:

> Monument Valley was an incredible, utterly fantastic place when we first saw it on August 2, 1908. A thin Navaho trail crossed through the middle. Sandstone buttes thrust upward one thousand feet, more or less; others, dozens of them, rose hazily in the dim distance. Excepting an occasional, sparrow-like bird startled from its shaded perch beneath a clump of rabbit brush, we saw no living thing, no sign of life. There were no trees on the sandy plain; no shrubs worthy of the name. The valley was empty and silent. . . . Our black-and-white snapshots scarcely portray the mystic beauty of the place as we first saw it. Monument Valley was a fairyland then, and it will always remain so despite motels, divided highways, and speeding autos.[4]

College students constituted the backbone of the crews that Ansel Hall recruited for the RBMV Expedition. They paid roughly $3.50 a day for the opportunity to participate in a scientific project led by professionals, many of whom were college professors volunteering during summer vacation. Some of the students even worked as cooks or laborers for the chance to go on the expedition.

The RBMV Expedition's emphasis on student participation was part of a growing movement in Southwestern archaeology. During the 1930s an increasing number of university-sponsored Southwestern field schools began training young archaeologists. This trend meant that "students became involved in the research goals of their institution or professor, and in some measure contributed to those goals."[5]

On campuses all over the country, young men heard of the RBMV Expedition and responded enthusiastically to Hall's bulletin board advertisements: "WANTED: 10 EXPLORERS!" "There was no lack of volunteers," the expedition's leading archaeologists later reported.[6] Hall interviewed student applicants in New York City at the Explorers' Club, of which he was a member. He also recruited students in California. The young men on the East and West Coasts formed two auto caravans and traveled together to the expedition headquarters in Kayenta—a ten-day drive from New York, and about half that long from California.

Top: Betatakin Ruins, c. 1910. Bottom left: Dwelling at
Betatakin, 1933. Bottom right: RBMV Expedition member
Paul Baldwin attempts to enter the upper dwellings at
Betatakin, 1933.

Besides recruiting, Ansel Hall masterminded a campaign of promotion, fund-raising, and public information for the expedition, working mainly from his Park Service desk. He used the student tuition fees to defray most of the expedition's expenses, including the salaries of guides, cooks, Navajo packers, and others. He also raised some money from private sources. By these means he financed "the largest self-supporting, multidisciplinary expedition ever conducted in North America."[7]

Hall had an equally fine talent for publicity; one archaeologist commented that he wrote "irresistible blurb."[8] He sent press releases to major newspapers and magazines, circulated articles by participants describing the RBMV Expedition's activities, and talked about it on national radio. Calling on his far-flung network of intellectual and business contacts, he made sure the expedition was supported by the worlds of business, academia, science, and museology, as well as the media.

Hall's ability to interest and involve the media resulted in copious film footage and thousands of still photographs of the expedition. By the end of the second season, Hall reported 17,000 feet of motion picture film had been shot, along with two hundred lantern slides and between fifteen hundred and two thousand photographs.[9]

Hall also persuaded the Ford Motor Company to contribute a small battalion of new, V-8 "woodie" station wagons and trucks for hauling men and gear on reservation dirt roads. Some of the film footage depicts scenes of archaeologists, Navajos, and students vigorously digging vehicles out of the sticky mud of Monument Valley after heavy rains.

Although no women students participated in the expedition, women did perform important peripheral jobs. Two served as expedition photographers; one of them, a pilot, provided valuable aerial shots. Ceramics expert Anna O. Shepard visited the camps to advise on pottery analysis. Other women visitors occasionally helped with fieldwork. The predominant perception of the time, however, was that the conditions and work on the expedition would be too harsh for women.

Once students arrived at the expedition's permanent camp at Marsh Pass, they were assigned to work crews, and sometimes sent to temporary camps in Tsegi Canyon. They were treated to what archaeologist Watson Smith called "a worm's eye view" of archaeological endeavors. Before being accepted, students had to agree to "carry out cheerfully any task ... whether it be field reconnaissance, 'wrangling' pack animals, running an instrument, building trails, recording scientific data — or even occasional kitchen duty."[10]

The journals and memoirs of the students and other expedition members are a treasure house of information about work, personalities, expedition politics, and common snafus. One entry, dated early July 1937, read:

Spent my first day in the field and, boy, was it a hard one. Started the day off wrong by leaving a thumb screw from my rod half way up to the top of the mesa. Before I got down from this height I managed to get stuck at a place where I couldn't get either up or down. After considerable time I managed to get back up to a level place where Kayatso, the dog, welcomed me back.[11]

Many of the students were so enthralled by the experience of living in the wilderness and doing scientific research that they went on to careers in archaeology or one of the natural sciences. Among those who trained with the expedition and later made significant contributions to the profession of archaeology were Omer C. Stewart, John B. Rinaldo, Richard S. MacNeish, and John W. Bennett, to name a few.

BESIDES ANSEL HALL, several others who knew and loved the Navajo country wanted to see it made into a national park. Among them was John Wetherill. The idea for the RBMV Expedition was conceived one night in the fall of 1932 as Ansel Hall sat before the fire at the Wetherill trading post in Kayenta. Hall later wrote: "Mr. John Wetherill, who has followed the frontier in that part of the desert Southwest for more than half a century, pointed out the value—the necessity, in fact—of thoroughly exploring the vast region lying north of Black Mesa and south of the San Juan and Colorado Rivers."[12]

John Wetherill was a younger brother of Richard Wetherill, who has been credited with the "discovery" of Cliff Palace at Mesa Verde. With Richard and his other brothers, Al, Winslow, and Clayton, John had spent many years exploring the Mesa Verde and Chaco Canyon country. Richard and Al began exploring Tsegi Canyon around 1890, and a few years later John looked for, and discovered, cliff houses there.[13]

In 1906, at the age of forty, John and his wife Louisa set up a trading post at Oljeto in Monument Valley, deep in the isolated fastness of the reservation. They moved with their two children four years later to Kayenta, Arizona, where, with their partner, Clyde Colville, they established the Wetherill and Colville Trading Post.

In 1909, when Navajo National Monument was established, John Wetherill became its custodian. The government paid him one dollar a month to oversee the monument, which encompassed numerous Indian ruins tucked into rock shelters in Tsegi and other canyons. Best-known among these sites were the beautiful cliff dwellings of Betatakin and Kiet Siel.

Wetherill was sixty-seven years old when the Rainbow Bridge–Monument Valley Expedition took to the field. By then he had been trader to the Navajos in the Kayenta–Monument Valley region for more than a quarter of a century. Out

An RBMV Expedition staff meeting at the Wetherill home in Kayenta, August 1933. Left to right: John Armstrong, Alonzo Pond, Robert Kissack, Ansel Hall, John Wetherill, Ben Wetherill, Tracy Kelley, Lyndon Hargrave.

of respect and affection, the Navajo people called him "Hosteen" John, a title denoting an older man of high status.

His steadiness and good nature made him a much appreciated part of the expedition, for which he served as a sort of walking encyclopedia on the back country. Archaeologist Neil Judd remarked that, once on the trail, Wetherill always kept on going:

> I had a deep admiration for John Wetherill. I had known him at Oljeto in 1908 and 1909, when northern Arizona was young and the Navahos were wild. He had guided the Cummings-Douglass party to discovery of Rainbow Bridge on August 14, 1909; he had been my chief reliance during restoration of Betatakin for the Interior Department in the late winter of 1917. A Quaker by birth and inclination, he could shoe a mule without swearing, and he could lead a pack train where a pack train had never gone before. The Clay Hills country was unmapped and virtually untraveled, but I knew that John Wetherill could take me there if anyone could.[14]

During its first two years, the RBMV Expedition used the Wetherill Trading Post at Kayenta as its base. Archaeologists, surveyors, geologists, biologists, paleontologists, entomologists, zoologists, herpetologists, and botanists all reconnoitered on the shady porch overlooking Louisa Wetherill's lawn, an oasis

Above: Group picture of RBMV crew and staff at Dunn's Place, July 1933. In the front row, starting at far right, are Ansel F. Hall, Benjamin Wetherill, John Wetherill, and Lyndon Hargrave. Right: Ben Wetherill examining corrugated pottery, 1933.

in the desert, before heading into the outback. Navajo and Anglo cooks and packers also gathered at the post.

In his role of expedition outfitter, guide, and advisor, Hosteen John helped Ansel Hall work out the overall plan for covering the enormous targeted area in Navajo country. Wetherill, though physically declining, followed the expedition's movements and archaeological activities closely and participated occasionally. In return for his active interest, support, and participation, Hall eventually appointed him associate director of the expedition.

Wetherill turned most of the strenuous fieldwork over to two younger family members—his son, Ben, and nephew, Milton. Each season Ben acted as guide and Navajo interpreter. During the 1933–34 season, he also served as an expedition archaeologist; in 1935 he was chief of archaeology; and in 1936–37 he held the title of associate field director. Milt Wetherill was "a big and enormously strong man," with "hands like two hams ... he could crush two of yours when he grasped them."[15] Milt was the expedition's man-of-all-trades.

Hosteen John spoke out sharply if he suspected the inexperienced student crew members of mishandling artifacts or taking them illegally (which they occasionally did). The students were warned against private collecting. At one point, Hall reported, "the whole archeological party—and the expedition in general—is 'in bad' with the Wetherills" because "a big bag of beautiful potsherds" scavenged from the Kiet Siel ruin had appeared in camp.[16] An archaeological historian looking back on the problem wrote, "While private collecting occurred frequently enough to create headaches for archaeological staff, it was not likely to have caused serious damage to the archaeological record of the region."[17]

Outfitters and government officials had become more aware of the value of archaeology. More rigorous federal and state legal restrictions protected archaeological sites and the collections gathered at them. The whole area covered by the expedition was federally controlled, and removing prehistoric artifacts required an antiquities permit. Hall took care of getting the permits, which "stipulated that all collected artifacts be placed in public museums."[18] Arrangements were made to store the expedition's collections, first at the Museum of Northern Arizona and later at the University of California, Los Angeles (UCLA).

Indian tribes had learned that they had a say in any archaeological work taking place on their land. Ansel Hall also obtained permission from the Navajo Council for the RBMV Expedition to work on tribal lands.

Many Navajos, who had known the Wetherills for years, participated as guides and packers and supplied animals to the pack trains. Years later expedition members remembered playing games with the Navajos at summer celebrations such as the Fourth of July. There were tug-of-wars, foot races, and horse races. Sometimes the men attended Navajo events. Once, at a mud dance, enthusiastic Indian dancers dunked an expedition photographer and several students in slippery mud baths.

Each season, as part of the expedition's archaeological and scientific reconnaissance, some participants spent a few weeks rafting along the San Juan River and in Glen Canyon on the Colorado River. On these boat trips they searched for otherwise inaccessible archaeological sites and gathered biological specimens that might prove important to setting the boundaries for a national park. The trips also supported one of Hall's expeditionary goals: to increase students' self-reliance and appreciation of nature. Ben Wetherill guided some of these river trips, and during the first season John Wetherill—"Uncle John" to most expedition members—went along as cook.

Three subjects dominated the journal entries of students who took part in these river trips: storms on the river, the excitement of discovery, and food. One crew member wrote to Hall of his overland trip to the launching point on the San Juan River and the subsequent boat trip:

> The Wetherills had said the trail [to the river] was a rough one, but the Wetherills are not the type to avoid a trail because of its roughness. . . . Thomas who drove the truck said that his machine consumed one gallon of gasoline every two and one-half miles, by which figures you can estimate the amount of radiator boiling and sand plowing we had to do. . . .
>
> Our crew was as willing, perspiring, and loyal as one could desire. At a few minutes before four in the afternoon we launched the seven tiny vessels upon the chocolate flood and began our fight with the rollicking sand waves. . . .
>
> [During a storm] a small canyon opposite us was transformed in five minutes from a dry wash into a squirming dragon of red mud and foam which belched tons of frothy filth into a giant whirlpool.[19]

MANY YOUNG SCIENTISTS found in Hall's elaborate yet loosely structured expedition an opportunity to begin carving their own professional niches. Among these was Lyndon Hargrave, a studious, feisty, and occasionally tormented man. Though physically small, he expressed himself vigorously and was capable of powerful leaps of intellect. "Hargrave was a natural scientist," one archaeologist commented.[20]

Like many others, Hargrave stumbled across the profession of archaeology serendipitously after training for another field. Graduating from a North Carolina teachers' college in 1917, Hargrave had planned to work at a school in the South. First, though, family connections led to his working for several years as a hydrographer at Roosevelt Dam in Arizona. There he began to explore and make notes on Indian ruins. Impressed by his work, pioneer archaeologist and anthropologist Dean Byron Cummings of the University of Arizona urged him to study the new disciplines as a second career. Hargrave took his advice.

Much of Hargrave's work in archaeology focused on the two most important ways of dating sites—tree-ring studies and ceramic analyses. Along with stratigraphic excavation techniques, these had become, in the first three decades of the twentieth century, the backbone of the Southwestern archaeologist's tool kit. Hargrave used all of these techniques, especially ceramic analyses, in imaginative and original ways on the RBMV Expedition and in his other research projects.

In 1929, with fellow student archaeologist Emil Haury, Hargrave had found a vital chunk of prehistoric wood, labeled "HH-39" (the acronym "HH" stood for "Haury-Hargrave"). It was this find that enabled astronomer A. E. Douglass to fill in the "missing link" in the Southwest's tree-ring chronology, closing the gap that had existed in the sequence of tree-rings extending from modern times into prehistory.

Birds were one of Hargrave's great passions. Combining his archaeological and ornithological interests, he pioneered the study of prehistoric bird bones and feathers at archaeological sites. His studies of bird remains provided archaeologists with knowledge related to such subjects as the changes in the environment and possible prehistoric trade links with Mexico.

John Wetherill preparing his famous hot biscuits at Warm Creek Camp, August 1933.

Lyndon Hargrave
examining wood specimens
in the field, 1933.

In February 1929 Hargrave began working for Dr. Harold S. Colton, the wealthy and scientifically influential archaeologist and founder of the Museum of Northern Arizona in Flagstaff. Under Colton, Hargrave searched for tree-ring specimens in the Hopi area and pioneered studies of potsherds, work that eventually resulted in several landmark publications.

Ansel Hall heard about Hargrave's talents from Jesse Nusbaum, then consulting archaeologist for the Department of the Interior, and arranged with Dr. Colton to borrow Hargrave for the RBMV Expedition. As director of fieldwork during the first expedition season, when over seventy men participated, Hargrave brought essential scientific focus to the survey. That year he did not excavate. Instead, his survey crews located and mapped some two hundred prehistoric sites in previously unexplored areas of Tsegi Canyon.

Hargrave had the crews collect samples of pottery sherds from the surface of every site for later analysis. The distinctive, decorated gray, white, or orange pottery of the Kayenta Anasazi soon became familiar to the students. Hargrave knew about the technique of collecting random samples of surface sherds, used in the seriation work done at Zuni by A. L. Kroeber and Leslie Spier. A. V. Kidder had pioneered the method, and teams of archaeologists working for Harold Gladwin at Gila Pueblo in Arizona had also adopted it in their extensive survey of the Southwest. Hargrave's adoption of random surface sherd collection added an important dimension to the expedition's scientific scope.

A careful recording process devised by Colton and Hargrave allowed tracking of every sherd. Each site was given an "NA" number, which added it to the site-numbering system of the Museum of Northern Arizona. Then each sherd was numbered according to the site on which it was found.

Hargrave connected the relative dates he obtained through sherd analysis with precise tree-ring dates from two hundred pieces of wood and charcoal taken from beams in the ancient cliff dwellings. Using these ceramic and tree-ring data, he was able to piece together the history of the construction of individual cliff houses as well as their relationships to each other over time.

To integrate his interests in ceramics, architecture, and dating methods with the animal and plant remains found at the sites, Hargrave pioneered a concept he called "human ecology." This approach aimed to create "a more thorough understanding of the environmental factors which contributed to the shaping of the early cultures in the region."[21] Hargrave had a formative influence on the study of culture as an adaptation to the environment, an approach now widely used.

Hargrave's ecological interests were augmented by the work of RBMV Expedition scientists from other disciplines, including two men who also had been part of the Awatovi expedition: Harvard geologist John Hack and University of Michigan ethnobotanist Volney Jones. Hack's studies of arroyo cutting and its relationship to Tsegi Canyon prehistoric agriculture, and Jones's analyses of prehistoric cultivated and uncultivated plants in the RBMV area, became appendices to the final report on the expedition.

Hargrave occasionally assisted the various scientists by working as a professional liaison, writing letters to request expert opinions about expedition finds. He corresponded with authorities in ornithology, avian paleontology, and other specialized branches of zoology. Scientists from the University of California and other institutions helped him to identify fossilized bones found in caves and geological formations. Among the discoveries were extinct species of horses, snails, and other long-vanished creatures.

The first season the discovery of dinosaur bones in a finger of Tsegi Canyon "turned out to be the most remarkable find of the whole summer,"[22] according to Ansel Hall. He went on to describe the discovery's scientific significance: "The first definite organic remains ever found in the continental Jurassic rocks of the Southwest—formations which cover thousands of square miles."[23] Dinosaur footprints were also discovered in Mesozoic rocks.

Besides working with the other scientists, Hargrave assisted the expedition's neophyte archaeologists. He visited their temporary "fly camps" in the canyon to give lectures on the rudiments of archaeology. For the students, the experience blended scientific challenge and pure, romantic adventure. They explored untouched places where ruins and artifacts lay scattered in hidden alcoves and canyon grottos. Potsherds might lie near a softly bubbling spring concealed among sweet-smelling wild honeysuckle vines and lush berry bushes.

During the second field season, in the summer of 1934, the archaeologists focused on Dogoszhi Biko (Greasewood Canyon) and its tributaries—the main eastern finger of Tsegi Canyon. Although Hargrave was not able to be present the entire time, for a few weeks he supervised all the work, which included excavations in Water Lily Canyon of a Basketmaker cave, a prehistoric granary of a later period, and a cliff dwelling called Len-a Ki.

In spite of the beautiful setting and the intriguing lessons in archaeology, problems with the students did crop up. Some found the conditions too harsh or discovered that archaeology was not to their liking. Conflicts between the educational mission of the expedition and its research goals continued throughout the endeavor. Andrew Christenson, the expedition's biographer, wrote:

> One of the disadvantages of a self-funding expedition is the necessity of accepting inexperienced personnel to keep a project afloat. Occasionally this can be disastrous, as with the young man whom Lyndon Hargrave described as "irresponsible, unreliable, indolent, careless to the extreme, and apparently without a permanent interest in anything." More often, however, it simply meant that crews did not operate at top efficiency. At the end of the 1934 season, Hargrave complained that his crew lacked a basic knowledge of southwestern archaeology and was unaccustomed to hard work and difficult living conditions. He had to spend much time giving lectures, training men in the use of tools and equipment, and generally keeping a close eye on everyone.[24]

Hargrave faced a mountain of scientific reporting after the second season. On top of this tough job, he struggled with a heavy workload at his regular museum post as well as the demands of his first marriage, which took place before the second field season. In a letter to Hall, he said, "I will not have the time I used to have before I was married but I will promise that certain reports will be forthcoming shortly."[25]

After the 1934 season he wrote to Hall explaining that Dr. Colton "has refused me Museum time to write this [1934 RBMV Expedition archaeological] report." He added, "These remarks should impress you with the fact that field data takes longer to study and report than it does to gather and that the Expedition is now more than a year behind."[26]

By December of that year Hargrave's wife was in the hospital. Although she eventually recovered, the emotional pressures and financial difficulties associated with her illness added to Hargrave's burdens.

Relations between Colton and Hall remained cordial, but Colton did not spare Hargrave to participate directly in the expedition's subsequent seasons. In appreciation of his significant contributions during the first two seasons, Hall recognized Hargrave "as a member of the field staff even though he may not have time to take active part in the field work."[27]

Although he sometimes ran behind schedule, Hargrave produced various scientific reports on his expedition findings. The high quality of his work helped offset some scholars' tendency to disparage the entire RBMV project as a light-weight concoction of Ansel Hall.

I N 1936, after seeing Watson Smith's work on RBMV surveys in Tsegi Canyon, Hargrave wrote to Hall,

> Watson Smith would be an excellent assistant for you this summer. ...
> I cannot recommend him too highly. Never have I seen anyone grasp
> the problems as has he and even now I value his opinion more highly
> than I do the opinion of most so-called southwestern archaeologists. I
> expect great things from him in the future.[28]

True to Hargrave's prediction, "Wat" Smith became a crucial figure in the development of Southwestern archaeology, and especially in the reporting of data. He also became a beloved friend of many archaeologists, appreciated "for the modest, witty, complex, inspiring, and delightful Edwardian personality that he is."[29]

A self-made archaeologist in the process of teaching himself the discipline, Smith was in his late thirties during his 1935–37 stint with the RBMV Expedition. His tenacity and his gift for synthesizing data into clear conclusions led Smith to become one of the archaeologists who took responsibility for writing the final report on the Rainbow Bridge–Monument Valley work. He would later do the same for two other major Southwestern expeditions—Awatovi and Hawikuh.

A Midwesterner trained in law at Harvard, Smith had fulfilled a long-standing dream by coming to the Southwest to participate in Paul S. Martin's dig at Lowry Ruin in Colorado. He wrote of this adventure in his memoirs: "In the spring of 1933, when the revolving doors of Destiny came full circle again ... [they] spewed me outward upon a westward-flying carpet toward new horizons in a Southwestern land of mystery and legend."[30]

Smith's participation in the RBMV Expedition began in the summer of 1935. That same year he moved to temporary accommodations in Flagstaff and began working at the Museum of Northern Arizona as editorial assistant to Colton and Hargrave. Also, beginning in 1936 and continuing for several summers, the

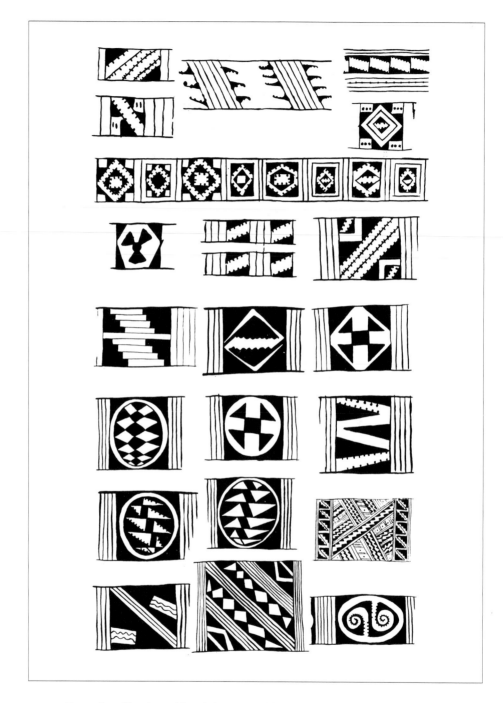

Examples of horizontal band designs on black-on-white pottery. Figure 24 in "Archaeological Studies in Northeast Arizona," by Ralph L. Beals, George W. Brainerd, and Watson Smith (1945).

Pueblo III (Tsegi) orange-ware jars and pitchers from site RB 568 and Tsegi
Canyon sites. Figure 67 in "Archaeological Studies in Northeast Arizona," by
Ralph L. Beals, George W. Brainerd, and Watson Smith (1945).

energetic lawyer-turned-archaeologist spent part of each field season, after his RBMV duties ended, working with the Awatovi expedition.

Three other young archaeologists destined for significant careers — George W. Brainerd, Edward T. Hall, and John B. Rinaldo — joined the RBMV Expedition in 1935, participating in an important archaeological survey in the Tsegi area, which was directed by Ansel Hall. Whereas Hargrave had focused on unexplored side-canyons, Hall and his crew looked for sites along the floor of the Long Canyon branch of the main Tsegi Canyon. "Theirs was the first effort to systematically examine the canyon floor and to record all sites."[31]

Brainerd and Smith described the survey method in their final report:

> Each morning one or more small parties would leave camp on foot to survey a definitely defined area. The group was always led by an experienced archaeologist and might consist of from two to six men. The ideal was to cover every square yard of ground so thoroughly that no prehistoric remains could possibly be overlooked. ...
>
> Whenever any member of the surveying party came upon a prehistoric site, as evidenced by the presence of potsherds, flint chips, masonry remains, or charcoal concentrations, he immediately made a collection of sherds and worked flint from the surface and painted a site number on a rock as nearly [sic] the center of the site as feasible. Usually the group leader went to each site located and entered descriptive field notes on a standard site card.[32]

Though the archaeological survey teams focused mainly on Tsegi Canyon, they also explored remote regions such as Skeleton Mesa at the northern end of the Tsegi, and the Kaiparowits Plateau (also called "Wild Horse Mesa") in Utah. Altogether the expedition surveyed more than a thousand sites, developing survey and mapping techniques that Field Director Ralph Beals credited in large part to the thinking and planning of Ansel Hall.[33] By the end of the expedition, the archaeologists had surveyed and mapped sites dating from 250 BC (Basketmaker II) to AD 1300 (Pueblo III).

In addition to directing surveys, Smith supervised a dig at a Pueblo II site on Black Mesa numbered "RB [for RBMV Expedition] site 551." One of the expedition's most important excavations, it was the site used to identify the characteristic Pueblo II pottery types in the region.[34] Work at RB 551 added pieces to the pottery jigsaw puzzle that archaeologists were attempting to solve in order to picture the lifeways and population movements of the Kayenta Anasazi.

Brainerd directed another important excavation from 1935 through 1938 at RB 568, an artifact-rich burial site near Kayenta, Arizona. Located in

Above: George Brainerd, at left, c. 1935, examining a collection of wood specimens (photo from Watson Smith's scrapbook). Left: Watson Smith (in trench) and Roy Crawford digging a refuse dump at a site near Marsh Pass, 1935.

shifting sands, the prehistoric graveyard told much about the early stages of the Pueblo III period in the RBMV region.

Although Rinaldo and Edward Hall participated only in 1935, Smith remained with the expedition through its 1937 season and Brainerd through 1938. Both were seasoned hands when, in 1937, a new field director arrived. Each year Ansel Hall had appointed a field director in charge of the expedition's wilderness operations. Several men held this position over the years, including Hargrave, Ben Wetherill, and Charles Amsden. In 1937 anthropologist Ralph Beals took command and, despite his lack of experience in archaeological field methods, directed the project to a successful conclusion.

As the expedition drew to a close, Ansel Hall arranged for George Brainerd and Watson Smith to assist Beals, then in the department of psychology at UCLA, in the preparation and production of a scientific report on the expedition. Smith wrote, "This was fine for George and me because it provided us with the opportunity to learn and to write and to get out a publication. It was good for Ralph because it gave him a little something to talk about in the university hierarchy, and of course it appealed to the romantic delusions of Ansel Hall."[35]

Beals, Brainerd, and Smith worked together in Los Angeles through the winter of 1937–38, and Smith and Brainerd finished the work in the winter of 1939 at Columbus, Ohio, where Brainerd had joined the faculty at Ohio State University. The three became friends and shared enough moments of levity to keep them going through the tedious months of data analysis and writing. Beals remembered, "With many student volunteers, we had to number, catalog, and type many tens of thousands of potsherds from survey and excavation. We sorted, counted, classified, reclassified, and recounted. Then we put everything back into the original site boxes."[36] Smith later remembered that they broke up the routine at UCLA by sipping milkshakes and watching starlets at Schwab's Drugstore in Hollywood.

Finally the three young archaeologists created a publication that would be valued and used for decades. Christenson commented, "They went to a level of detail that nobody had done before in that [Kayenta Anasazi] region, especially in ceramics. They measured details such as line widths [of painted designs]."[37]

This meticulous study was largely the result of Brainerd's scientific method. Brainerd applied sophisticated methods of statistical analysis to seriation of the RBMV Expedition's surface collections of pottery, presenting his results in elaborate charts published in the final report. Describing Brainerd's analytical work, Smith wrote, "His ingenuity and imagination were shown in many ways: by the invention of instruments to measure hardness of pottery, to calculate

RBMV crew excavating a Basketmaker site in Monument Valley, 1936.

vessel sizes from sherds, and by his clear grasp of a very complex problem and his capacity to marshal an overwhelming mass of data."[38]

Smith's legal training was evidenced in his demand for critical analysis of details, his deft use of language, and his insistence that all statements be backed by proof and thorough documentation. Beals provided a mature perspective and acted as the team's professional overseer.

In 1945 the University of California published their report, *Archaeological Studies in Northeast Arizona*. Walter Taylor, critic of Southwestern archaeology, praised the work where he had harshly judged the more descriptive works of A. V. Kidder and other earlier attempts to present ceramic data. Agreeing with favorable comments on the work made by J. O. Brew, Taylor wrote, "I heartily concur with Brew's enthusiasm for their results."[39]

For Watson Smith, as for many others, the Rainbow Bridge–Monument Valley Expedition was an opportunity to become part of an increasingly complex and fascinating discipline. For forty years after the publication of the RBMV Expedition report, Smith would work at writing, or encouraging others to write, the final reports essential to the growth of archaeology as a science.

The sun sets on an archaeological
exploring party, Rainbow
Bridge–Monument Valley, 1933.

From Grand Adventure
to Modern Science

WORLD WAR II BROUGHT DOWN THE CURTAIN on the first fifty years of archaeology in the Southwest. The days of romantic, adventuresome excavations led by individualistic pioneers in archaeology and anthropology ended as far-reaching technological, economic, and societal changes redefined the face of scientific research.

No longer would archaeologists in the Southwest conduct large-scale excavations that aimed to uncover as much as possible of a site, simply in order to find out what was there. Likewise digging merely to obtain artifacts, and to record their numbers and types, became scientifically passé. In the second half of the twentieth century, archaeologists began to redefine and focus the scope of their work, adopting a highly specialized, problem-solving orientation.

Fact-gathering became an increasingly scientific, methodical, technologically assisted process. Artifacts were carefully scrutinized in laboratories, where tests were performed to determine not only their age but their chemical make-up and the types of fossil pollen adhering to them.

A number of new, more precise dating techniques allowed archaeologists to pinpoint prehistoric events. Besides tree-ring dating, which became increasingly accurate during and after the 1950s, radiocarbon dating (used to date materials over 2,000 years old) and archaeomagnetic dating expanded the archaeologist's chronological hindsight into distant millennia.

While increasing their technological controls, archaeologists also took giant intellectual steps in data analysis and the creation of theories about prehistory. As their data base and theories proliferated they interpreted and reinterpreted ten thousand years of Southwestern prehistory. The Basketmaker and Pueblo time periods first sketched out by Kidder and his colleagues at the 1927 Pecos Conference were reexamined; remarkably, the chronological framework established by the early pioneers proved generally sound.

Archaeologists went beyond the refinement of such developmental periods to grasp the fundamental processes of major human phenomena. Based on excavations at sites such as Bat Cave and Tularosa Cave, and limited digging at Mesa Verde, Chaco, and elsewhere, they mapped out the sequence of events that led to the rise of agriculture in the Southwest, the evolution of the region's cultures, its migration and settlement patterns, and the growth of regional trade systems.

They began to develop "research designs," that is, scientific plans accompanied by questions that would enable them to use excavated artifacts and architecture as evidence in formulating theories about the development of prehistoric society. Gradually the focus of archaeology moved from finding and categorizing artifacts, to trying to understand the patterns and processes of prehistoric life, which might in turn tell modern society more about itself. During the late 1960s and early 1970s, the heyday of an academic movement called the New Archeology, some archaeologists began to look at the process of change itself, examining human evolution in new ways.

Many discoveries emerged from the more focused methods of excavation, backed by scientific dating methods and sophisticated analysis. Among them was the delineation of another distinct Southwestern prehistoric culture, known as Mogollon, based in the central Arizona–New Mexico highlands. Also developed were postulations about the existence of a Chacoan regional system, indicated by the discovery of numerous outlying settlements connected by a web of prehistoric roads to the immense ruins at Chaco Canyon itself.

Increasingly sophisticated studies examined migration and settlement patterns over time in the Anasazi world, from its origins at small Basketmaker villages to the complex, cohesive, large Pueblo towns that grew after 1300. The connections between population growth, increased cultural specialization, and competition for resources were studied, as were cultural phenomena—the factors leading to the creation of rituals, pottery styles, language groups, trade patterns, and so on.

While archaeology was moving toward more sophisticated scientific data gathering and theoretical work, it was also facing increasing pressures that inhibited pure research. The era of "salvage" archaeology that began in the 1950s led archaeologists to investigate proposed sites of dams, pipelines, highways, and other construction projects. Their mission was to record prehistoric remains before they were lost forever.

Also referred to as "contract" archaeology, work of this kind was commissioned by clients seeking to fulfill specific legislative requirements. Archaeologists in such situations have had to work under clearcut deadlines and financial constraints—a far cry from the days when excavations could continue for season after season before any measurable findings were produced.

Another pressure on archaeologists was the need to reach an understanding with Native American peoples. At the turn of the century, many Southwestern archaeologists believed that modern Native Americans had not been in the region long. It was thought that Mesoamerican groups to the south had formerly inhabited the Southwest and had created the region's most spectacular ruins, such as those at Chaco. However, during the 1940s and 1950s, finds dating back thousands of years at hunting sites such as Ventana Cave in Arizona and Clovis, New Mexico, augmented evidence provided by the 1926 discovery at Folsom of the antiquity of man in the Americas.

At the other end of the prehistoric chronological spectrum, findings at late prehistoric Pueblo and Hohokam ruins were combined with ethnological data to suggest links between prehistoric lifeways and those of modern Native American tribes. Today many, though not all, archaeologists acknowledge possible connections between prehistoric Anasazi and Hohokam peoples, who created the Southwest's remarkable ancient architecture, and modern Native American groups.

Archaeologists have also learned to honor Native American claims to land and property rather than setting them aside in the name of research. No longer is there rampant digging of Indian burials, nor are ruins on reservation land automatically presumed to be rightful subjects of archaeologists' investigations. Enhanced cultural awareness on the part of archaeologists, increased political activism among Native Americans, and stronger federal and state laws protecting sites have worked together to transform the way archaeology is done today.

Though it has changed dramatically since the early days, in one respect archaeology has remained the same: It is an art as well as a science—and a social science at that. "It is not the tools or instruments which constitute science, but rather the way a researcher uses whatever tools he has available," pointed out one professor of archaeology in the 1990s.

Regarding methods of scientific investigation, and the goals of the discipline itself, it often seems that archaeologists are destined to permanent disagreement. Today the Southwest is one of the most thoroughly explored, archaeologically rich areas of the United States. With the growth of the data base, disagreements among archaeologists have proliferated as if contention were the profession's intellectual life's blood. Perhaps "disagreement is structurally built into the profession because an original viewpoint is necessary to achieve status," as one knowledgeable observer commented.

Much of modern Southwestern archaeology appears to involve the creation of a pool of competing ideas about the physical remains of the prehistoric Southwest, from which no single theory emerges completely victorious. Perhaps, in the end, this situation fosters a healthy skepticism, which in turn may encourage more valuable research.

Those who will forge the next decades of Southwestern archaeology certainly are confronted with many challenges. As the twenty-first century approaches we are in dire need of greater understanding of ourselves as a species, of how to live together peacefully, and how to adapt successfully to the natural environment. Increased interdisciplinary studies may be one key to acquiring such knowledge. Perhaps the twenty-first century will see archaeology evolve in ways that Kidder and the other pioneers envisioned. Kidder himself wrote,

> The archeologist is thus abruptly hailed from the comforting shade of his trenches to the glare of the existing world, and there he stands bewildered. He surveys the environment of today to find that its complexities are utterly beyond his power to comprehend. He looks at the very simplest of modern peoples; their life proves unbelievably involved. But if he be willing to face the situation and not pop mole-like back into his burrow, he will find that other sciences are grappling with the problems of plants and animals, of weather and rocks, of living men and existing social orders; collecting, classifying, winnowing detail, and gradually formulating the basic laws which render this perplexing universe understandable. Beside and with them the archeologist must work if his results are to be more than the putterings of the antiquary.[1]

As Kidder intuited, the future success of archaeology seems inevitably linked to the willingness of archaeologists to use their knowledge to attack problems of modern society and to raise an active voice in human affairs. Educating young archaeologists to share their results through print and visual media may thus become as vital as teaching them to follow sound scientific methodology.

At field schools today, young Southwestern archaeologists work in the rich laboratory of the region's prehistoric remains. Their future task will be to define their studies and their evolving discipline so that the goals of basic and applied research dovetail with the needs of society. By striving to attain these ends, the next generation of archaeologists will be carrying out the intellectual trajectory set in motion by Kidder and other pioneers nearly a century ago.

Notes

Notes to Chapter 1

1. Maurine S. Fletcher (ed.). *The Wetherills of Mesa Verde: Autobiography of Benjamin Alfred Wetherill.* University of Nebraska Press, Lincoln, 1977, pp. 110–11.

2. Fletcher, p. 130.

3. Fletcher, p. 181.

4. Frederick Chapin, paper read before the Appalachian Mountain Club, Feb. 13, 1890. In Jesse Walter Fewkes, *Antiquities of the Mesa Verde National Park: Cliff Palace.* Bulletin 51, Bureau of American Ethnology, Washington, D.C., 1911, pp. 14, 15.

5. John Otis Brew, *The Archaeology of Alkali Ridge, Southeastern Utah.* Papers of the Peabody Museum of American Archaeology and Ethnology 21, Peabody Museum, Cambridge, MA, 1946, p. 21.

6. Nathalie F. S. Woodbury, "Women's Money and the 'Study of Man': The Hemenway Expeditions, Part II," *Anthropology Newsletter,* vol. 29, no. 4, April 1988, p. 12.

7. Jesse Walter Fewkes, *Antiquities of the Mesa Verde National Park: Cliff Palace.* Bulletin 51, Bureau of American Ethnology, Washington, D.C., 1911, p. 12.

8. David Breternitz, note to the author, May 21, 1993.

9. Fewkes, manuscript, Smithsonian Institution, quoted in Robert H. Lister, "They All Worked at Mesa Verde," in *Camera, Spade and Pen,* Marnie Gaede (ed.), University of Arizona Press, Tucson, 1980, p. 42.

10. Attendance records for year ending Sept. 30, 1935. Park Archaeologist's (Naturalist's) Monthly Reports, file no. 207–03.1, on file at the Park Museum, National Park Service, Mesa Verde National Park.

11. Emil W. Haury, interview with the author, Feb. 12, 1988.

12. Alden C. Hayes, interview with the author, Feb. 13, 1988.

13. Jenny L. Adams, *Pinto Beans and Prehistoric Pots: The Legacy of Al and Alice Lancaster.* Arizona State Museum Archaeological Series 183, University of Arizona Press, Tucson, 1994, p. 27.

14. Al Lancaster, interview with the author, June 25, 1988.

15. Jack Smith, interview with the author, June 23, 1988.

16. Adams, p. 65.

17. Adams, p. 80.

18. Citation for Distinguished Service: James Allen Lancaster. On file at the Research Center, Mesa Verde National Park.

19. Larry V. Nordby, interview with the author, June 20, 1988.

NOTES TO CHAPTER 2

1. Gordon Willey, in an interview with Alfred Vincent Kidder, unpublished transcript, 1957, part 2, p. 2. National Park Service files, Pecos National Historical Park, Pecos, NM.

2. Alfred Vincent Kidder, *Pecos, New Mexico: Archaeological Notes.* Papers of the Robert S. Peabody Foundation for Archaeology, vol. 5, Phillips Academy, Andover, MA, 1958, p. 3.

3. Richard B. Woodbury, *Alfred V. Kidder.* Columbia University Press, New York, 1973, p. 30.

4. Gordon R. Willey, "Alfred Vincent Kidder, October 29, 1885–June 11, 1963," *National Academy of Sciences Biographical Memoirs* 39. Columbia University Press, New York, 1967, pp. 293–94.

5. Alfred Vincent Kidder, "Reminiscences in Southwest Archaeology: I," *The Kiva,* vol. 25, no. 4 (April 1960), p. 1.

6. Florence C. Lister and Robert H. Lister, *Earl Morris and Southwestern Archaeology.* University of New Mexico Press, Albuquerque, 1968, p. 19.

7. Willey, *Biographical Memoirs* 39, 1967, p. 297.

8. Alfred V. Kidder, "The Peabody Expedition to the Mimbres Valley, New Mexico, Season of 1927," p. 9. Manuscript (bound volume) on file at the Laboratory of Anthropology, Santa Fe.

9. Ann Axtell Morris, *Digging in the Southwest.* Doubleday/Cadmus Books/E. M. Hale and Co., Chicago, 1933, p. 86.

10. Kidder in Woodbury, 1973, p. 186.

11. Watson Smith, "One Man's Archaeology," privately published manuscript, "second printing," Tucson, 1984, p. 403. On file at the library, School of American Research, Santa Fe. A condensed version of this manuscript, also titled "One Man's Archaeology," appeared in *The Kiva,* vol. 57, no. 2, 1992.

12. Kidder, 1958, p. xiv.

13. Rosemary Nusbaum, *Tierra Dulce: Reminiscences from the Jesse Nusbaum Papers.* Sunstone Press, Santa Fe, 1980, p. 55.

14. Stephen H. Lekson, personal communication, March 31, 1994. After investigating mounds at Chaco Canyon that may have had particular significance, Lekson and John R. Stein wrote of prehistoric burial practices on page 97 of an article titled "Anasazi Ritual Landscape": "Because we are willing to conclude that the Anasazi put the remains of their loved ones out with the trash, we argue that the content of the mound, including what might otherwise be considered to be refuse, was largely symbolic in nature." Although the Chaco mounds were different from the midden at Pecos, the point appears relevant. The article appears in *Anasazi Regional Organization and the Chaco System,* David Doyel (ed.), Anthropological Papers no. 5, Maxwell Museum, Albuquerque, 1992, pp. 97–100.

15. Kidder in Woodbury, 1973, p. 110.

16. Kidder in Woodbury, 1973, p. 109.

17. Douglas R. Givens, *Alfred Vincent Kidder and the Development of Americanist Archaeology.* University of New Mexico Press, Albuquerque, 1992, p. 61.

18. Alfred V. Kidder, in an interview with Gordon Willey, unpublished transcript, 1957, part 1, pp. 43–44. National Park Service files, Pecos National Historical Park, Pecos, NM.

19. Walter W. Taylor, "A Study of Archeology," *American Anthropologist,* vol. 50, no. 3, pt. 2, American Anthropological Association Memoir No. 69, July 1948, p. 16.

20. Robert L. Schuyler, "The History of American Archeology: An Examination of Procedure," *American Antiquity,* vol. 36, no. 4 (1971), pp. 384, 385.

21. Letter dated Feb. 2, 1960 from Nelson to Richard B. Woodbury, quoted in Woodbury, "Nelson's Stratigraphy," *American Antiquity,* vol. 26, no. 1 (July 1960), p. 98.

22. Richard B. Woodbury, "Nels C. Nelson and Chronological Archaeology," *American Antiquity,* vol. 25, no. 3 (January 1960), pp. 400–401.

23. Kidder in Woodbury, 1973, p. 111.

24. Alfred Vincent Kidder, in an interview with Gordon Willey, unpublished transcript, 1957, part 1, pp. 37–38. National Park Service files, Pecos National Historical Park, Pecos, NM.

25. Barbara Kidder Aldana, "The Kidder Pecos Expedition, 1924–1929: A Personal Memoir," *The Kiva,* vol. 48, no. 4 (1983), pp. 244–45.

26. Alfred V. Kidder in an interview with Gordon Willey, unpublished transcript, 1957, part 1, p. 3. National Park Service files, Pecos National Historical Park, Pecos, NM.

27. Neil Judd, *Men Met Along the Trail: Adventures in Archaeology.* University of Oklahoma Press, Norman, 1968, p. 94.

28. Alfred Vincent Kidder, field notes. National Park Service files, Pecos National Historical Park, Pecos, NM. Original notebook on file at the Laboratory of Anthropology, Santa Fe.

29. Alfred Vincent Kidder, *The Pottery of Pecos, Vol. I: The Dull-Paint Wares.* Yale University Press, New Haven, 1931, p. 15.

30. Aldana, 1983, p. 245.

31. Aldana, 1983, p. 248.

32. Alfred Vincent Kidder, *An Introduction to the Study of Southwestern Archaeology, with a Preliminary Account of the Excavations at Pecos, and a Summary of Southwestern Archaeology Today, by Irving Rouse.* New Haven: Yale University Press, 1924 (rev. ed. 1962), pp. 101–102.

33. Kidder, 1924, p. 105.

34. Kidder, 1958, p. 63.

35. Kidder, 1958, p. 71.

36. Kidder, 1958, p. 68.

37. Willey, *Biographical Memoirs* 39, p. 299.

38. Carl E. Guthe, book review, *El Palacio,* vol. 66, no. 1 (Feb. 1959), p. 35.

39. Smith, 1984, pp. 411–12.

40. Taylor, 1948, p. 46.

41. Paul S. Martin, "Early Development in Mogollon Research," in Gordon R. Willey (ed.), *Archaeological Researches in Retrospect,* Winthrop Publishers, Cambridge, MA, 1977, p. 5.

NOTES TO CHAPTER 3

1. Florence C. Lister and Robert H. Lister, *Earl Morris and Southwestern Archaeology.* University of New Mexico Press, Albuquerque, 1968, p. 13.

2. Earl H. Morris, *Archaeological Studies in the La Plata District: Southwestern Colorado and Northwestern New Mexico.* Carnegie Institution of Washington Publications 519, Washington, D.C., 1939, p. iii.

3. Earl H. Morris, *The Aztec Ruin.* Anthropological Papers of the American Museum of Natural History, vol. 26, part 1, American Museum of Natural History, New York, 1919, p. 10.

4. Walter W. Taylor, "Southwestern Archeology: Its History and Theory," *American Anthropologist,* vol. 56 (1954), p. 566.

5. Taylor, 1954, p. 566.

6. Robert H. Lister, interview with the author, Oct. 27, 1988, transcript, p. 18, side *b*.

7. Ann Axtell Morris, *Digging in the Southwest*. Doubleday/Camus Books, E. M. Hale and Co., Chicago, 1933, pp. 167–68.

8. Ann Morris, 1933, p. 168.

9. Ann Morris, 1933, p. 127.

10. Neil M. Judd, *Men Met Along the Trail: Adventures in Archaeology*. University of Oklahoma, Norman, 1968, p. 94.

11. Watson Smith, "One Man's Archaeology," privately published manuscript, "second printing," Tucson, 1984, p. 401. On file at the library, School of American Research, Santa Fe. A condensed version of this manuscript, also titled "One Man's Archaeology," appeared in *The Kiva*, vol. 57, no. 2, 1992.

12. Smith, 1984, p. 401.

13. Robert H. Lister, interview with the author, Oct. 27, 1988, transcript, p. 3, side *b*.

14. Lister and Lister, 1968, p. 15.

15. Frederick W. Lange and Diana Leonard (eds.), *Among Ancient Ruins: The Legacy of Earl H. Morris*. University of Colorado Museum, Johnson Books, Boulder, CO, 1985, p. 3.

16. Lister and Lister, 1968, p. 36.

17. Earl H. Morris, *Notes on Excavations in the Aztec Ruin*. Anthropological Papers of the American Museum of Natural History, vol. 26, part 5, American Museum of Natural History, New York, 1928, p. 418.

18. Lister and Lister, 1968, p. 26.

19. Robert H. Lister and Florence C. Lister, *Aztec Ruins National Monument: Administrative History of an Archeological Preserve*. Southwest Cultural Resources Center, Professional Papers 24, Santa Fe: National Park Service, 1990, p. 19.

20. Lister and Lister, 1990, p. 30.

21. Lister and Lister, 1990, p. 20.

22. Earl H. Morris, *The Temple of the Warriors*. Charles Scribners Sons, New York, 1931, p. 8.

23. Lister and Lister, 1990, p. 30.

24. Lister and Lister, 1990, p. 30.

25. Lister and Lister, 1990, p. 35.

26. Lister and Lister, 1990, p. 43.

27. Robert H. Lister, interview with the author, Oct. 27, 1988, transcript, p. 18.

28. Lister and Lister, 1990, p. 44.

29. George Ernest Webb, *Tree Rings and Telescopes: The Scientific Career of A. E. Douglass*. University of Arizona, Tucson, 1983, pp. 115–16.

30. Lister and Lister, 1990, p. 56.

31. Robert H. Lister and Florence C. Lister, *Aztec Ruins on the Animas: Excavated, Preserved, and Interpreted*. University of New Mexico Press, Albuquerque, 1987, p. 60.

32. Earl Morris, *Burials in the Aztec Ruin: The Aztec Ruin Annex*. Anthropological Papers of the American Museum of Natural History, vol. 26, parts 3 and 4, American Museum of Natural History, New York, 1924, pp. 155–56.

33. Lister and Lister, 1968, p. 27.

34. Clyde Kluckhohn, *Beyond the Rainbow*. Christopher Publishing House, Boston, 1933, p. 226.

35. Lister and Lister, 1990, p. 50.

36. Robert H. Lister, interview with the author, Oct. 27, 1988, transcript, pp. 7, side *b*-9.

37. Alfred Vincent Kidder in an interview with Gordon Willey, unpublished transcript, 1957, part 1, p. 1. National Park Service files, Pecos National Historical Park, Pecos, NM.

38. Morris, 1928, p. 417.

39. Morris, 1928, p. 267.

40. Morris, 1928, p. 420.

41. Lange and Leonard (eds.), 1985, p. 55.

42. Alden Hayes, interview with the author, Feb. 13, 1988.

NOTES TO CHAPTER 4

1. Richard B. Woodbury, "A Century of Zuni Research," in David Grant Noble (ed.), *Zuni and El Morro, Past and Present. Exploration,* Annual Bulletin of the School of American Research, Santa Fe, 1983, p. 10.

2. Neil M. Judd, M. R. Harrington, and S. K. Lothrop, "Frederick Webb Hodge—1864–1956," *American Antiquity,* vol. 22, no. 4 (April 1957), p. 403.

3. James K. Flack, quoted in Jesse Green (ed.), "Introduction," in *Zuñi: Selected Writings of Frank Hamilton Cushing,* University of Nebraska Press, Lincoln, 1979, p. 31, n. 24.

4. Watson Smith, Richard B. Woodbury, and Nathalie F. S. Woodbury, *The Excavation of Hawikuh by Frederick Webb Hodge: Report of the Hendricks-Hodge Expedition 1917–1923.* Museum of the American Indian, Heye Foundation, New York, 1966, p. 135.

5. F. W. Hodge, "The First Discovered City of Cibola," *American Anthropologist,* vol. 8, no. 2 (April 1895), p. 152.

6. Smith, Woodbury, and Woodbury, 1966, p. 135.

7. Watson Smith, "One Man's Archaeology," privately published manuscript, "second printing," Tucson, 1984, p. 353. On file at the library, School of American Research, Santa Fe. A condensed version of this manuscript, also titled "One Man's Archaeology," appeared in *The Kiva,* vol. 57, no. 2, 1992.

8. Smith, 1984, p. 357.

9. A. L. Kroeber, *Zuni Potsherds.* Anthropological Papers of the American Museum of Natural History, vol. 28, part 1, American Museum of Natural History, New York, 1916, p. 21.

10. Woodbury, in Noble, 1983, pp. 11–12.

11. Brenda L. Shears, "The Hendricks-Hodge Archaeological Expedition Documentation Project: Preparing a Museum Collection for Research." Masters thesis, Hunter College, The City University of New York, 1989, pp. 12–13.

12. Victor Mindeleff, "A Study of Pueblo Architecture in Tusayan and Cibola," in J. W. Powell, *Eighth Annual Report of the Bureau of Ethnology, 1886–'87,* Washington, D.C., Government Printing Office, 1891, p. 80.

13. Rosemary Nusbaum, *Tierra Dulce: Reminiscences from the Jesse Nusbaum Papers.* Sunstone Press, Santa Fe, 1980, p. 57.

14. F. W. Hodge, *Explorations and Field-Work of the Smithsonian Institution in 1917: Excavations at Hawikuh, New Mexico.* Smithsonian Miscellaneous Collections, vol. 68, no. 12, Smithsonian Institution, Washington, D.C., June 1918, p. 64.

15. Fred Plog, "Prehistory: Western Anasazi," in Alfonso Ortiz (vol. ed.), *Handbook of North American Indians,* vol. 9, *Southwest.* William C. Sturtevant (gen. ed.), Smithsonian Institution, Washington, D.C., 1979, p. 109.

16. Shears, 1989, pp. 69–71.

17. Shears, 1989, p. 70.

18. Smith, Woodbury, and Woodbury, 1966, p. 12.

19. Smith, Woodbury, and Woodbury, 1966, p. 6.

20. Smith, Woodbury, and Woodbury, 1966, p. 8.

21. Hodge in Smith, Woodbury, and Woodbury, 1966, p. 167.

22. Smith, Woodbury, and Woodbury, 1966, pp. 48–49.

23. Hodge in Smith, Woodbury, and Woodbury, 1966, p. 142.

24. Hodge, *Smithsonian,* June 1918, pp. 70–71.

25. Smith, Woodbury, and Woodbury, 1966, p. 173.

26. F. W. Hodge, "Excavations at the Zuñi Pueblo of Hawikuh in 1917," *Art and Archaeology,* vol. 7, no. 9, Washington, D.C., 1918, p. 374.

27. Hodge, *Art and Archaeology,* 1918, p. 377.

28. Smith, Woodbury, and Woodbury, 1966, p. 70–71.

29. F. W. Hodge, "Recent Excavations at Hawikuh," *El Palacio,* Museum of New Mexico, Santa Fe, vol. 12, no. 1 (Jan. 1, 1922), p. 11.

30. Mindeleff in Powell, 1891, p. 81.

31. Smith, Woodbury, and Woodbury, 1966, p. 7.

32. Neil M. Judd, *Men Met Along the Trail: Adventures in Archaeology.* University of Oklahoma, Norman, 1968, p. 117.

33. Watson Smith, interview with the author, Feb. 13, 1988.

34. Watson Smith, interview with the author, Feb. 13, 1988.

35. Fay-Cooper Cole, "Frederick Webb Hodge 1864–1956," *American Anthropologist,* vol. 59, no. 3 (June 1957), p. 520.

36. Smith, Woodbury, and Woodbury, 1966, p. 78.

37. F. W. Hodge, *History of Hawikuh, New Mexico: One of the So-Called Cities of Cíbola.* Southwest Museum, Los Angeles, 1937, p. 42.

38. Hodge, *Art and Archaeology,* 1918, p. 379.

39. Evelyn Brew, interview with the author, March 1988.

NOTES TO CHAPTER 5

1. Neil M. Judd, *The Material Culture of Pueblo Bonito.* Smithsonian Miscellaneous Collections, vol. 124, Smithsonian Institution, Washington, D.C., Dec. 29, 1954, p. vii.

2. Robert H. Lister and Florence C. Lister, *Chaco Canyon: Archaeology and Archaeologists.* University of New Mexico, Albuquerque, 1981, p. 36.

3. Donald D. Brand, "Introduction," in Brand, Florence M. Hawley, and Frank C. Hibben, *Tseh So, A Small House Ruin, Chaco Canyon, New Mexico,* University of New Mexico Bulletin, Whole Number 308, Anthropological Series, vol. 2, no. 2, Albuquerque, June 15, 1937, p. 23.

4. Neil M. Judd, "Everyday Life in Pueblo Bonito," *National Geographic Magazine,* vol. 48, no. 3 (Sept. 1925), p. 258.

5. Neil M. Judd, "Reminiscences in Southwest Archaeology: II," *The Kiva,* vol. 26, no. 1 (Oct. 1960), p. 4.

6. N. C. Nelson, "Notes on Pueblo Bonito," in George H. Pepper, *Pueblo Bonito,* Anthropological Papers of the American Museum of Natural History, vol. 27, New York, 1920, p. 383.

7. Judd, October 1960, p. 1.

8. Besides learning archaeology from Cummings, in 1910 Judd attended a field school led by Hewett on the Pajarito Plateau at today's Bandelier National Monument. However, Judd "didn't like Hewett so he didn't talk about it," according to archaeologist Stephen Lekson (note to the author, May 27, 1993).

9. Judd, Oct. 1960, p. 3.

10. Judd, Oct. 1960, p. 3.

11. Waldo R. Wedel, "Neil Merton Judd, 1887–1976," *American Antiquity,* vol. 43, no. 3 (1978), p. 399. See also Stephen C. Jett, "The Great 'Race' to 'Discover' Rainbow Natural Bridge in 1909," *The Kiva,* vol. 58, no. 1, pp. 3–66.

12. Neil M. Judd, *Men Met Along the Trail: Adventures in Archaeology.* University of Oklahoma Press, Norman, 1968, p. 125.

13. Alfred V. Kidder, quoted in Gordon Vivian and Tom W. Mathews, "Introduction," in *Kin Kletso: A Pueblo III Community in Chaco Canyon, New Mexico,* Technical Series, vol. 6, part 1, Southwestern Parks and Monuments Association (third printing), 1977, p. 1.

14. Judd, 1968, p. 122.

15. Vivian and Mathews, 1977, p. 1.

16. Vivian and Mathews, 1977, p. 1.

17. Neil M. Judd, *The Architecture of Pueblo Bonito.* Smithsonian Miscellaneous Collections, vol. 147, no. 1, Smithsonian Institution, Washington, D.C., June 30, 1964, p. iv.

18. Judd, Sept. 1925, p. 231.

19. Judd, 1968, p. 122.

20. Nelson in Pepper, 1920, p. 389.

21. George Ernest Webb, *Tree Rings and Telescopes: The Scientific Career of A. E. Douglass.* University of Arizona, Tucson, 1983, p. 131.

22. Judd, 1968, pp. 124–25.

23. Judd, 1968, p. 133.

24. Judd, 1968, p. 134.

25. Judd, 1954, p. 9.

26. Judd, 1964, p. v.

27. Judd, 1964, p. 16.

28. Judd, 1964, p. 141.

29. Richard B. Woodbury, *Sixty Years of Southwestern Archaeology: A History of the Pecos Conference.* University of New Mexico Press, Albuquerque, 1993, p. 14.

30. Judd, 1968, p. 130.

31. Judd, 1954, p. 9.

32. Judd, 1964, p. 8.

33. Judd, Sept. 1925, p. 230 (caption).

34. Judd, 1964, pp. 9–10.

35. Judd, 1964, p. 11.

36. Judd, 1964, p. 12.

37. Judd, 1964, p. 11.

38. Judd, 1964, p. 13.

39. Judd, 1964, p. 14.

40. Judd, 1964, p. 41.

41. Judd, 1964, p. 14.

42. Judd, Sept. 1925, p. 227.

43. Judd, 1964, p. 58; p. 45.

44. Judd, Sept. 1925, p. 227.

45. Judd, Sept. 1925, p. 238.

46. Judd, Sept. 1925, pp. 240–41.

47. Judd, 1964, p. 141.

48. Stephen H. Lekson, "Sedentism and Aggregation in Anasazi Archaeology," in *Perspectives on Southwestern Prehistory,* Paul E. Minnis and Charles L. Redman (eds.), Westview Press, Boulder, CO, 1990, p. 337.

49. Judd, 1964, p. 19.

50. Judd, 1964, p. 21.

51. Judd, 1964, p. 3.

52. Judd, 1954, p. 3.

53. Judd, 1954, p. 3.

54. Frances Joan Mathien, *Environment and Subsistence of Chaco Canyon, New Mexico.* Publications in Archaeology 18E, Chaco Canyon Studies, National Park Service, Albuquerque, 1985, p. 4.

55. Judd, 1968, p. 129.

56. Webb, 1983, p. 144.

57. Andrew Ellicott Douglass, "The Secret of the Southwest Solved by Talkative Tree Rings," *National Geographic Magazine,* vol. 56, no. 6 (Dec. 1929), pp. 737–38.

58. Wedel, 1978, p. 401.

59. Gilbert Grosvenor, "Preface," in Judd, 1954, p. iv.

60. Judd, 1964, p. 41.

61. Judd, 1964, p. 41.

62. Mathien, 1985, p. 4.

63. Judd, October 1960, p. 6.

NOTES TO CHAPTER 6

1. Emil W. Haury, *The Hohokam: Desert Farmers and Craftsmen: Excavations at Snaketown, 1964–1965.* University of Arizona Press, Tucson, 1976, p. 5.

2. Walter W. Taylor, "Southwestern Archeology: Its History and Theory," *American Anthropologist,* vol. 56 (1954), p. 563.

3. Frank Pinkley, letter to Stephen T. Mather, Feb. 1, 1919, National Park Service files, Casa Grande National Monument, Coolidge, AZ.

4. Quoted in Emil W. Haury and J. Jefferson Reid, "Harold Sterling Gladwin, 1883–1983," *The Kiva,* vol. 50, no. 4, 1985, p. 273.

5. Watson Smith, "One Man's Archaeology," privately published manuscript, "second printing," Tucson, 1984, pp. 362–63. On file at the library, School of American Research, Santa Fe. A condensed version of this manuscript, also titled "One Man's Archaeology," appeared in *The Kiva,* vol. 57, no. 2, 1992.

6. Stewart Peckham, interview with the author, Jan. 22, 1988.

7. Katharine Bartlett, interview with the author, Aug. 9, 1988.

8. John Otis Brew, *Archaeology of Alkali Ridge, Southeastern Utah.* Papers of the Peabody Museum of American Archaeology and Ethnology, Harvard University, no. 21, Peabody Museum, Cambridge, MA, 1946, p. viii.

9. Harold S. Gladwin, *Excavations at Snaketown, Part II: Comparisons and Theories.* Medallion Papers, no. 26, Gila Pueblo, Globe, AZ, 1937 ("Preface," without page number).

10. Harold Sterling Gladwin, *Men Out of Asia.* Whittlesey House, McGraw-Hill, New York, 1947, pp. 20–21.

11. Linda S. Cordell, *Prehistory of the Southwest.* A School of American Research Book, Academic Press/Harcourt Brace Jovanovich, Orlando, FL, 1984, p. 277.

12. Harold S. Gladwin et al., *Excavations at Snaketown: Material Culture.* Medallion Papers 25, Gila Pueblo, Globe, AZ, 1937, p. 1.

13. Gladwin, 1937, no. 25, p. 7.

14. Gladwin, 1937, no. 25, p. 6.

15. Gladwin, 1937, no. 25, p. 4.

16. Gladwin, 1937, no. 25, p. 7.

17. Julian Hayden, "Talking with the Animals: Pinacate Reminiscences," *Journal of the Southwest,* vol. 29, no. 2 (summer 1987), p. 226.

18. Haury, 1976, p. 8.

19. Emil W. Haury, "Reflections: Fifty Years of Southwestern Archaeology," *American Antiquity,* vol. 50, no. 2 (April 1985), p. 393.

20. Emil W. Haury, interview with the author, Feb. 12, 1988.

21. Watson Smith, interview with the author, Feb. 13, 1988.

22. J. Jefferson Reid and David E. Doyel (eds.), *Emil W. Haury's Prehistory of the American Southwest.* University of Arizona Press, Tucson, 1986, p. 8.

23. David E. Doyel, interview with the author, May 8, 1989.

24. Emil W. Haury, interview with the author, Feb. 12, 1988.

25. Emil W. Haury, interview with the author, Feb. 12, 1988.

26. Herbert W. Dick and Albert H. Schroeder, "Lyndon Hargrave, a Brief Biography," in *Collected Papers in Honor of Lyndon Lane Hargrave,* Papers of the Archaeological Society of New Mexico, no. 1, Museum of New Mexico Press, Santa Fe, 1968, p. 3.

27. Haury, April 1985, p. 390.

28. Emil W. Haury, interview with the author, Feb. 12, 1988.

29. Emil W. Haury, interview with the author, Feb. 12, 1988.

30. Julian Hayden, interview with the author, Feb. 14, 1988.

31. Gladwin, 1937, no. 25, p. 11.

32. Emil W. Haury, interview with the author, Feb. 12, 1988.

33. Gladwin, 1937, no. 25, p. 6.

34. Gladwin, 1937, no. 25, p. 7.

35. Gladwin, 1937, no. 25, p. 9.

36. Gladwin, 1937, no. 25, p. 7.

37. Haury in Gladwin et al., 1937, no. 25, p. 23.

38. Haury in Gladwin et al., 1937, no. 25, p. 23.

39. Julian Hayden, interview with the author, Feb. 14, 1988.

40. Emil W. Haury in Gladwin et al., 1937, no. 25, p. 33.

41. David E. Doyel, "Pueblo Grande National Landmark Celebrates a Centennial," *Masterkey,* vol. 60, no. 4 (1987), p. 3.

42. Neil M. Judd, "Arizona's Prehistoric Canals from the Air," *Explorations and Field-Work of the Smithsonian Institution in 1930,* Smithsonian Institution, Washington, D.C., 1931, pp. 157–66.

43. Emil W. Haury, *The Excavation of Los Muertos and Neighboring Ruins in the Salt River Valley, Southern Arizona: Based on the Work of the Hemenway Southwestern Archaeological Expedition of 1887–1888.* Papers of the Peabody Museum of American Archaeology and Ethnology, Harvard University, vol. 24, no. 1, Peabody Museum, Cambridge, MA, 1945, p. 12.

44. Richard B. Woodbury, "The Hohokam Canals at Pueblo Grande, Arizona," *American Antiquity,* vol. 26, no. 2 (Oct. 1960), p. 267.

45. Woodbury, Oct. 1960, p. 267.

46. Emil W. Haury, interview with the author, Feb. 12, 1988.

47. Emil W. Haury in Gladwin et al., 1937, vol. 25, p. 136.

48. Harold S. Gladwin and Winifred Gladwin, *A Method for Designation of Cultures and Their Variations.* Medallion Papers, no. 15, Gila Pueblo, Globe, AZ, 1934, pp. 9–10.

49. Brew, 1946, p. 60.

50. Richard B. Woodbury, *Sixty Years of Southwestern Archaeology: A History of the Pecos Conference.* University of New Mexico Press, Albuquerque, 1993, p. 123.

51. Watson Smith, "Emil Haury's Southwest," *Journal of the Southwest,* vol. 29, no. 1 (1987), p. 117.

52. Haury, 1976, p. 3.

53. Emil W. Haury, interview with the author, Feb. 12, 1988.

54. Jonathan Gell, appendix 1, "The Cartography of Snaketown," in Haury, 1976, p. 361.

55. Julian Hayden, interview with the author, Feb. 14, 1988.

56. One of Lancaster's colleagues, Alden Hayes, wrote to the author (Dec. 19, 1992): "Lancaster had great respect for Emil and found the archeology interesting enough, but he didn't like the desert and never felt at home with the Hohokam. He preferred working in what he called the 'magoo'—the red loess of the Mesa Verde country."

57. Emil W. Haury, interview with the author, February 12, 1988.

58. Jeffrey S. Dean, "Thoughts on Hohokam Chronology," in George J. Gumerman (ed.), *Exploring the Hohokam: Prehistoric Desert Peoples of the American Southwest*, University of New Mexico Press, Albuquerque, 1991, p. 61.

59. Cordell, 1984, p. 112.

60. Cordell, 1984, p. 162.

61. Emil W. Haury, interview with the author, Feb. 12, 1988.

62. Cordell, 1984, p. 210.

63. Haury, 1976, p. 9.

64. Haury, 1976, p. xii.

65. Smith, 1984, p. 411.

66. Smith, 1987, p. 117.

67. Smith, 1987, p. 107.

68. David Breternitz, interview with the author, April 10, 1988.

NOTES TO CHAPTER 7

1. J. Walter Fewkes, "A-Wa'-To-Bi: An Archeological Verification of a Tusayan Legend," *American Anthropologist*, vol. 6, no. 4 (Oct. 1893), p. 373.

2. Alfred V. Kidder, in an interview with Gordon Willey, unpublished transcript, 1957, part 1, p. 46. National Park Service files, Pecos National Historical Park, Pecos, NM.

3. Raymond H. Thompson, "And Then There Was Watson Smith," in *When Is A Kiva? And Other Questions About Southwestern Archaeology*, by Watson Smith (Raymond H. Thompson, ed.), University of Arizona Press, Tucson, 1990, p. 1.

4. Watson Smith, interview with the author, Feb. 13, 1988.

5. Letter from Watson Smith to the author, May 30, 1993.

6. Evelyn Brew, interview with the author, Sept. 19, 1990.

7. J. O. Brew, "The Excavation of Awatovi," in *Camera, Spade and Pen: An Inside View of Southwestern Archaeology*, Marnie Gaede (ed.) and Marc Gaede (photog.), University of Arizona Press, Tucson, 1980, p. 107.

8. Watson Smith, "One Man's Archaeology," privately published manuscript, "second printing," Tucson, 1984, p. 128. On file at the library, School of American Research, Santa Fe. A condensed version of this manuscript, also titled "One Man's Archaeology," appeared in *The Kiva*, vol. 57, no. 2, 1992.

9. J. O. Brew, "Preface," in Ross Gordon Montgomery, Watson Smith, and John Otis Brew, *Franciscan Awatovi: The Excavation and Conjectural Reconstruction of a 17th-Century Spanish Mission Establishment at a Hopi Indian Town in Northeastern Arizona*. Papers of the Peabody Museum, vol. 36, Reports of the Awatovi Expedition, no. 3, Peabody Museum, Cambridge, MA, 1949, p. vii.

10. Brew in Gaede and Gaede, 1980, p. 106.

11. J. O. Brew, "The First Two Seasons at Awatovi," *American Antiquity*, vol. 3, no. 2 (Oct. 1937), p. 124–25.

12. Watson Smith, *Painted Ceramics of the Western Mound at Awatovi*. Papers of the Peabody Museum of Archaeology and Ethnology, vol. 38, Reports of the Awatovi Expedition, no. 8, Peabody Museum, Cambridge, MA, 1971, p. 16.

13. Brew, "The First Two Seasons at Awatovi," Oct. 1937, p. 132.

14. Brew, "The First Two Seasons at Awatovi," Oct. 1937, p. 136.

15. Watson Smith, *Kiva Mural Decorations at Awatovi and Kawaika-a: With a Survey of Other Wall Paintings in the Pueblo Southwest.* Papers of the Peabody Museum, vol. 37, Reports of the Awatovi Expedition, no. 5, Peabody Museum, Cambridge, MA, 1952, table 1, p. 10.

16. Penny Davis Worman, interview with the author, Sept. 20, 1990.

17. Brew, "Introduction," in Montgomery, Smith, and Brew, 1949, p. xix.

18. Katharine Bartlett, interview with the author, Aug. 9, 1988.

19. Brew, "Introduction," in Montgomery, Smith, and Brew, 1949, pp. xix–xx.

20. Brew, abstract of part II, "The Excavation of Franciscan Awatovi," in Smith, Montgomery, and Brew, 1949, p. 48.

21. J. O. Brew, "Camp Journal, Awatovi, 1939," manuscript, Peabody Museum, Harvard University, p. 12.

22. J. O. Brew, "Preliminary Report of the Peabody Museum Awatovi Expedition of 1937," *American Antiquity,* vol. 5, no. 2 (Oct. 1939), p. 105.

23. Smith, 1971, p. 599.

24. Evelyn Brew, interview with the author, Sept. 19, 1990.

25. Richard B. Woodbury, interview with the author, Sept. 20, 1990.

26. Smith, 1984, p. 169.

27. Pages 193–202 of the 1984 unpublished version of Smith's "One Man's Archaeology" present an entertaining description of this wedding, an occasion of great revelry. In a letter to the author (May 30, 1993), Watson Smith wrote, "I feel sorry that the rather long account of the wedding at Awatovi was omitted for lack of room from the *Kiva* presentation" [condensed version of "One Man's Archaeology," published in *The Kiva,* vol. 57, no. 2, 1992].

28. Smith, 1984, p. 36.

29. For more information on the Indian Reorganization Act see "The Wheeler-Howard (Indian Reorganization) Act" and "Indian Reorganization," pp. 957–97 in Francis Paul Prucha, *The Great Father: The United States Government and the American Indians,* vol. 2, University of Nebraska Press, Lincoln, 1984.

30. Evelyn Brew, interview with the author, Sept. 19, 1990.

31. Brew, "Camp Journal, Awatovi, 1939," p. 9.

32. Watson Smith, interview with the author, Feb. 13, 1988.

33. In a letter to the author (Dec. 19, 1992), Alden Hayes wrote, "Brew's failure to describe the architecture and stratigraphy greatly diminished the value of the Awatobi Expedition. Hack's and Wat Smith's contributions were the most valuable. I believe Jo's much smaller scale Alkali Ridge job had a greater impact on SW archeology." Comments such as this one reflect views of the subsequent generation of Southwestern archaeologists, who criticized Brew, Earl Morris, and other pioneers for lack of reporting.

34. Brew in Gaede and Gaede, 1980, p. 107.

35. J. O. Brew, "Foreword," in Smith, 1971, p. xvii.

36. Richard B. Woodbury, *Prehistoric Stone Implements of Northeastern Arizona.* Papers of the Peabody Museum of American Archaeology and Ethnology, vol. 34, Reports of the Awatovi Expedition, no. 6, Peabody Museum, Cambridge, MA, 1954, p. 5.

37. Brew in Montgomery, Smith, and Brew, 1949, p. xx.

38. Brew in Montgomery, Smith, and Brew, 1949, p. 22.

39. Watson Smith, *Prehistoric Kivas of Antelope Mesa, Northeastern Arizona.* Papers of the Peabody Museum, vol. 39, no. 1, Peabody Museum, Cambridge, MA, 1972, pp. 70–75.

40. Christy G. Turner II and Nancy T. Morris, Abstract of "A Massacre at Hopi," *American Antiquity,* vol. 35, no. 3 (1970), p. 320.

41. Turner and Morris, 1970, p. 330.

1. Watson Smith, "One Man's Archaeology," privately published manuscript, "second printing," Tucson, 1984, p. 47. On file at the library, School of American Research, Santa Fe. A condensed version of this manuscript, also titled "One Man's Archaeology," appeared in *The Kiva,* vol. 57, no. 2, 1992.

2. Ralph L. Beals, George W. Brainerd, and Watson Smith, *Archaeological Studies in Northeast Arizona.* University of California Publications in American Archaeology and Ethnology 44 (1), University of California Press, Berkeley and Los Angeles, 1945, p. iii.

3. Stephen C. Jett, Abstract, "The Great 'Race' to 'Discover' Rainbow Natural Bridge in 1909," *The Kiva,* vol. 58, no. 1 (1992), p. 3.

4. Neil M. Judd, *Men Met Along the Trail: Adventures in Archaeology.* University of Oklahoma Press, Norman, 1968, pp. 28–29.

5. Carol A. Gifford and Elizabeth A. Morris. "Digging for Credit: Early Archaeological Field Schools in the American Southwest." *American Antiquity,* vol. 50, no. 2 (April 1985), p. 395.

6. Beals, Brainerd, and Smith, 1945, p. iii. See also the handwritten journal by Arthur W. Nelson, Jr. "My Experiences as A Member of the Rainbow Bridge–Monument Valley Expedition Summer of 1936," p. 1, on file at the Museum of Northern Arizona Library, Flagstaff.

7. Andrew L. Christenson, "The Last of the Great Expeditions: The Rainbow Bridge/Monument Valley Expedition, 1933–38," *Plateau,* vol. 58, no. 4 (1987), Museum of Northern Arizona, Flagstaff, p. 30.

8. Smith, 1984, p. 56.

9. Ansel Hall, "Explorer News Letter No. 1," Feb. 18, 1934, pp. 1 and 7. Colton Collection, Expeditions: Rainbow Bridge–Monument Valley, 1933, Museum of Northern Arizona Library, Flagstaff.

10. "Memorandum of Agreement Under Which Expedition Members Are Accepted." Colton Collection, Expeditions: RBMV, 1934. Museum of Northern Arizona Library, Flagstaff.

11. Diary of Shepard J. Crumpacker, Jr., 1937 field season, typed excerpt on file with the author, p. 6.

12. Ansel Franklin Hall, foreword in Lyndon Hargrave, *Report on Archaeological Reconnaissance in the Rainbow Plateau Area of Northern Arizona and Southern Utah: Based Upon Fieldwork by the Rainbow Bridge–Monument Valley Expedition of 1933,* University of California Press, Berkeley, 1935, p. 5.

13. In a letter to the author (Dec. 19, 1992), Alden Hayes wrote, "Lyndon Hargrave told me that he and another member of RBMV spent a couple of days at repeated, and finally successful, attempts to get into a small, precariously perched cliff site in the Tsegi. When they finally poked their heads above the ledge, they were confronted by a shake on which was written in charcoal, 'Oh, what fools we mortals be! [signed] John Wetherill.'"

14. Judd, 1968, p. 95.

15. Smith, 1984, p. 108.

16. Letter from Ansel Hall to Lyndon Hargrave, dated only "Monday noon." Colton Collection, Expeditions: Rainbow Bridge–Monument Valley, 1933, 1934, Museum of Northern Arizona Library, Flagstaff.

17. Andrew L. Christenson, "The Archaeological Investigations of the Rainbow Bridge–Monument Valley Expedition, 1933–1938," in Helen K. Crotty, *Honoring the Dead: Anasazi Ceramics from the Rainbow Bridge–Monument Valley Expedition,* University of California, Los Angeles, Museum of Cultural History Monograph Series no. 22, p. 18.

18. Christenson in Crotty, monograph series no. 22, p. 18.

19. Bayne Beauchamp. "Second River Trip," report of July 21, 1935, from The Great Bend, San Juan River. Colton Collection, Expeditions: Rainbow Bridge-Monument Valley, 1935, Museum of Northern Arizona Library, Flagstaff.

20. David Breternitz, interview with the author, April 10, 1988.

21. Ansel Franklin Hall, *General Report: Rainbow Bridge-Monument Valley Expedition of 1933*. University of California Press, Berkeley, n.d. (ca. 1934), p. 23.

22. Ansel Hall, Explorer News Letter No. 1, February 18, 1934, p. 6. Colton Collection, Museum of Northern Arizona Library, Flagstaff.

23. Hall, General Report, p. 21.

24. Christenson in Crotty, monograph series no. 22, p. 18.

25. Letter from Lyndon Hargrave to Ansel Hall, Oct. 15, 1934. Colton Collection, Museum of Northern Arizona Library, Flagstaff.

26. Letter from Lyndon Hargrave to Ansel Hall, Oct. 18, 1934. Colton Collection, Museum of Northern Arizona Library, Flagstaff.

27. Letter from Ansel Hall to Harold Colton, April 23, 1935. Colton Collection, Museum of Northern Arizona Library, Flagstaff.

28. Letter from Lyndon Hargrave to Ansel Hall, March 21, 1936. Colton Collection, Museum of Northern Arizona, Flagstaff.

29. Raymond H. Thompson, "Preface," in *When Is A Kiva? and Other Questions About Southwestern Archaeology*, by Watson Smith (Raymond H. Thompson, ed.), University of Arizona Press, Tucson, 1990, p. xi.

30. Smith, unpublished bound volume stamped "Compiled Appendices" (a sequel to his memoir, "One Man's Archaeology,"), p. 3 of a section titled "Blankets by Beacon," August 1985, on file with the author.

31. Christenson, "The Expedition's Accomplishments," *Plateau*, 1987, p. 29.

32. Beals, Brainerd, and Smith, 1945, pp. 7–9.

33. Ralph Beals, taped speech to the Rainbow Bridge-Monument Valley Symposium, University of California at Los Angeles, Nov. 6, 1983. Copy of tape on file with the School of American Research.

34. Richard B. Woodbury, "Watson Smith and Southwestern Archaeology," in Smith, (R. H. Thompson, ed.), 1990, pp. 9–11.

35. Smith, 1984, p. 102.

36. Beals, speech, Nov. 6, 1983.

37. Andrew Christenson, interview with the author, March 12, 1988.

38. Watson Smith, "George Walton Brainerd—1909–1956," *American Antiquity*, vol. 22, no. 2 (Oct. 1956), p. 166.

39. Walter W. Taylor, "A Study of Archeology," *American Anthropologist*, vol. 50, no. 3, part 2, American Anthropological Association Memoir 69, July 1948, p. 130.

Notes to Epilogue

1. Robert Wauchope, "Alfred Vincent Kidder, 1885–1963," *American Antiquity*, vol. 31, no. 2 (Oct. 1965), p. 157.

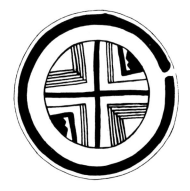

BIBLIOGRAPHY

Adams, Jenny L. *Pinto Beans and Prehistoric Pots: The Legacy of Al and Alice Lancaster.* Arizona State Museum Archaeological Series 183. Tucson: University of Arizona Press, 1994.

Aldana, Barbara Kidder. "The Kidder Pecos Expedition, 1924–1929: A Personal Memoir." *The Kiva* 48(4):243–50 (1983).

Arrhenius, Olof W. *Stones Speak and Waters Sing: The Life and Works of Gustaf Nordenskiöld.* Edited and annotated by Robert H. Lister and Florence C. Lister. Mesa Verde Museum Association, 1984.

Bandelier, Adolph F. *Report on the Ruins of the Pueblo of Pecos.* Papers of the Archaeological Institute of America, American Series 1(2). Boston: A. Williams, 1881.

Bartlett, Katharine. "How Don Pedro de Tovar Discovered the Hopi and Don Garcia Lopez de Cardenas Saw the Grand Canyon, with Notes Upon Their Probable Route." *Plateau* 12(3):37–45 (1940).

Beals, Ralph L. Speech to the Rainbow Bridge-Monument Valley Symposium, University of California, Los Angeles, Nov. 6, 1983. Tape on file with the School of American Research.

Beals, Ralph L., George W. Brainerd, and Watson Smith. *Archaeological Studies in Northeast Arizona.* University of California Publications in American Archaeology and Ethnology 44(1). Berkeley and Los Angeles: University of California Press, 1945.

Beauchamp, Bayne. "Further News From the River Exploration Party." Report of July 21, 1935, from the Great Bend, San Juan River. Colton Collection, Expeditions: Rainbow Bridge-Monument Valley, 1935. Flagstaff: Museum of Northern Arizona Library.

Bezy, John V., and Joseph P. Sanchez (eds.). *Pecos: Gateway to Pueblos and Plains: The Anthology.* Tucson: Southwestern Parks and Monuments Association, 1988.

Bishop, Ronald L., and Frederick W. Lange (eds.). *The Ceramic Legacy of Anna O. Shepard.* Niwot: University Press of Colorado, 1991.

Blachly, Lou. Interviews with Marietta Wetherill. Transcripts of tapes 438, 440, and 441. Pioneers Foundation, Inc., tape recordings 1865-1952. Special Collections, Zimmerman Library, University of New Mexico, Albuquerque.

Brand, Donald D. Introduction to *Tseh So, A Small House Ruin, Chaco Canyon, New Mexico*, by Donald D. Brand, Florence M. Hawley, and Frank C. Hibben. University of New Mexico Bulletin 308, Anthropological Series 2(2). Albuquerque: University of New Mexico, 1937.

Breternitz, David. "Mesa Verde National Park: A History of Its Archaeology." *Essays and Monographs in Colorado History* 2. Denver: Colorado Historical Society, 1983.

Brew, John Otis. "The First Two Seasons at Awatovi." *American Antiquity* 3(2):122-37 (1937).

———. Camp Journal, Awatovi, 1939. Manuscript, Peabody Museum, Harvard University.

———. "Preliminary Report of the Peabody Museum Awatovi Expedition of 1937." *American Antiquity* 5(2):103-14 (1939).

———. "Preliminary Report of the Peabody Museum Awatovi Expedition of 1939." *Plateau* 13(3):37-48 (1941).

———. *The Archaeology of Alkali Ridge, Southeastern Utah*. Papers of the Peabody Museum of American Archaeology and Ethnology 21. Cambridge: Harvard University, 1946.

———. "Neil Merton Judd, 1887-1976." *American Anthropologist* 60(2):352-54 (1978).

Brew, John Otis, and John T. Hack. "Prehistoric Use of Coal by Indians of Northern Arizona." *Plateau* 12(1):8-14 (1939).

Brugge, David M. "A History of the Chaco Navajos." *Reports of the Chaco Center* 4. Albuquerque: National Park Service, Division of Chaco Research, 1980.

———. "The Chaco Navajos." In *New Light on Chaco Canyon*, David Grant Noble (ed.), pp. 73-92. Special volume in the School of American Research *Exploration* series. Santa Fe: School of American Research, 1984.

Bryan, Kirk. *The Geology of Chaco Canyon, New Mexico, in Relation to the Life and Remains of the Prehistoric Peoples of Pueblo Bonito*. Smithsonian Miscellaneous Collections 122(7), 1954.

Burgh, Robert F. "Earl Halstead Morris, 1889-1956." *American Anthropologist* 59(3):521-23 (1957).

Chapin, Frederick. Paper read before the Appalachian Mountain Club on February 13, 1890. In *Antiquities of the Mesa Verde National Park: Cliff Palace*, by Jesse Walter Fewkes. Bulletin 51:14-15. Washington, D.C.: Bureau of American Ethnology, 1911.

Chapman, Kenneth M., F. W. Hodge, Jesse L. Nusbaum, and Ina Sizer Cassidy. "Reminiscences of Four Oldtimers," tape-recorded conversations, September 9, 1955. Laboratory of Anthropology, Santa Fe.

Christenson, Andrew L. "The Archaeological Investigations of the Rainbow Bridge–Monument Valley Expedition, 1933-1938." In *Honoring the Dead: Anasazi Ceramics from the Rainbow Bridge Monument Valley Expedition*, by Helen Crotty. University of California, Los Angeles, Museum of Cultural History Monograph Series 22:9-22 (1983).

———. "The Last of the Great Expeditions: The Rainbow Bridge/Monument Valley Expedition, 1933-38." *Plateau* 58(4). Flagstaff: Museum of Northern Arizona, 1987.

Cole, Fay-Cooper. "Frederick Webb Hodge 1864–1956." *American Anthropologist* 59(3):517–20 (1957).

Colton, Harold S., and Lyndon L. Hargrave. *Handbook of Northern Arizona Pottery Wares.* Museum of Northern Arizona Bulletin 11. Flagstaff: Northern Arizona Society of Science and Art, 1937.

Cordell, Linda S. *Prehistory of the Southwest.* A School of American Research Book. Orlando: Academic Press/Harcourt Brace Jovanovich, 1984.

Crotty, Helen K. *Honoring the Dead: Anasazi Ceramics from the Rainbow Bridge Monument Valley Expedition.* Museum of Cultural History Monograph Series 22. Los Angeles: University of California, 1983.

Crumpacker, Shepard J., Jr. Diary of 1937 Rainbow Bridge–Monument Valley Expedition field season. On file with Andrew L. Christenson.

Dean, Jeffrey S. "Thoughts on Hohokam Chronology." In George J. Gumerman (ed.), *Exploring the Hohokam: Prehistoric Desert Peoples of the American Southwest.* Albuquerque: University of New Mexico, 1991.

Dick, Herbert W., and Albert H. Schroeder. "Lyndon Hargrave, a Brief Biography." Papers of the Archaeological Society of New Mexico 1. *Collected Papers in Honor of Lyndon Lane Hargrave.* Santa Fe: Museum of New Mexico Press, 1968.

Douglass, Andrew Ellicott. "The Secret of the Southwest Solved by Talkative Tree Rings." *National Geographic Magazine* 54(6):737–70 (1929).

———. *Dating Pueblo Bonito and Other Ruins of the Southwest.* National Geographic Society Technical Papers, Pueblo Bonito Series 1 (1935).

Doyel, David E. "Pueblo Grande National Landmark Celebrates a Centennial." *Masterkey* 60(4):3–11 (1987).

Doyel, David E. (ed.). *Anasazi Regional Organization and the Chaco System.* Anthropological Papers 5. Albuquerque: Maxwell Museum, University of New Mexico, 1992.

Ellis, Bruce. "Byron Cummings." *El Palacio* 57(11):362–64 (1950).

"Excavations at Aztec." *El Palacio* 6(13):214–15 (1919).

Fewkes, Jesse Walter. "A-Wa'-To-Bi: An Archeological Verification of a Tusayan Legend." *American Anthropologist* 6(4):363–75 (1893).

———. *Antiquities of the Mesa Verde National Park: Cliff Palace.* Bulletin 51. Washington, D.C.: Bureau of American Ethnology, 1911.

———. *Casa Grande, Arizona.* Twenty-eighth Annual Report of the Bureau of American Ethnology. Washington, D.C.: Smithsonian Institution, 1912.

———. "Fire Worship of the Hopi Indians." In *Annual Report of the Smithsonian Institution, 1920,* pp. 589–610. Washington, D.C.: Government Printing Office, 1922.

Fletcher, Maurine S. (ed.). *The Wetherills of Mesa Verde: Autobiography of Benjamin Alfred Wetherill.* Lincoln: University of Nebraska Press, 1977.

Gaede, Marnie (ed.), and Marc Gaede (photog.). *Camera, Spade and Pen: An Inside View of Southwestern Archaeology.* Tucson: University of Arizona Press, 1980.

Gifford, Carol A., and Elizabeth A. Morris. "Digging for Credit: Early Archaeological Field Schools in the American Southwest." *American Antiquity* 50(2):395–411 (1985).

Givens, Douglas. *Alfred Vincent Kidder and the Development of Americanist Archaeology.* Albuquerque: University of New Mexico Press, 1992.

Gladwin, Harold Sterling. *A Method for the Designation of Southwestern Pottery Types.* Medallion Papers 7. Globe, AZ: Gila Pueblo, 1930.

————. *Excavations at Snaketown, Part II: Comparisons and Theories.* Medallion Papers 26. Globe, AZ: Gila Pueblo, 1937.

————. *Excavations at Snaketown, Part III: Revisions.* Medallion Papers 30. Globe, AZ: Gila Pueblo, 1942.

————. *Men Out of Asia.* New York and London: Whittlesey House/McGraw-Hill, 1947.

————. *Excavations at Snaketown, Part IV: Reviews and Conclusions.* Medallion Papers 38. Globe, AZ: Gila Pueblo, 1948.

Gladwin, Harold S., and Winifred Gladwin. *A Method for Designation of Cultures and Their Variations.* Medallion Papers 15. Globe, AZ: Gila Pueblo, 1934.

Gladwin, Harold S., Emil W. Haury, E. B. Sales, and Nora Gladwin. *Excavations at Snaketown: Material Culture.* Medallion Papers 25. Globe, AZ: Gila Pueblo, 1937.

Green, Jesse (ed.). *Zuni: Selected Writings of Frank Hamilton Cushing.* Lincoln: University of Nebraska Press, 1979.

Guernsey, Samuel J., and Alfred V. Kidder. *Basket-Maker Caves of Northeastern Arizona.* Papers of the Peabody Museum of American Archaeology and Ethnology 8(2). Cambridge: Harvard University, 1921.

Guthe, Carl E. Review of A. V. Kidder's *Pecos, New Mexico: Archaeological Notes* (1958). In *El Palacio* 66(1):33–36 (1959).

Hall, Ansel Franklin. *General Report: Rainbow Bridge–Monument Valley Expedition of 1933.* Berkeley: University of California Press, n.d. (c. 1934).

————. Explorer News Letter No. 1. February 18, 1934. Colton Collection, Expeditions: Rainbow Bridge–Monument Valley, 1933. Flagstaff: Museum of Northern Arizona Library.

————. Explorers' News Letter, November 29, 1936. Colton Collection, Expeditions: Rainbow Bridge–Monument Valley, 1936. Flagstaff: Museum of Northern Arizona Library.

Hall, Ansel, and Lyndon Hargrave. Letters. Colton Collection, Expeditions: Rainbow Bridge–Monument Valley. Flagstaff: Museum of Northern Arizona Library.

Hargrave, Lyndon. *Report on Archaeological Reconnaissance in the Rainbow Plateau Area of Northern Arizona and Southern Utah: Based Upon Fieldwork by the Rainbow Bridge–Monument Valley Expedition of 1933.* Berkeley: University of California Press, 1935.

Haury, Emil W. *The Excavation of Los Muertos and Neighboring Ruins in the Salt River Valley, Southern Arizona: Based on the Work of the Hemenway Southwestern Archaeological Expedition of 1887–1888.* Papers of the Peabody Museum of American Archaeology and Ethnology 24(1). Cambridge: Harvard University, 1945.

————. *The Hohokam: Desert Farmers and Craftsmen: Excavations at Snaketown, 1964–1965.* Tucson: University of Arizona Press, 1976.

———. "Reflections: Fifty Years of Southwestern Archaeology." *American Antiquity* 50(2): 383–94 (1985).

Haury, Emil W., and J. Jefferson Reid. "Harold Sterling Gladwin, 1883–1983." *The Kiva* 50(4):271–83 (1985).

Hayden, Julian. "Talking with the Animals: Pinacate Reminiscences." *Journal of the Southwest* 29(2):222–27 (1987).

Hinsley, Curtis. "The Problem of Mr. Hewett: Academics and Popularizers in American Archeology, c. 1910." *History of Anthropology Newsletter* 7(1):7–10.

Hodge, F. W. "The First Discovered City of Cibola." *American Anthropologist* 8(2):142–52 (1895).

———. "Excavations at the Zuñi Pueblo of Hawikuh in 1917." *Art and Archaeology* 7(9):367–79. Washington, D.C., 1918.

———. *Explorations and Field-Work of the Smithsonian Institution in 1917: Excavations at Hawikuh, New Mexico.* Smithsonian Miscellaneous Collections 68(12):61–72. Washington, D.C.: Smithsonian Institution, 1918.

———. "Recent Excavations at Hawikuh." *El Palacio* 12(1):3–11 (1922).

———. *History of Hawikuh, New Mexico: One of the So-called Cities of Cíbola.* Los Angeles: Southwest Museum, 1937.

———. *Turquoise Work at Hawikuh, New Mexico.* Leaflet 2. New York: Museum of the American Indian, Heye Foundation, 1921.

Hooton, Earnest Albert. *The Indians of Pecos Pueblo: A Study of Their Skeletal Remains.* Papers of the Southwestern Expedition 4. New Haven: Yale University Press, 1930.

Hough, Walter. "Archaeological Field Work in Northeastern Arizona: The Museum–Gates Expedition of 1901." In *Annual Report of the U.S. National Museum, 1901*, pp. 287–358. Washington, D.C.: U.S. Government Printing Office, 1903.

———. *Antiquities of the Upper Gila and Salt River Valleys in Arizona and New Mexico.* Bureau of American Ethnology Bulletin 35. Washington, D.C.: Government Printing Office, 1907.

———. "Jesse Walter Fewkes." *American Anthropologist* 33(1):92–97 (1931).

Jett, Stephen C. "The Great 'Race' to 'Discover' Rainbow Natural Bridge in 1909." *The Kiva* 58(1):3–66.

Judd, Neil M. "The Pueblo Bonito Expedition of the National Geographic Society." *National Geographic Magazine* (March 1922):322–31.

———. "Pueblo Bonito, the Ancient." *National Geographic Magazine* (July 1923):99–108.

———. "The Everyday Life in Pueblo Bonito." *National Geographic Magazine* 47(3):227–62 (1925).

———. "Arizona's Prehistoric Canals from the Air." *Explorations and Field-work of the Smithsonian Institution in 1930*, pp. 157–66. Washington, D.C.: Smithsonian Institution, 1931.

———. "Byron Cummings, 1860–1954." *American Anthropologist* 56(5):871–72, 1954.

———. *The Material Culture of Pueblo Bonito.* Smithsonian Miscellaneous Collections 124. Washington, D.C.: Smithsonian Institution, 1954.

———. *Pueblo del Arroyo, Chaco Canyon, New Mexico.* Smithsonian Miscellaneous Collections 138(1). Washington, D.C.: Smithsonian Institution, 1959.

———. "Reminiscences in Southwest Archaeology: II." *The Kiva* 26(1):1–6 (1960).

———. *The Architecture of Pueblo Bonito.* Smithsonian Miscellaneous Collections 147(1). Washington, D.C.: Smithsonian Institution, June 30, 1964.

———. *The Bureau of American Ethnology: A Partial History.* Norman: University of Oklahoma Press, 1967.

———. *Men Met Along the Trail: Adventures in Archaeology.* Norman: University of Oklahoma Press, 1968.

Judd, Neil M., M. R. Harrington, and S. K. Lothrop, "Frederick Webb Hodge—1864–1956." *American Antiquity* 22(4):401–4 (1957).

Kessell, John. *Kiva, Cross, and Crown: The Pecos Indians and New Mexico, 1540–1840.* Washington, D.C.: National Park Service, 1979.

Kidder, Alfred Vincent. *An Introduction to the Study of Southwestern Archaeology, with a Preliminary Account of the Excavations at Pecos, and a Summary of Southwestern Archaeology Today, by Irving Rouse.* New Haven: Yale University Press, 1924. (Rev. ed. 1962)

———. "The Peabody Expedition to the Mimbres Valley, New Mexico, Season of 1927." Laboratory of Anthropology, Santa Fe.

———. "Southwestern Archaeological Conference." *El Palacio* 23(22):554–61 (1927)

———. Field notes. National Park Service files, Pecos National Historical Park, Pecos, NM. Original notebook, 1927–29. Laboratory of Anthropology, Santa Fe.

———. "Colonel and Mrs. Lindbergh Aid Archaeologists." *The Masterkey* 3(6):4–17 (1930).

———. *The Pottery of Pecos. Vol. I: The Dull-Paint Wares.* Papers of the Southwestern Expedition 5. New Haven: Yale University Press, 1931.

———. *The Artifacts of Pecos.* Papers of the Southwestern Expedition 6. New Haven: Yale University Press, 1932.

———. "Pecos Pueblo." *El Palacio* 58(3):82–89 (1951).

———. "Earl Halstead Morris—1889–1956." *American Antiquity* 22(4):390–97 (1957).

———. *Pecos, New Mexico: Archaeological Notes.* Papers of the Robert S. Peabody Foundation for Archaeology 5. Andover, MA: Phillips Academy, 1958.

———. "Reminiscences in Southwest Archaeology: I." *The Kiva* 25(4):1–32 (1960).

Kidder, Alfred Vincent, and Samuel J. Guernsey. *Archaeological Explorations in Northeastern Arizona.* Bulletin of the Bureau of American Ethnology 65. Washington, D.C.: Smithsonian Institution, 1919.

Kidder, Alfred Vincent, and Anna O. Shepard. *The Pottery of Pecos. Vol. II.* New Haven: Yale University Press, 1936.

Kluckhohn, Clyde. *Beyond the Rainbow.* Boston: Christopher Publishing House, 1933.

Kroeber, A. L. *Zuni Potsherds.* Anthropological Papers of the American Museum of Natural History 28(1). New York: American Museum of Natural History, 1916.

Lange, Frederick W., and Diana Leonard (eds.). *Among Ancient Ruins: The Legacy of Earl H. Morris.* Boulder: University of Colorado Museum, Johnson Books, 1985.

Lekson, Stephen H. *Great Pueblo Architecture of Chaco Canyon, New Mexico.* Publications in Archaeology 18B, Chaco Canyon Studies. Albuquerque: National Park Service, 1984.

———. "Sedentism and Aggregation in Anasazi Archaeology." In *Perspectives on Southwestern Prehistory,* Paul E. Minnis and Charles L. Redman (eds.). Boulder: Westview Press, 1990.

Lister, Florence C., and Robert H. Lister. *Earl Morris and Southwestern Archaeology.* Albuquerque: University of New Mexico Press, 1968.

Lister, Robert H., and Florence C. Lister. *Anasazi Pottery: Ten Centuries of Prehistoric Ceramic Art in the Four Corners Country of the Southwestern United States.* Albuquerque: Maxwell Museum of Anthropology/University of New Mexico Press, 1978.

———. *Chaco Canyon: Archaeology and Archaeologists.* Albuquerque: University of New Mexico, 1981.

———. *Those Who Came Before: Southwestern Archaeology in the National Park System.* Globe, AZ: Southwest Parks and Monuments Association, 1983.

———. *Aztec Ruins on the Animas: Excavated, Preserved, and Interpreted.* Albuquerque: University of New Mexico Press, 1987.

———. *Aztec Ruins National Monument: Administrative History of an Archeological Preserve.* Professional Papers 24. Santa Fe: National Park Service, Southwest Cultural Resources Center, 1990.

Martin, Paul S. "Early Development in Mogollon Research." In *Archaeological Researches in Retrospect,* Gordon R. Willey (ed.), pp. 3–29. Cambridge, MA: Winthrop Publishers, 1977.

Mason, C. C. "The Story of the Discovery and Early Exploration of the Cliff Houses at the Mesa Verde." Given to the Colorado State Historical Society by Charles Mason, May 5, 1918. Typewritten copy at the National Park Service Research Center, Mesa Verde National Park.

Mathien, Frances Joan. *Environment and Subsistence of Chaco Canyon, New Mexico.* Publications in Archaeology 18E, Chaco Canyon Studies. Albuquerque: National Park Service, 1985.

McNitt, Frank. *Richard Wetherill: Anasazi.* (Rev. ed.) Albuquerque: University of New Mexico Press, 1966.

McNitt Collection. Hollinger Box I: file III: Stories, Paragraphs and Notes Taken from Files of Mancos Times. Hollinger Box I: file IV: Notes from Interviews with Marietta Wetherill. State Records Center and Archives, Santa Fe, New Mexico.

Memorandum of Agreement Under Which Expedition Members Are Accepted. File for 1934, Colton Collection, Expeditions: Rainbow Bridge–Monument Valley. Flagstaff: Museum of Northern Arizona Library.

Mindeleff, Victor. "A Study of Pueblo Architecture in Tusayan and Cibola." In *Eighth Annual Report of the Bureau of Ethnology, 1886–'87,* by J. W. Powell, pp. 13–228. Washington, D.C.: Government Printing Office, 1891.

Mobley-Tanaka, Jeannette L. "Don Carlos Takes the Cake: An Anecdote from the Hemenway Southwest Archaeological Expedition, 1888." In *Why Museums Collect: Papers in Honor of Joe Ben Wheat*, Meliha S. Duran and David T. Kirkpatrick (eds.), pp. 183–93. The Archaeological Society of New Mexico 19. Albuquerque: Archaeological Society of New Mexico, 1993.

Montgomery, Ross Gordon, Watson Smith, and John Otis Brew. *Franciscan Awatovi: The Excavation and Conjectural Reconstruction of a 17th-Century Spanish Mission Establishment at a Hopi Indian Town in Northeastern Arizona*. Papers of the Peabody Museum 36, Reports of the Awatovi Expedition 3. Cambridge, MA: Peabody Museum, 1949.

Monthly Reports of the Park Archaeologist and Naturalist. File no. 207-03.1. Park Museum, National Park Service, Mesa Verde National Park.

Morris, Ann Axtell. *Digging in the Southwest*. Chicago: Doubleday/Camus Books, E. M. Hale and Co., 1933.

Morris, Earl H. *The Aztec Ruin*. Anthropological Papers of the American Museum of Natural History 26(1). New York: American Museum of Natural History, 1919.

———. "Further Discoveries at the Aztec Ruin." *El Palacio* 6(2):19–26 (1919).

———. *The House of the Great Kiva at the Aztec Ruin*. Anthropological Papers of the American Museum of Natural History 26(2). New York: American Museum of Natural History, 1921.

———. *Burials in the Aztec Ruin; The Aztec Ruin Annex*. Anthropological Papers of the American Museum of Natural History 26(3&4). New York: American Museum of Natural History, 1924.

———. *Notes on Excavations in the Aztec Ruin*. Anthropological Papers of the American Museum of Natural History 26(5). New York: American Museum of Natural History, 1928.

———. *The Temple of the Warriors*. New York: Charles Scribner's Sons, 1931.

———. Notes and Photos of Stabilization Projects at Mesa Verde National Park, 1934–35. National Park Service files, Research Center, Mesa Verde National Park.

———. *Archaeological Studies in the La Plata District: Southwestern Colorado and Northwestern New Mexico*. Washington, D.C.: Carnegie Institution of Washington Publications 519, 1939.

Nelson, Arthur W., Jr. "My Experiences as a Member of the Rainbow Bridge–Monument Valley Expedition, Summer of 1936." Handwritten journal. Flagstaff: Museum of Northern Arizona Library.

Nelson, N. C. "Notes on Pueblo Bonito." In *Pueblo Bonito,* by George H. Pepper. Anthropological Papers of the American Museum of Natural History 27. New York: American Museum of Natural History, 1920.

Nordenskiöld, Gustaf. *The Cliff Dwellers of the Mesa Verde*. Translated by D. Lloyd Morgan. Stockholm and Chicago: P. A. Norstedt and Söner, 1893.

Nusbaum, Rosemary. *Tierra Dulce: Reminiscences from the Jesse Nusbaum Papers*. Santa Fe: Sunstone Press, 1980.

Ortiz, Alfonso (vol. ed.). *Handbook of North American Indians,* vol. 9, *Southwest* (William C. Sturtevant, gen. ed.). Washington, D.C.: Smithsonian Institution, 1979.

Pepper, George H. *Pueblo Bonito*. Anthropological Papers of the American Museum of Natural History 27. New York: American Museum of Natural History, 1920.

Pinkley, Frank. Correspondence. National Park Service files, Casa Grande National Monument, Coolidge, Arizona.

Plog, Fred. "Prehistory: Western Anasazi." In *Handbook of North American Indians*, vol. 9, *Southwest*, Alfonso Ortiz (ed.). Washington, D.C.: Smithsonian Institution, 1979.

Plog, Stephen. "Regional Perspectives on the Western Anasazi." *American Archeology* 4(3): 162–70 (1984).

Prucha, Francis Paul. *The Great Father: The United States Government and the American Indians*, vol. 2. Lincoln: University of Nebraska Press, 1984.

Reed, Erik K. "Cultural Areas of the Pre-Spanish Southwest." *New Mexico Quarterly* (Winter): 428–39 (1951).

———. "Human Skeletal Material from Site 59, Chaco Canyon National Monument." *El Palacio* 69(4):240–47 (1962).

Reid, J. Jefferson, and David E. Doyel (eds.). *Emil W. Haury's Prehistory of the American Southwest*. Tucson: University of Arizona Press, 1986.

Roberts, Frank H. H. *Shabik'eshchee Village: A Late Basketmaker Site in Chaco Canyon, New Mexico*. Bureau of American Ethnology Bulletin 92. Washington, D.C.: Smithsonian Institution, 1929.

Schuyler, Robert L. "The History of American Archaeology: An Examination of Procedure." *American Antiquity* 36(4):383–409 (1971).

Schroeder, Albert H. *The Hakataya Concept and Origin of Its Group*. Museum of New Mexico Archaeological Notes 47. Santa Fe: Office of Archaeological Studies, 1991.

Scott, Douglas D. "Pioneering Archaeology in Southwestern Colorado: The Kidder and Morley Years." In *Why Museums Collect: Papers in Honor of Joe Ben Wheat*. Meliha S. Duran and David T. Kirkpatrick (eds.), pp. 203–11. The Archaeological Society of New Mexico 19. Albuquerque: The Archaeological Society of New Mexico, 1993.

Shears, Brenda L. "The Hendricks-Hodge Archaeological Expedition Documentation Project: Preparing a Museum Collection for Research." M.A. thesis, Hunter College, the City University of New York, 1989.

Smith, Jack E. *Mesas, Cliffs, and Canyons: The University of Colorado Survey of Mesa Verde National Park, 1971–1977*. Mesa Verde National Park: Mesa Verde Museum Association, 1986.

Smith, Watson. *Kiva Mural Decorations at Awatovi and Kawaika-a: With a Survey of Other Wall Paintings in the Pueblo Southwest*. Papers of the Peabody Museum 37, Reports of the Awatovi Expedition 5. Cambridge, MA: Peabody Museum, 1952.

———. "George Walton Brainerd—1909–1956." *American Antiquity* 22(2):165–68 (1956).

———. *Painted Ceramics of the Western Mound at Awatovi*. Papers of the Peabody Museum of Archaeology and Ethnology 38, Reports of the Awatovi Expedition 8. Cambridge: Peabody Museum, 1971.

———. *Prehistoric Kivas of Antelope Mesa, Northeastern Arizona*. Papers of the Peabody Museum 39(1). Cambridge: Peabody Museum, 1972.

———. "One Man's Archaeology," privately published manuscript, second printing. Tucson, 1984. Catherine McElvaine Library, School of American Research, Santa Fe, New Mexico.

———. "Blankets by Beacon" in "Compiled Appendices," a sequel to "One Man's Archae-ology," August 1985. On file with the author.

———. "Emil Haury's Southwest." *Journal of the Southwest* 29(1):107–20 (1987).

———. "One Man's Archaeology" (condensed version). *The Kiva* 57(2), 1992.

Smith, Watson. Raymond H. Thompson (ed.). *When Is A Kiva? And Other Questions About Southwestern Archaeology.* Tucson: University of Arizona Press, 1990.

Smith, Watson, Richard B. Woodbury, and Nathalie F. S. Woodbury. *The Excavation of Hawi-kuh by Frederick Webb Hodge: Report of the Hendricks-Hodge Expedition 1917–1923.* New York: Museum of the American Indian, Heye Foundation, 1966.

Spier, Leslie. *An Outline for a Chronology of Zuni Ruins.* Anthropological Papers of the American Museum of Natural History 28(3). New York: American Museum of Natural History, 1917.

Stein, John R., and Stephen H. Lekson. "Anasazi Ritual Landscapes." In *Anasazi Regional Organization and the Chaco System,* David E. Doyel (ed.). Anthropological Papers 5:87–100. Albuquerque: Maxwell Museum, University of New Mexico, 1992.

Stuart, David. "Canyon Harbors Secret of the Ancients." *New Mexico Magazine* 65(10):52–56 (1987).

Taylor, Walter W. "A Study of Archeology." *American Anthropologist* 50(3, pt. 2), American Anthropological Association Memoir 69, 1948.

———. "Southwestern Archeology: Its History and Theory." *American Anthropologist* 56:561–75 (1954).

Torres-Reyes, Ricardo. "Mesa Verde National Park: An Administrative History, 1906–1970." National Park Service, Office of History and Historic Architecture, Washington, D.C., 1970. On file at the Park Museum, Mesa Verde National Park.

Turner, Christy G., II, and Nancy T. Morris. Abstract of "A Massacre at Hopi." *American Antiquity* 35(3):320–31 (1970).

Vivian, Gordon, and Tom W. Mathews. Introduction to *Kin Kletso: A Pueblo III Community in Chaco Canyon, New Mexico.* Technical Series 6(1). Globe, AZ: Southwest Parks and Monuments Association, 1977.

Vivian, Gordon, and Paul Reiter. *The Great Kivas of Chaco Canyon and Their Relation-ships.* School of American Research Monograph 22. Albuquerque: University of New Mexico Press, 1960.

Waters, Frank. *The Book of the Hopi.* New York: Ballentine, 1969.

Wauchope, Robert. "Alfred Vincent Kidder, 1885–1963." *American Antiquity* 31:2(1):149–71 (1965).

Webb, George Ernest. *Tree Rings and Telescopes: The Scientific Career of A. E. Douglass.* Tucson: University of Arizona, 1983.

Wedel, Waldo R. "Neil Merton Judd, 1887–1976." *American Antiquity* 43(3):399–404 (1978).

Willey, Gordon R. Interview with Alfred Vincent Kidder, 1957. Transcript, parts I and II. Pecos, NM: National Park Service files, Pecos National Historical Park.

————. "Alfred Vincent Kidder, October 29, 1885–June 11, 1963." *National Academy of Sciences Biographical Memoirs 39*, pp. 292–322. New York: Columbia University Press, 1967.

Willey, Gordon R., and Jeremy Sabloff. *A History of American Archaeology* (2nd ed.). San Francisco: W. H. Freeman, 1980.

Wilson, John P. "Awatovi—More Light on a Legend." *Plateau* 44(3):125–30 (1972).

Woodbury, Nathalie F. S. "Women's Money and the 'Study of Man': The Hemenway Expeditions, Part II." *Anthropology Newsletter* 29(4):12 (1988).

Woodbury, Richard B. *Prehistoric Stone Implements of Northeastern Arizona.* Papers of the Peabody Museum of American Archaeology and Ethnology 34, Reports of the Awatovi Expedition 6. Cambridge, MA: Peabody Museum, 1954.

————. "Nels C. Nelson and Chronological Archaeology." *American Antiquity* 25(3):400–401 (Jan. 1960).

————. "Nelson's Stratigraphy." *American Antiquity* 26(1):98–99 (July 1960).

————. "The Hohokam Canals at Pueblo Grande, Arizona." *American Antiquity* 26(2):267–70 (Oct. 1960).

————. *Alfred V. Kidder.* Leaders in Modern Anthropology Series. New York: Columbia University Press, 1973.

————. "A Century of Zuni Research." In *Zuni and El Morro, Past and Present.* David Grant Noble (ed.), pp. 9–14. *Exploration,* Annual Bulletin of the School of American Research. Santa Fe: School of American Research, 1983.

————. "Looking Back at the Pecos Conference." *The Kiva* 48(4):251–65 (1983).

————. "John Otis Brew, 1906–1988." *American Antiquity* 55(3):452–59 (1990).

————. *Sixty Years of Southwestern Archaeology: A History of the Pecos Conference.* Albuquerque: University of New Mexico Press, 1993.

Picture Credits

The beginnings of archaeology in the American Southwest coincided with the early use of the camera in documenting the dramatic landscapes of the region and the work of its scientific explorers. Early on, the camera became an indispensable tool recording the activities of, and the peoples and places visited by, the researchers whose work is described in this book. Every archaeological expedition or field study had, and still has, its accompanying photographer—often, several. Thus, the visual resources available, though not always of the best technical quality, are vast.

In selecting photographs for use in *Great Excavations,* the author and publisher have sought to illustrate the major figures involved in early Southwestern archaeology, the sites they explored, the cultural materials they studied, and the methods they used for excavation. Certain contemporary concerns about the depiction of sensitive cultural and archaeological materials were taken into account. It was decided, for example, not to use photographs of skeletal materials, despite their value in providing information about the ways in which burials were excavated in these early days of scientific archaeology. Photographs of sensitive burial or ritual materials unearthed in the excavations also were avoided. Individuals pictured in the field photographs are identified whenever possible. We welcome feedback from readers who may be able to identify friends or relatives who appear in these images, especially those that illustrate the crucial role played by Native American guides and excavation crews, who participated in virtually all of the archaeological studies in this book.

The author and publisher want to thank the institutions and collections listed below for their assistance in the often challenging task of finding historic photographs and for generously allowing us to reproduce them in this book. Our thanks go to Mrs. J. O. (Evelyn) Brew; Ted Bundy, Arizona State Museum; Willow Roberts Powers and Sibel Melik, Laboratory of Anthropology; Arthur Olívas and Richard Rudisill, Museum of New Mexico; Kim Walters, Southwest Museum, Los Angeles; Donna Dickerson and Martha LaBell, Peabody Museum, Harvard University; Richard Woodbury; Carol Burke, Museum of Northern Arizona; Faith Kidder Fuller; Paul Saavadra, New Mexico State Records Center & Archives; Ramona Hutchinson, Mesa Verde National Park; Paula Fleming, National Anthropology Archives; Laura Nash, National Museum of the American Indian; April Goebel, National Geographic Society; and R. David Wells, American Museum of Natural History. And very special thanks to SAR Press picture researcher Baylor Chapman.

ABBREVIATIONS

ASM/UA	Arizona State Museum, University of Arizona, Tucson
CHS	Colorado Historical Society
DLS/AMNH	Department of Library Services, American Museum of Natural History
MIAC/LA	Museum of Indian Arts and Culture/Laboratory of Anthropology, Santa Fe
MNA/PA	Museum of Northern Arizona Photo Archives
MNM	Museum of New Mexico
MOMA	Museum of Modern Art, New York
NGS	National Geographic Society, Neil Judd Collection

NMAI/SI   National Museum of the American Indian, Smithsonian Institution
NPS/ARNM   National Park Service, Aztec Ruins National Monument
NPS/MVNP   National Park Service, Mesa Verde National Park
PM/HU   Peabody Museum, Harvard University
RBMV   Rainbow Bridge–Monument Valley Expedition Collection
SAR/CC   School of American Research, Chapman Collection
SI   Smithsonian Institution
SMLA   Southwest Museum, Los Angeles
SRC&A   State Records Center & Archives, 404 Montezuma, Santa Fe, NM
UA/DPC   University of Arizona, Special Library Collections, Douglass Papers Collection
UCM   University of Colorado Museum, Boulder

T: page top   B: page bottom   L: page left   R: page right   C: page center

Cover: All photos © Bruce Hucko; **Frontispiece:** NGS 29-SJ389 CC 1481; **Prologue:** SI, Neil Judd Collections; Map by Carol Cooperrider (based on a map in Lister and Lister 1983:21).

Chapter 1: Cliff Palace

2: Photo by William Henry Jackson, CHS, no. T-4254; **6TL:** SRC&A, McNitt Collection, no. 8615; **6TR:** NPS/MVNP, no. 4946; **6BR:** SRC&A, McNitt Collection, no. 8616; **8–9:** Photo by Jesse L. Nusbaum, MNM, no. 77777; **12:** Pl. 44 in *The Cliff Dwellers of the Mesa Verde* by Gustaf Nordenskiöld (1893), copy photo by Ted Rice; **13:** Pl. 31 in *The Cliff Dwellers of the Mesa Verde* by Gustaf Nordenskiöld (1893), copy photo by Ted Rice; **14:** SRC&A, McNitt Collection, no. 8621; **16T:** Photo by Jesse L. Nusbaum, MNM, no. 60513; **16BR:** Photo by Jesse L. Nusbaum, MNM, 60531; **18L:** NPS/MVNP, no. 4068; **18R:** SRC&A, McNitt Collection, 8649; **21:** NPS/MVNP, no. 4155; **22:** Photo by Watson, NPS/MVNP.

Chapter 2: Pecos Pueblo

24: Photo by Jesse L. Nusbaum, MNM, no. 41024; **29:** Courtesy Faith Kidder Fuller; **32:** Photo by Jesse L. Nusbaum, MNM, no. 41010; **33T:** Photo by Charles A. Lindbergh, MNM, no. 13028; **33B:** Drawing by Singleton Peabody Moorehead from *Pecos, New Mexico: Archaeological Notes*, by A. V. Kidder (1958), courtesy Robert S. Peabody Museum of Archaeology, Phillips Academy, Andover, MA, copy photo by Ted Rice; **36:** MIAC/LA Archives, Kidder Collection, no. 432a; **38L:** Photo by Jesse L. Nusbaum, MNM, no. 41022; **38R:** MNM, no. 47893; **40:** From *The Artifacts of Pecos* by Alfred Vincent Kidder, published for Phillips Academy by Yale University Press, © Yale University Press, 1932, copy photo by Ted Rice; **41:** From *The Pottery of Pecos, vol. I, The Dull-Paint Wares,* by Alfred Vincent Kidder, published for Phillips Academy by Yale University Press, © Yale University Press, 1931, copy photo by Ted Rice; **43:** All courtesy Faith Kidder Fuller; **44T:** MIAC/LA Archives, Kidder Collection, no. 931; **44B:** MIAC/LA Archives, Kidder Collection, no. 392; **46:** MIAC/LA Archives, Kidder Collection, no. 103; **49:** Courtesy Faith Kidder Fuller; **50:** ASM/UA, ASM neg. no. 58298.

Chapter 3: Aztec Ruin

52: Photo by Earl H. Morris, DLS/AMNH, no. 119535; **55:** Photo by Earl H. Morris, UCM; **57L:** MNM, no. 7380; **57C:** Photo by E. M. Meyer, DLS/AMNH, no. 283468; **57R:** MNM, no. 139070; **60T:** Photo by Watson Smith, MNA/PA, no. 72.535; **60B:** UCM; **62T:** Photo by Earl H. Morris, DLS/AMNH, no. 119733. **62B:** Photo by Earl H. Morris, DLS/AMNH, no. 119554; **64:** From *Aztec Ruins on the Animas: Excavated, Preserved, and Interpreted* by Robert H. Lister and Florence C. Lister, © University of New Mexico Press, 1987, copy photo by Ted Rice; **65:** From *Notes on Excavations in the Aztec Ruin* by Earl H. Morris, Anthropological Papers of the American Museum of Natural History, vol. 26, part V, © American Museum of Natural History, New York, 1928, copy photo by Ted Rice; **68:** Photo by Earl H. Morris, DLS/AMNH, no. 119550; **69:** NPS/ARNM; **70:** MNM, no. 58304; **72:** Photo by Paul Logsdon, courtesy Marcia Logsdon; **74T:** MNM, no. 46723; **74B:** Photo by Earl H. Morris, DLS/AMNH, no. 119747; **75:** Photo by Earl H. Morris, DLS/AMNH, no. 119672.

Chapter 4: Hawikuh

78: From *History of Hawikuh, New Mexico: One of the So-Called Seven Cities of Cibola* by F. W. Hodge (1937); courtesy NMAI/SI, copy photo by Ted Rice; **81L:** SI, no. 80-9479; **81R:** MNM, no. 7296; **82:** Photo by Stowell, Albuquerque, SI, no. 2342A; **84T:** SMLA, no. P.39324 N.41927; **84B:** Photo by Jesse L. Nusbaum, MNM, no. 139191; **87T:** SMLA, no. N29482; **87B:** Courtesy Faith Kidder Fuller; **89:** NMAI/SI, no. 6813; **90T:** NMAI/SI, no. 7448; **90B:** NMAI/SI, no. 7442; **93:** Drawing by Ross Montgomery, fig. 33 in *The Excavation of Hawikuh by Frederick Webb Hodge: Report of the Hendricks-Hodge Expedition 1917–1923*, by Watson Smith, Richard B. Woodbury, and Nathalie Woodbury (1966), NMAI/SI, copy photo by Ted Rice; **95:** SMLA, N.42017; **96:** From F. W. Hodge, *Turquoise Work at Hawikuh, New Mexico*, Leaflet 2, Museum of the American Indian, Heye Foundation, New York, 1921, NMAI/SI, copy photo by Ted Rice; **97:** From *The Excavation of Hawikuh by Frederick Webb Hodge: Report of the Hendricks-Hodge Expedition 1917–1923*, by Watson Smith, Richard B. Woodbury, and Nathalie Woodbury (1966), NMAI/SI, copy photo by Ted Rice.

Chapter 5: Pueblo Bonito

102: Photo by Neil M. Judd, © NGS, no. 18654-A; **105T:** SAR/CC, no. 1419. **105B:** DLS/AMNH, no. 411882; **106:** DLS/AMNH, no. 411970; **107:** DLS/AMNH, no. 411912; **108:** Photo by Charles F. Lummis, SMLA, no. P.23820 N.41926; **110:** PM/HU; **112:** MNM, no. 81128; **113:** DLS/AMNH, no. 412026; **115T:** Photo by O. C. Havens, © NGS, no. 32368-A; **115B:** Photo by O. C. Havens, © NGS, no. 32363-A; **116:** Photo by NGS, PM/HU, N33301 **118:** Photo by O. C. Havens, © NGS, no. 28369-A; **119:** MNM, no. 48551; **120:** MNM, no. 80594; **123:** MNM, no. 80837; **126:** From *The Material Culture of Pueblo Bonito* by Neil M. Judd (1954), SI, copy photo by Ted Rice; **127:** From *The Material Culture of Pueblo Bonito* by Neil M. Judd (1954), SI, copy photo by Ted Rice.

Chapter 6: Snaketown

132: ASM/UA, no. 78311; **135:** ASM/UA, no. 13313; **139:** ASM/UA, no. 79300; **142L:** ASM/UA, no. 70552; **142R:** Courtesy Special Collections, University of Arizona Library; **144:** ASM/UA, no. 70366; **146:** ASM/UA, neg. no. 70196; **148:** ASM/UA, copy photo by Ted Rice; **149:** ASM/UA, copy photo by Ted Rice; **150:** ASM/UA, copy photo by Ted Rice; **151:** ASM/UA, no. 70770; **153:** ASM/UA, no. 70575; **154L:** Photo by E. B. Sayles, ASM/UA, no. 2205; **154R:** Photo by Helga Teiwes, ASM/UA; **159T:** Photo by Helga Teiwes, ASM/UA, no. 80621; **159B:** ASM/UA, no. 80376.

Chapter 7: Awatovi

162: PM/HU, N33302, cat. no. 10-58; **165:** Photo by P. Hobler, ASM/UA, no. 7879; **166:** Fig. 6a in Watson Smith, *Painted Ceramics of the Western Mound at Awatovi*. Papers of the Peabody Museum of Archaeology and Ethnology, vol. 38. Copyright 1971 by the President and Fellows of Harvard College; cat. no. 17-36; **169T:** PM/HU, cat. no. H-81; **169B:** PM/HU, cat. no. H-49; **171:** Photo by F. P. Orchard, PM/HU, photo. no. 38-401; **173T:** N33303, cat. no. 10-58; **173B:** Fig. 38c in Watson Smith, *Kiva Mural Decorations at Awatovi and Kawaika-a*. Papers of the Peabody Museum of Archaeology and Ethnology, vol. 37. Reprinted courtesy of the Peabody Museum of Archaeology and Ethnology, Harvard University; N39-133; **175:** From Ross Gordon Montgomery, Watson Smith, and John Otis Brew, *Franciscan Awatovi*. Papers of the Peabody Museum of Archaeology and Ethnology, vol. 36. Copyright 1949 by the President and Fellows of Harvard College. Drawing by Ross Montgomery, copy photo by Ted Rice; **176:** From Watson Smith, *Painted Ceramics of the Western Mound at Awatovi*. Papers of the Peabody Museum of Archaeology and Ethnology, vol. 38. Copyright 1971 by the President and Fellows of Harvard College. Copy photo by Ted Rice; **179:** "General View of Antelope Mesa Looking West," PM/HU; **182, 183:** From Ross Gordon Montgomery, Watson Smith, and John Otis Brew, *Franciscan Awatovi*. Papers of the Peabody Museum of Archaeology and Ethnology, vol. 36. Copyright 1949 by the President and Fellows of Harvard College. Copy photos by Ted Rice; **184:** Photo by Albert Fenn, MOMA 12,538. **186:** Photo by Lowell Lurvey, ASM/UA.

Chapter 8: Rainbow Bridge–Monument Valley

188: Photo by Grace E. Hoover, MNA/PA, RBMV 1072; **192T:** Photo by Robert Branstead, MNA/PA, RBMV 122; **192B:** Photo by E. Beckwith, MNA/PA, RBMV 2213; **196T:** Photo by H. F. Robinson,

MNM, no. 37394 **194BL:** Photo by Robert Branstead, MNA/PA, RBMV 12; **194BR:** Photo by Robert Branstead, MNA/PA, RBMV Expedition 15; **197:** Photo by Robert Branstead, MNA/PA, RBMV 236; **198T:** Photo by Robert Branstead, MNA/PA, RBMV 103; **198R:** Photo by Robert Branstead, MNA/PA, RBMV 233; **201:** Photo by L. W. Lowery, MNA/PA, RBMV 648; **202:** Photo by Robert Branstead, MNA/PA, RBMV 73; **206:** © University of California Press, copy photo by Ted Rice; **207:** © University of California Press, copy photo by Ted Rice; **209T:** Photo by Watson Smith, copy photo by Marc Gaede, MNA/PA 72563; **209L:** Photo by Clifford Bond, MNA/PA, RBMV 1659; **211:** Photo by Clifford Bond, MNA/PA, RBMV 1927.

Epilogue
212: MNA/PA, MV 385.

INDEX